Contents

A Cautionary Note

This guidebook is not a legal document. It is intended to provide accurate information about the subject matter. It is sold with the understanding that the publisher and author are not engaged in rendering legal or other professional services. Specifically, the recommendations contained herein are only guidelines, not legal advice, and the publisher and author do not warrant, in any manner, their suitability for any particular usage. If legal advice or other expert assistance is required, the services of an attorney or other competent professional, with knowledge of all laws pertaining to the reader and the jurisdiction, should be sought.

Preface

As a special education resource specialist, I received many questions regarding the various exceptionalities of children. Most questions are about children with physical or mental disabilities. I have found a general lack of understanding and much misinformation about children with special needs. Unfortunately, much of this misinformation gets passed on to others. This, in turn, creates problems for not only children with disabilities, but also others in their ultimate understanding and acceptance of such children.

While teaching at the university level, I found that most students entering my classes were also misinformed about exceptional children. As student teachers, they wanted to better understand such children, but they needed more information about specific disabilities to eradicate their misconceptions. I was motivated to write this book about children with disabilities in the hope of correcting the myths, misunderstandings, and misinformation about young students with special needs. It is only through knowledge that attitudes will change and educators will become less apprehensive about teaching students with disabilities.

The terminology for children with exceptional needs has been in constant change. The Education of the Handicapped Act refers to "handicapped" individuals. More recently, the Individuals with Disabilities Education Act (IDEA) used the term *disability* instead of handicap. Regardless of terminology, the challenges and issues faced by those affected are much the same.

The term *exceptional* refers to any child or youth who shows significant discrepancy between ability and achievement and may require specialized services to meet that child's educational needs (Pierangelo & Jacoby, 1996). The focus of this book is on students with physical disabilities, mental disabilities, or both.

Teachers are often unprepared to work with students with disabilities who are placed in the regular classroom. This book provides information about the nature and characteristics of the disabilities a teacher is likely to encounter, and it suggests practical strategies that educators can use to promote good learning experiences for all students in a regular classroom. The book is intended as a handy reference for a teacher's desk, principal's office, or school library.

Many books have been written about disabilities, and it can be very time consuming to research a specific exceptionality. Because most educators have huge time constraints, the major disabilities in this book are arranged alphabetically from "aphasia" to "visual processing dysfunction." This provides a quick, easy way for educators to access information about a specific disability.

The manifestation of characteristics for any given disability will vary greatly from individual to individual. So, while one student may be significantly impaired by a particular condition, another with the same disability might manifest no evidence of it whatsoever or might have a degree of impairment so slight that the student has no special needs and would not be considered a student with a disability. Clearly, not everyone with a disability discussed in this book requires special education.

WHAT'S NEW IN THIS EDITION

New sections of interest have been added to this edition. Chapter 1 includes a section on IDEA 2004 Reauthorization followed by No Child Left Behind and Postsecondary Transition. Bipolar disorder has been added to Chapter 4. The same format as used with the other disabilities in this section provides a wealth of information about the disorder. The new Resource E compares the similarities and differences between ADHD and bipolar disorder.

Since telephone numbers and addresses are never static, all of the telephone numbers and addresses have been verified or corrected if needed. Additional information has been added to most of the disabilities addressed in this book. More books and Web sites are included for your convenience.

Acknowledgments

The author gratefully acknowledges the assistance of Lawrence B. Trygstad, a Los Angeles attorney specializing in law relating to education, for reviewing and providing additional information for Chapter 1. The author appreciates the assistance received from Janet Canning, Consultant, and Victor Hackett, Special Education Office Assistant, at the California Department of Education, Special Education Division, Sacramento, California.

Publisher's Acknowledgments

Corwin Press gratefully acknowledges the contributions of the following reviewers:

Joseph Staub
Resource Specialist Teacher
Thomas Starr King Middle
  School
Los Angeles, CA

Joyce Williams Bergin, EdD
Professor, Department of Special
  and Adult Education
Armstrong Atlantic State
  University
Savannah, GA

Debi Gartland, PhD
Professor of Special Education
Towson University
Towson, MD

Nicole Guyon
Special Educator
Westerly School Department
Cranston, RI

Vicki McFarland
Special Education Director
Learning Matters Educational
  Group
Phoenix, AZ

About the Author

 **Lee (Leona) Brattland Nielsen** received her Bachelor of Arts degree from the University of Minnesota and studied voice at the Minneapolis College of Music. She took postgraduate studies at the University of Florida; California State University, Northridge; University of California, Berkeley; and California Lutheran University. Her California teaching credentials include a Lifetime Standard Credential, a Special Education Learning Handicapped Credential, and a Special Education Resource Specialist Credential. She has also held teaching credentials in Arizona and Florida.

She has taught for more than 25 years at the elementary, secondary, and university levels. While teaching at California Lutheran University, she taught Mainstreaming the Exceptional Student to teachers and students who were working toward their teaching credentials.

She founded WTHS, Dade County's educational broadcasting station in Miami, Florida, and she worked for 2 years as the program director. During this period, she coordinated all the educational programming.

During her teaching experience, she has worked with many children with many types of exceptionalities. As a resource specialist teacher, she taught students with learning disabilities in the Los Angeles Unified School District. She believes in a positive approach to learning, with emphasis on building self-esteem in all students.

1

What Educators Need to Know About the Law

Educators and parents need to be aware that individuals with disabilities have rights and protections that are guaranteed under the law. This brief overview of the law is by no means complete. Rather, it is intended to provide a basic understanding of the laws affecting children with disabilities and their families.

Before the 1970s, children with disabilities had no federally guaranteed legal right to a public education. Many persons with disabilities were excluded from public education or employment and often confined to institutions or kept at home. In some states, such as Alaska, laws provided for the exclusion from school of children who might have physical or mental incapacities. These laws were based on the belief that children with disabilities would not benefit from education and that their presence in school would have a detrimental effect on other students. We now know that these beliefs are erroneous. Laws have since been passed to give rights to and protect the rights of children with disabilities.

What the Law Provides

Although there are some differences between the laws, Section 504 of the Rehabilitation Act of 1973 and Pub. L. No. 94-142 (PL 94-142), more properly known as the Education for All Handicapped Children Act (EAHCA) of 1975 and subsequently renamed the Individuals with Disabilities Education Act (IDEA) in 1990, mandate that all children with disabilities are entitled to a free, appropriate public education in the "least restrictive environment" (LRE) in light of a student's educational needs. If a disability is so severe that a student's needs cannot be met in the regular education classroom even with the use of supplementary aids and services, a different, more restrictive placement must be considered (Alper, Schloss, Etscheidt, & Macfarlane, 1995).

Section 504 and the IDEA, although similar, do differ in some important ways. For example, the IDEA covers students ages 3 to 21. Section 504 covers students and school staff of all ages, including those who may not be covered under the IDEA. In addition, the IDEA does not limit the amount of money a school district must be required to spend to provide services. However, Section 504 does allow a school district to discontinue services if it determines such services to be too costly. The IDEA has provisions that school districts be reimbursed for a portion of their costs associated with special education, but Section 504 has no such funding provisions. Although Congress still lacks the constitutional power to directly regulate the public school systems, federal funding does give the government a degree of leverage in dictating educational policy. What is more, current laws require that a recipient of federal funds has an obligation not to discriminate against any adult or child who has a disability. Schools receiving this funding are required to prevent discrimination in the "school district's employment practices, access to school buildings and other facilities, and the design of new construction."

The stated purposes of the IDEA are to

> assure that all children with disabilities have available to them within the time periods specified . . . a free appropriate public education which emphasizes special education and related services designed to meet their unique needs; to assure that the rights of children with disabilities and their parents or guardians are protected; to assist States and localities to provide for the education of all children with disabilities; and to assess and assure the effectiveness of efforts to educate children with disabilities. (20 U.S.C. § 1400[c])

The IDEA provides for procedures to ensure that individuals with exceptional needs are given opportunities to interact to the "maximum extent" possible in the LRE with children without disabilities, unless the severity of the disability is such as to preclude such an arrangement. Thus, if a child, even with support, has a disability that prevents attendance within the regular school program, a free, appropriate public education that still includes special education and related services for the child must be arranged. Related services are defined as

> transportation, and such developmental, corrective, and other supportive services (including speech pathology and audiology, psychological services, physical and occupational therapy, recreation, including therapeutic recreation, social work services, counseling services, including rehabilitation counseling, and medical services, except that such medical services shall be for diagnostic and evaluation purposes only) as may be required to assist a child with a disability to benefit from special education, and includes the early identification and assessment of disabling conditions in children. (20 U.S.C. § 1401[a]17)

Procedural safeguards in the IDEA expanded on the safeguards already adopted by Congress as part of the Education Amendments of 1974. Moreover, state and local school districts must adopt procedures that guarantee parents' rights. These include rights to "(a) inspect all the educational records of the child, (b) obtain an independent educational evaluation of the child, (c) obtain prior notice of their rights, (d) file complaints and have them resolved by an impartial due process hearing, and (e) have a State review of the hearing held at the local level" (Johnson, 1986, p. 40).

Alper et al. (1995) clearly summarize the major implications of IDEA and other federal laws that dictate how learners with disabilities are identified, assessed, placed, and taught:

1. Special education services suitable to the needs of the disabled student must be provided at no cost to the student or family.

2. Parents must receive written notification prior to the school's conducting a case study evaluation that may determine eligibility for special education services.

3. Individualized, comprehensive, and nondiscriminatory assessment must be provided for the purpose of identifying the learner's unique characteristics and needs.

4. An individualized education program (IEP) must be developed annually for students with disabilities. The IEP must contain a statement of current performance levels, annual goals, and short-term objectives, specific services to be provided, extent of participation in regular education settings, projected date for initiation of services, expected duration of services, objective criteria, and evaluation procedures.

5. An individualized family service plan (IFSP) must be provided to children with disabilities who are 3 to 5 years of age. The IFSP must contain the child's current performance levels, family strengths and weaknesses, anticipated outcomes, necessary services, time lines for initiating and completing services, the name of the service manager, and methods for transitioning the child to appropriate services.

6. An individual transition plan (ITP) must be included with the IEPs of adolescents and young adults. The ITP is developed with the assistance of community-based vocational rehabilitation personnel. It complements the IEP by adding skills and services needed to support the transition from school to work.

7. Beyond specific educational services, students with disabilities are entitled to receive necessary related services. These include developmental, corrective, and other support services needed for the child or youth to benefit fully from the educational program. They may include transportation, counseling, medical evaluation, and physical, occupational, and recreation therapy.

8. Educational services must be provided in the least restrictive setting appropriate to the student's educational needs.

9. Finally, parents and guardians are entitled to due process when disputes regarding the appropriateness of the educational program occur. (pp. 8–9)

The IDEA Amendments of 1997 strengthened parents' roles. The amendments require that parents of children with disabilities are included on the individualized education program (IEP) team and given opportunities to become active participants in the education of their children. Previously, no requirement existed for reporting to the parents of children with disabilities as to the progress of their children. IDEA 1997 requires schools to report progress, or lack of progress, as often as reports are given to parents of children without disabilities.

Emphasis is placed on providing children with disabilities meaningful access to the general curriculum to the maximum extent possible. Supplementary aids and support services are to be made available to assist and support their participation in the general education curriculum. In cases in which a student is a nonparticipant, an explanation is required to be stated on the IEP document as to why and how the disability of the student affects actual participation in the general education program or extracurricular activities.

Before the passage of the IDEA Amendments of 1997, no requirement existed for students with disabilities to participate in state and district assessments. Students with disabilities are now required to meet the same standards and assessments as students without disabilities. If this is not an appropriate expectation for a particular student with disabilities, it must be stated on the IEP as to how the disability would affect a student's performance. In this regard, special accommodations can be taken into consideration for the assessment process, such as cognitive abilities, behavior, language needs, communicative needs, use of Braille, and the need for assistive technology. If accommodations are going to be used for testing, they must be stated on the IEP. Suggested testing accommodations are shown in Table 1.1.

Although it is not required, a 3-year evaluation meeting can be called to serve the best interests of a child with a disability. It is not necessary to wait for 3 years, but changes can be made during the school year to best serve the student's needs without formal testing. Parents and guardians are involved and informed as to why the changes may be needed.

Table 1.1 Advisory on Inclusion of Students

Flexible Scheduling	
Extension of Time	May use the entire testing window if needed
Testing Duration	Specify the amount of time a student will work without a break, for example, 30-minute blocks of time
Successive Administration	Administer the test or section over two or more testing sessions
Multiple Days	Administer the test or section over several days
Flexible Setting	
Individual Administration	Administer tests individually and in separate locations
Small-Group Administration	Administer tests to small groups of students in separate locations
Adaptive or Special Equipment Test Setting	Provide special lighting in regular test setting
Adaptive or Special Equipment in Separate Test Location	Provide special acoustics, minimize noise, etc.
Revised Test Format	
Braille Editions or Transcriptions	Provide Braille materials
Large-Print Editions	Provide large-print editions
Changes in Presentation Questions/Items	Increase spacing between test items, reduce number of items on a page
Changes in Space for Answers/ Vertical Format, etc.	Increase size of answer bubbles or blocks; arrange items in multiple choice

(Continued)

Table 1.1   (Continued)

Revised Test Directions	
Rewriting or Reformatting	Simplify language in directions; provide additional examples or cues such as arrows on answer form
Emphasizing Key Words/Directions	Highlight or underline key words or verbs in instructions
Reading Standard Directions	Read directions to student; reread directions for each page
Use of Aids and/or Classroom Assistants to Interpret the Test Items	
Special Equipment	Use of magnification, auditory amplification, auditory tape of the test, "masking" of test protocol, use of markers to maintain place
Proctor/Reader	Repeat oral comprehension items more than in standard test demonstration, read or sign test passage (if not a test of reading comprehension), questions, items, and multiple-choice responses to student. Cue on-task behavior
Equipment to Record	Use tape recorders, typewriters, word processors, pointers, communication
Responses	Boards, adaptive writing devices

SOURCE: California Department of Education.

The importance of transition plans has always been addressed in the IDEA. Since 1990 ITPs were a requirement of IDEA for students who were 16 years or older, but with the reauthorization of IDEA in 1997, a statement of transition service needs is now required at age 14 for students with disabilities. The 1997 Amendments state, "The purpose of the requirement is to focus attention on how the child's educational program can be planned to help the child make a successful transition to his or her goals for life after secondary school" (H. Rep. No. 105-95 [1997], pp. 101–102; S. Rep. No. 105-17 [1997], p. 22).

Typically, members of the IEP team handle the development of an ITP for a student with disabilities. The student and his or her family are the core members of the team. Other members on the IEP team include transition specialists who are well informed about resources and adult services in the community, related services support personnel, and representatives of any outside agency assisting the student.

The purpose of the team is to discuss the transition needs of the student to develop goals and activities that will provide a successful transition from secondary education to adulthood. Working collaboratively, the team draws on the expertise and knowledge of the different members to make recommendations and decisions for the student. The linguistics of the parents are taken into consideration, and if their language is other than English, an interpreter is provided. The parents can also request a written translation of the IEP document.

Beginning at age 14, the team examines the student's course of study to determine whether the coursework is educationally preparing the student for the transition. At this time, the team may consider other courses that might be more relevant for the student's goals in life. At age 16, or younger if appropriate, an important facet in the ITP is a consideration of the student's preferences and interests. The student's service needs, educational experiences, and interagency linkages are addressed. Emphasis is placed on postschool education, vocational training, and employment. When the student with disabilities is nearing graduation or culmination, the team arranges for the student to have actual links with the community or workplace. If appropriate, daily living skills are also addressed. The ITP is a legal document and is reviewed annually, or as needed, to address the changing needs of the student.

When a student with disabilities has reached the age of majority, as stated under state law, IDEA 1997 has outlined procedures for the transfer of parental rights to the student who must receive this notification at least one year before reaching the age of maturity. Parents are also given this notification of any transfer of rights. This notification must be noted on the student's IEP. If a student has been determined to be incompetent, the rights remain with the parents. In some cases, students may not have been determined by law to be incompetent but still do not have the ability or competence to give consent with respect to their educational program. Their transfer of rights is still protected under IDEA 1997. For these students, states are required to establish procedures for appointing parents or other individuals to represent the students' educational interests.

Discipline and Students With Disabilities

One of the most frequently misunderstood areas that educators face when dealing with students with disabilities is discipline. Consistent with the U.S. Supreme Court's ruling in *Honig v. Doe* (1988), a school district may not unilaterally change the placement of a child with a disability for misbehavior that is a manifestation of that student's disability. At issue in *Honig* was a situation in which a school district suspended two children with disabilities for more than 10 days—an action that violated the so-called "stay put" provision of the IDEA. This means that although a school district may discipline children with disabilities who present dangers to themselves or others, any exclusion from school for more than 10 days violates the heart of the IDEA.

Properly understood, however, this does not leave school officials help-less. Rather, it means that educators must first consult with parents and seek to amend a child's IEP to find a more appropriate, and often more restrictive, placement before removing a child with a disability who misbehaves from the classroom (*Honig v. Doe*, 484 U.S. 305 [1988]).

The reauthorization of IDEA 1997 addresses the serious concerns of teachers and school administrators regarding the issue of disci-pline of students with disabilities while at the same time preserving school safety. The changes in IDEA gives school districts increased flexibility to maintain a safe learning environment for all students as well as to protect the rights of students with disabilities. This amend-ment provides for due process hearings so that the rights of students with disabilities are protected.

If the IEP team determines that the student's misconduct was not a manifestation of the student's disability, the student is subject to the same disciplinary actions as are applied to students without disabili-ties. Short-term removals for misconduct are permitted to the same extent as are applied to students without disabilities. Overall, if the misconduct is of a less serious nature, a student with disabilities can be removed from that student's current placement multiple times for 10 consecutive days or less for separate incidents of misconduct. The 1997 IDEA gives school officials the right to remove a student with a disability from that student's current placement for up to 10 days without the parents' consent (§ 300.520[a][1]).

There are no specific limits on the number of days a student with disabilities can be removed from that student's current placement. If a student is removed for more than 10 cumulative days in a year, however, services must be provided to continue that student's prog-ress in attaining the goals of the IEP and the education curriculum (§ 300.524). It is the responsibility of the special education teacher of the child and school personnel to determine the extent and if services may be needed for the student (§ 300.121[d]).

If the removal constitutes a pattern of removals culminating in more than 10 days in a school year, a change of placement for a stu-dent with disabilities may be indicated. Factors such as "the length of the removal, the total amount of time the child is removed, and the proximity of the removals to one another" (§ 300.519) are taken into consideration. The IEP team determines what interim alternative educational setting may be needed. If a student is placed in an alter-native setting, the goals, services, and modifications stated in that student's IEP are continued.

The amendment to IDEA allows a school district to protect teachers and students from a dangerous student, even if the student is classified as a student with a disability. The amendment provides that a local educational agency may place a student with a disability in an alternative educational setting for up to 45 days for conduct that poses a serious danger to the safety of other students or school personnel.

If a student has brought a weapon to school, possessed or used drugs, or solicited the sale of controlled substances while at school or at a school function (§ 300.520[a][2]), school authorities are allowed to remove the student from that student's regular placement for up to 45 days at a time. This does not require the parents' consent, even though they may disagree to a disciplinary change of placement for their child.

At the end of the 45-day placement, if school officials feel that the child would still be a threat if returned to that child's regular placement, another request to extend the time for up to an additional 45 days can be made to an impartial hearing officer (§ 300.521). School officials can also seek to obtain a court order to remove a student from that student's regular placement to protect the right to have a safe learning environment for all students and teachers.

This amendment provides for due process hearings so that the rights of students with disabilities are protected. At the same time, it enables school districts to remove violent students, even if they have disabilities, so that teachers and other students are protected (Amendment to Education for All Handicapped Children Act, 20 U.S.C., § 1415 [e]).

IDEA 2004 Reauthorization

The IDEA has been updated about every 5 years. The reason for updating the law after a period of time is to provide enough time to see how the law actually works out in practice. If changes in the law are necessary to achieve the purpose of IDEA, the law can be amended and revised.

On December 3, 2004, President George W. Bush signed IDEA 2004 (PL 108-446) and stated, "All students in America can learn. That's what all of us up here believe. All of us understand we have an obligation to make sure no child is left behind in America. So I'm honored to sign the Individuals with Disabilities Education Improvement Act of 2004, and once again thank the members for being here."

IDEA 2004 continued the policy of LRE or mainstreaming requiring school districts to educate students with disabilities, including children in public or private institutions or other care facilities, with their nondisabled peers to the maximum extent appropriate. The purpose of mainstreaming is to prevent schools from segregating students with disabilities from the general education students. At this time, the term *inclusion* was not used in IDEA.

Special classes, separate schooling, or other removal of children with disabilities from the regular educational environment occurs only if the nature or severity of the disability is such that education in regular classes with the use of supplementary aids and services cannot be achieved satisfactorily.

A few of the new changes follows but these changes do not reflect the many changes in the new Individuals with Disabilities Education Improvement Act. Previously, schools have been required to wait until a child fell considerably below grade level before becoming eligible for special education services. This requirement changed with the new law. School districts are no longer required to follow the discrepancy regulation, but are given more leeway in the identification of children with disabilities. Determining if a child has a learning disability is to be based on a child's response to scientific research-based interventions. Educators cannot rely on a single procedure to determine if a child is eligible for special education services.

Other changes were made in the Individuals with Disabilities Education Improvement Act. In grades K–12, children who had not been identified as needing special education services, but who are in need of intervening support to succeed in general education classes, can receive this support. This eliminates the need for a formal identification and allows the child to receive behavioral and academic support. School districts are allowed to use 15% of the federal money granted for these services.

This act also addresses the need for making IEPs more relevant to student progress. The long-term goals are required to be measurable and functional. There is no longer a requirement to have the short-term objectives addressed on the IEP. There is, however, an exception to this requirement. Schools must provide short-term objectives for students with significant disabilities, which represents only a small percentage—less than one percent—as stated in the Individuals with Disabilities Education Improvement Act.

The students with significant disabilities will be able to have alternate achievement standards. When an alternate assessment is deemed necessary for a student, it must be stated in their IEP, including why alternate assessment is needed and why a particular assessment is chosen for the student.

Previously, transition was addressed at age 14. The Individuals with Disabilities Education Improvement Act increased the age to 16 to address transition. The law also states, however, that transition can be addressed earlier than age 16 if necessary.

When minor changes are deemed necessary for a student with disabilities, there is greater flexibility. Changes can be made to the IEP without reconvening the IEP team. Parents and school professionals can make minor changes to the IEP of a student with disabilities giving additional flexibility to all concerned. The Individuals with Disabilities Education Improvement Act also increases the parental involvement in the IEP process. They can now use teleconferencing, videoconferencing, and other alternative means for participation in the IEP process.

Early intervention for infants and toddlers is stressed. When there is a need, intervention referrals are to be made. Infants and toddlers who are abused, drug exposed, neglected, or have suffered family violence will need intervention.

The law requirements that "highly qualified" teachers should teach special education students became effective immediately upon President Bush's signature.

Only a few of the changes made in the new Individuals with Disabilities Education Improvement Act have been addressed, but there are many. These changes and amendments can be found on the official U.S. government Web site: http://idea.ed.gov. A print version of the Individuals with Disabilities Education Improvement Act can be ordered on the following Web site: http://www.gpoaccess.gov.

U.S. Secretary of Education Rod Paige expressed the importance of this law upon the approval of a House–Senate conference committee of legislation to reauthorize IDEA. Secretary Paige stated, "This is a giant step toward promoting educational excellence for America's 6.8 million children and youth with disabilities."

No Child Left Behind

The No Child Left Behind (NCLB) Act of 2001 reauthorized the Elementary and Secondary Education Act (ESEA) of 1965, which was the federal law affecting education from kindergarten to high school. The ESEA was to help educate disadvantaged children, but 40 years later, only 32% of fourth graders could read at grade level. Many minority children and those who lived in poverty made up the remaining 68% who cannot read well. Congress added benchmarks, measurements, and sanctions to ESEA and renamed it the NCLB. President Bush signed it on January 8, 2002. Now NCLB is up for reauthorization, which was scheduled for November 2007. Since it was deemed necessary to improve the scope of the law, Congress introduced and passed the Higher Education Extension Act of 2007 in order to provide time to make changes in the act. The Higher Education Extension Act of 2007 was signed into law. It will keep NCLB on the books up through April 30, 2008, allowing additional time to address the concerns about NCLB.

Since reauthorization of NCLB is forthcoming, only a few of the changes made will be addressed here. Briefly, schools are accountable for adequate yearly progress (AYP) toward meeting state proficiency goals. It is a standards-based education reform, which was formerly known as outcome-based education. This reform is based on high expectations and setting of goals and requires states to develop criterion-based assessments in certain grades. If a school does not attain these proficiency goals, over time the school will be subject to improvement, corrective action, and restructuring measures. Schools that meet these goals are eligible for State Academic Achievement Awards.

If students attend a school that does not meet state minimum achievement standards for 2 or 3 years, the school must offer the student choices. These include transferring to a higher performing local school, receiving free tutoring, or attending afterschool programs.

Parents of students in schools failing to meet AYP goals must be given detailed report cards on their child with explanations on the AYP performance. The parents also need to be informed if their student is being taught by a paraprofessional teacher who does not meet the "highly qualified" requirements. A teacher who is "highly qualified" has fulfilled the state's certification and licensure requirements.

Another change that should be mentioned concerns support for state and local efforts to keep our schools safe and drug free. It ensures that students who have been victims of school violence on school grounds or students who are in a persistently dangerous school will be allowed to transfer to a safe school. Schools are also required to report school safety statistics on a school-by-school basis.

Local education agencies (LEAs) must use Federal Safe and Drug-Free Schools and Communities funding to implement drug and violence prevention programs.

Postsecondary Transition

Postsecondary transition presents many problems and is fraught with concern for all who are entering adult life. It is especially difficult for children with disabilities. IDEA regulations, however, relieve them of many concerns and help make the transition smoother. If a student drops out or ages out of school, the law has no absolute guarantee that they will continue to receive services.

In IDEA, the term *transition services* means a coordinated set of activities that is designed to be within a results-oriented process for a child with a disability—that is, focused on improving the academic and functional achievement of the child with a disability to facilitate the child's movement from school to postschool activities, including postsecondary education, vocational education, integrated employment (including supported employment), continuing and adult education, adult services, and independent living or community participation and is based on the individual child's needs, taking into account the child's strengths, preferences, and interests.

An evaluation is not required before the termination of a child's eligibility if it is due to graduation from a secondary school with a regular high school diploma or if the child exceeds the age of eligibility. If this is the case, the LEA must provide the child with a summary of his or her academic achievement and functional performance, including recommendations on how to assist the child in meeting postsecondary goals.

Children who are receiving special education services must have transition goals in their IEPs starting at age 16 or earlier if needed. Postsecondary goals must address transition services beginning no later than the first IEP to be in effect when the child reaches 16 or earlier and should be based upon transition assessments, training education, employment, independent living skills, if appropriate, and transition services needed to reach the goals.

Transition services include the following:

1. Transition services means a coordinated set of activities for a child with a disability that is designed to be within a results-oriented process that is focused on improving the academic and functional achievement of the child with a disability to facilitate the child's movement from school to postschool activities including postsecondary education, vocational education, integrated employment (including supported employment),

community and adult education, adult services, independent living, or community participation.

2. [It i]s based on the individual child's needs, taking into account the child's strengths, preferences, and interests. (20 U.S.C. § 1401)

To make a successful transition from high school, various options should be addressed. The Virginia State Department of Education listed a few of the options, such as "community colleges, four-year colleges, on-the-job training, apprenticeships, military service, adult education, technical schools, and independent living skills. Assisting in helping a student make satisfactory correct decisions is essential for the transition from high school to adult life."

Many who have disabilities plan to continue their education into college. Their rights are protected from discrimination by Section 504 and Title I. A postsecondary school is required to provide appropriate adjustments, and if the school provides housing for students who are not disabled, it must also provide convenient housing for students with disabilities at the same cost. If the requirements for admission to a college are met, there can be no discrimination because of a disability. It is not necessary for a student to inform the school of having a disability unless there is a need for accessible facilities. The disclosure of having a disability is always voluntary.

Academic adjustments in college are determined by the disability and individual needs. These adjustments may include auxiliary aids and modifications to academic requirements. Examples of this are reduction of academic course load, electronic devices, sign language interpreters, and computers with screen reading, voice recognition, or other devices to assist a student with a disability. The postsecondary school does not have to provide personal attendants, individually prescribed devices, or tutoring. To receive this additional help, it is necessary for a student to inform the school of the disability. The request for an academic adjustment can be made at any time, but it is best if it is requested as early as possible. If the academic adjustments are not working, it is important that the student notify the school as soon as possible to make a satisfactory college experience.

The Collaborative Team

Educating students with disabilities is a shared, collaborative team effort. Depending on the student's IEP and personal needs, the team may include a special education teacher, regular education teacher, school nurse or other health care professional, school psychologist, social worker, speech pathologist, physical therapist, occupational therapist, other professionals and consultants, building principal, and parents. The regular classroom teacher may call on one or more of these individuals for information and assistance, as needed.

The team membership for both elementary and secondary schools is generally the same. This team is commonly referred to as a Student Success Team (SST), but individual school districts often use many different titles for the team. Regardless of the title given to the team, their purpose remains the same—to help students achieve.

Teachers can make a referral to the SST for support and assistance with students who are experiencing difficulties in areas of academics, behavior, attendance, or other school-related issues. Because referrals to the SST are not referrals for special education services, the team is not subject to the restrictions and time lines of special education. Before a student is referred to the SST, documented interventions and modifications for the student need to have been incorporated in the general education class.

When a referral is made to the SST, a meeting is scheduled to address the concerns and needs of the student. The collaborative efforts of the team identify the student's strengths, weaknesses, and results of the modifications already attempted. Based on the team's discussion, a plan of action is developed along with systematic monitoring of the student's progress. A follow-up meeting is scheduled to review and evaluate the results of the plan. The team's responsibility is to differentiate between those students whose needs can be met in the general education program with further modifications and those students who may need a referral for special education assessment under IDEA. See the Process Flow Chart (Figure 1.1).

Some students may not meet the eligibility requirements for special education services under IDEA, but they may have a disability that requires accommodations within the regular education program. Individuals between the ages of 3 and 21 who meet the requirements under Section 504 may qualify for services. The U.S. Department of Education Regulation (34 C.F.R. § 104.3[j]) states that eligibility for services under Section 504 is an "individual with a disability" who

1. has a physical or mental impairment which substantially limits one or more major life activities;

2. has a record of such disability; or

3. is regarded as having such a disability.

If a disability does not substantially limit a major life activity (i.e., caring for oneself, walking, hearing, seeing, learning, breathing, performing manual tasks, working, etc.), the individual is not considered disabled.

A referral is given to a Section 504 team composed of members similar to that of the SST. The Section 504 team reviews the nature of the disability and how it affects the student's education. The team members evaluate the student's attendance, relevant medical records, and cumulative records as well as the documents and records provided by the parents. Determination is made as to the accommodations needed by the student to reach that student's potential in the general education program. All pertinent information and decisions made by the team are required to be documented.

As stated in Section 504 of the Rehabilitation Act of 1973, "No otherwise qualified individual with a disability, shall solely by reason of her or his handicap, be excluded from participation, be denied the benefits of, or be subjected to discrimination under any program activity receiving Federal financial assistance" (29 U.S.C. § 794[a], 1973).

A student with a disability may be placed in a regular classroom on a part-time or a full-time basis, with consultative or other assistance provided by special educators. The curriculum for a student with a disability may parallel the regular curriculum, but the regular teacher will need to modify teaching techniques and pace, course content, and evaluation methods to fit the student's special learning needs. Special educators can provide guidance to regular teachers on strategies to use with students with special needs (Alper et al., 1995).

Figure 1.1   Process Flow Chart

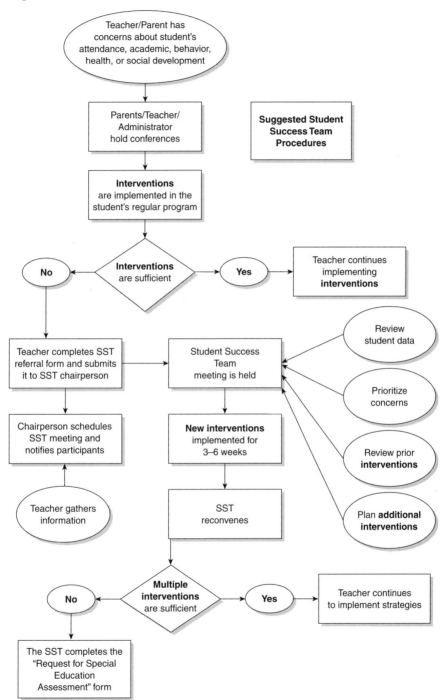

SOURCE: California Department of Education.

For Further Information

Books

Buzzeo, T. *Collaborating to meet standards: Teacher/librarian partnerships for K-6.*

Buzzeo, T. *Collaborating to meet literacy standards: Teacher/librarian partnerships for K-2.*

Cramer, S. F. *Special educator's guide to collaboration.*

Demchak, M. A., & Greenfield, R. G. *Transition portfolios for students with disabilities.*

Kimmelman, P. *Implementing NCLB.*

Levinson, E. M. (Ed.). *Transition from school to post-school life for individuals with disabilities.*

Miller, R. J., Lombard, R. C., & Corbey, S. A. *Transition assessment: Planning transition and IEP development for youths with mild to moderate disabilities.*

Smith, D. D. *Introduction to special education: Making a difference.*

Smith, D. D *Introduction to special education: Teaching in the age of opportunity, IDEA 2004.*

Sunderman, G. L., Kim, J. S., & Orfield, G. G. *NCLB meets school realities: Lessons from the field.*

Turnbull, H. R., Turnbull, A. P., Stowe, M., Wilcox, B. L., & Turnbull, H. R., III, *Free appropriate public education.*

Wilmshurst, L., & Brue, A. W. *A parent's guide to special education.*

Wright, P. W. D., & Wright, P. D. *Wrightslaw: Special education law.*

Wright, P. W. D., Wright, P. D., & Heath, S. W. *Wrightslaw: No child left behind.*

Yell, M. L. *The law and special education.*

Ysseldyke, J., Algozzine, B., & Thurlow, M. L. *Critical issues in special education.*

Organizations and Agencies

Council for Exceptional Children (CEC)
1110 N. Glebe Road
Arlington, VA 22201-5704
800-328-0272
E-mail: cecpubs@cec.sped.org
http://www.sped.org

National Center on Secondary Education and Transition
Institute on Community Integration
6 Pattee Hall
150 Pillsbury Drive SE
Minneapolis, MN 55455
612-624-2097
Fax: 612-624-9344
E-mail: ncset@umn.edu
http://www.ncset.org

The National Early Childhood Technical Assistance Center
Campus Box 8040, UNC-CH
Chapel Hill, NC 27599-8040
919-962-2001
TDD: 919-843-3269
Fax: 919-966-7463
E-mail: nectac@unc.edu
http://www.nectac.org

U.S. Department of Education
400 Maryland Avenue SW
Washington, DC 20202
800-USA-LEARN (800-872-5327)
http://www.ed.gov/offices/OSERS/IDEA

2

How Teachers
Can Create a
Positive Learning
Environment

Whenever feasible, students with disabilities should be placed in the least restrictive environment (LRE):

> To the maximum extent appropriate, children with disabilities, including children in public or private institutions or other care facilities, are educated with children who are nondisabled, and that special classes, separate schooling or other removal of children with disabilities from the educational environment occurs only when the nature or severity of the disabilities is such that education in general education classes with the use of supplementary aides and services cannot be achieved satisfactorily. (IDEA, 34 C.F.R., § 300.550; 20 U.S.C. 1412[5][B], 1414[a][1][c][iv])

In keeping with the law, a student with disabilities who is primarily educated in a self-contained special education class can be mainstreamed for specific subjects and activities in the general education programs. This is in conjunction with that student's placement in the special education class and has to be addressed on that student's individual education plan (IEP). Mainstreaming is not necessarily for all students with disabilities. Although there are students with disabilities who could benefit from participating in the learning environment of general education classes, there are also students with severe disabilities who need a self-contained class to meet their educational and physical needs.

The student who is being mainstreamed has opportunities to interact with that student's chronologically age-appropriate peers without disabilities. Being able to participate in academic, nonacademic, and extracurricular activities can have a positive influence on the student's social development and reduce feelings of isolation inherent in a special education self-contained class.

The option of mainstreaming a student with disabilities requires parental approval and willingness of the student to be mainstreamed. If a student is being mainstreamed, it is noted on the IEP. Careful planning and preparation by the special education teacher and the support service providers of the student being mainstreamed is essential. Their ongoing responsibility for the student remains the same. Inclusion or mainstreaming for specific classes requires open communication between the parents or guardians, teachers, and support personnel if the experience is to be successful.

In contrast to mainstreaming, inclusion generally refers to the placement of students with disabilities in the same general education classroom that they would attend if they did not have disabilities. IDEA does not use the term *inclusion*. Consequently, the Department of Education has not defined the term and, as such, the interpretation of inclusion practices is continually evolving. Usually, inclusion of a student with disabilities in the general education class is a service delivery option for students with disabilities in the context of the regular education setting. Inclusion requires bringing the appropriate support services and supplementary aids to the student with disabilities in the regular education environment and is so stated on the IEP.

Advocates of inclusion feel that all students with disabilities, regardless of their handicap, should be placed in regular general education classrooms where support services are brought to the students in that setting. Unfortunately, some supportive services are not always available in every school.

Proponents of inclusion feel that students placed in a separate class are denied the opportunity to interact with students without disabilities and that being in separate classrooms only emphasizes the differences between students. Inclusive settings also enable students to learn about the complexity and diversity of human characteristics and that shared traits and needs exceed differences (Alper et al., 1995). Appreciating the many similarities and interests between the students with disabilities and their peers without disabilities often leads to lasting friendships.

A student's placement must be individually determined as to whether placement in a regular education class best meets the unique needs of the student or if a more restrictive environment is indicated. All placement options are to be considered and based on a well-developed IEP. Whatever the placement, the student's individual educational needs and a continuum of services are required if a student is to reach his or her individual potential.

Creating an Inclusive Environment

The educational environment has a tremendous influence on students with disabilities, as well as students without disabilities. In the process of including students with disabilities in the regular education classroom, the teacher must convey positive feelings and a caring attitude toward them. The attitudes of the teacher are quickly picked up and emulated by other students. Creating a positive and comfortable environment is essential if the educational experience is to be successful and rewarding for all students.

The language one uses in referring to a student with a disability can impart negative attitudes toward the student and hinder the development of self-esteem. The teacher must avoid any language that has a negative connotation. For example, two very commonly used words are *afflicted* and *unfortunate. Afflicted* is very negative because it suggests the person has been singled out or cursed, and *unfortunate* implies that the person with a disability is unlucky or to be pitied. Other words considered inappropriate and to be avoided include *handicapped, crippled, deformed, diseased, burdensome, spastic, incapacitated,* and *disadvantaged.*

Arranging for a student who has been in a restrictive setting to enter into a less restrictive setting requires advance preparation on the part of teachers and others involved. It must be a cooperative effort by all. A conference of the administrators and all educators who are responsible for the education of a student with a disability is essential to provide properly for the inclusion of the child in the regular classroom. The regular education teacher should also be provided with information regarding the present skills and objectives of the student along with that student's strengths and weaknesses. All education personnel who are responsible for the physical and educational needs of a student must share the responsibility for meeting those needs.

Educators need to learn about the disabling condition of a student placed in a regular classroom. The special education teacher can provide much of that information. The general education teacher should also check the student's medical and other school records. This information will guide the teacher in making appropriate modifications to the room environment and in using strategies that will best fit the educational and physical needs of the student.

The furniture and equipment of the room may need to be changed to accommodate students with disabilities. It is helpful if students with disabilities have an opportunity to become familiar with the room environment without other students being present. Prior orientation to the room will help the students to adjust and to feel comfortable and secure in the room.

Depending on the particular disability, the special education teacher can work with the regular teacher to ensure that all needed assistance devices are available for the student. These might include rubber thumbs to turn pages, pencil grips, large-type texts, or other devices that are currently available. Many professionals are available to assist the regular teacher. The teacher should check on supportive personnel services that are available. For example, psychologists, interpreters, tutors, and aides are generally available at the school site or through the district office to help the teacher. Many organizations dedicated to helping students with disabilities can also provide assistance to the teacher. (See Resource B for the list of public agencies.)

Teaching Students About Disabilities

Students without disabilities should be given accurate information, in advance, about the disability of a student who is being placed in their class. The teacher, although mindful of the need for privacy, should provide enough background information about the disability to allay any fears or misconceptions the other students may have. Students need to be made aware of the strengths of the student with disabilities as well as that student's limitations. Having general education students participate in simulated disabling activities gives them an opportunity to better understand the problems faced by the student who has a disability. Students should also be given the opportunity to learn about people with disabilities who have achieved success. Many books, films, and other audiovisual materials about people who have overcome their disabilities are available.

Positive interaction between students without disabilities and students with disabilities depends on the teacher's attitude and ability to promote a positive environment. One way of achieving this is by using cooperative learning to facilitate small-group interaction. A supportive atmosphere is created when everyone is cooperating to achieve group goals and is primarily concerned with the success of the group as a whole. When working together cooperatively, students tend to give more praise, encouragement, and support to students with disabilities. These positive experiences provide an opportunity for social and emotional growth for everyone involved.

Including Parents and Guardians

Parents and guardians also have to be involved if their child is to have a rewarding experience. The teacher, before placing a child with a disability in a general education class, should invite the parents or guardians to visit the class and confer about their child. It is important to open the lines of communication. Thereafter, the general education teacher needs to communicate with the parents or guardians on a regular basis to keep them informed of the student's progress, homework and daily assignments, and any future projects that are planned. Parental or guardian involvement in the educational process and the special assistance given to the student with a disability will contribute to the student's academic success. On occasion, a teacher may offer guidance to parents or guardians on ways to help their children. For example, a teacher may tactfully encourage parents or guardians to outwardly show their affection and support for their child as that child embarks on a new experience or achieves a new goal.

A student with a disability has the same basic needs as a student without a disability. Stressing the similarities is essential if positive interactions among all students are to be achieved. To grow emotionally and socially, students with disabilities need the support and acceptance of their peers, their teachers, and their parents or guardians.

For Further Information

Books

Biklin, D., Ferguson, D., & Ford, A. *Schooling and disability (Pt. 2): Eighty-eighth yearbook of the National Society for the Study of Education.*
Clutterbuck, P. *Bright ideas for managing the positive classroom.*

Cowley, S. *You can create a calm classroom for ages 7–11.*

Giangreco, M. F., Cloniger, C. J., & Iverson, V. S. *Choosing outcomes and accommodations for children.*

Goodlad, J. I., & Lovitt, T. C. (Eds.). *Integrating general and special education.*

Pearpoint, J., Forest, M., & Snow, J. *The inclusion papers: Strategies to make inclusion work.*

Salend, S. J. *Effective mainstreaming: Creating inclusive classrooms.*

Williams, R. B. *36 tools for building spirit in learning communities.*

Organizations and Agencies

California Department of Education
Positive Environments, Network Trainers
Diagnostic Center
4339 State University Drive
Los Angeles, CA 90032

Council for Exceptional Children
1110 North Glebe Road, Suite 300
Arlington, VA 22201
888-232-7733
TTY: 866-915-5000
Fax: 703-264-9494
www.cec.sped.org

National Dissemination Center for Children
    with Disabilities (NICHCY)
P.O. Box 1492
Washington, DC 20013-1492
800-695-0285
E-mail: nichcy@aed.org
www.nichcy.org

National Professional Resources, Inc.
25 South Regent Street
Port Chester, NY 10573
800-453-7461 (USA and Canada)
914-937-8879 (other areas)
Fax: 914-937-9327
E-mail: service@nprinc.com
www.nprinc.com

National Technical Assistance Center
Positive Behavioral Interventions and Support
1235 University of Oregon
Eugene, OR 97403-1235
541-346-2505
Fax: 541-346-5517
www.pbis.org

3

Understanding the Parents of Exceptional Children

Parents of exceptional children are confronted with numerous challenges and many difficult situations that other parents never have to experience. The child with a disability—especially a severe disability—may have a profound effect on the family, and the interactions can often lead to great anxiety and frustration. Undue strain may be placed on the family structure. Relationships may either grow stronger or disintegrate because of the considerable stress of coping with the unanticipated obligations. Some parents are able to realistically and successfully adapt, whereas others are less prepared to accept the challenge of having a child with a disability in the family.

To effectively communicate with parents of children with disabilities, a teacher must be aware of the wide spectrum of emotions parents go through when they discover that their child has a disability. This myriad of emotions affects the behavior of both the parents and child. It has a direct influence on the dynamics of the total family unit. Not only must the parents deal with the inherent obligations of parenting but also with the many responsibilities that are associated with a child with disabilities.

Parents of children with disabilities often go through certain stages of feelings. These stages include shock, denial, anger, resignation, and acceptance, followed by a return to a normalized life pattern. Inflexible emphasis on the stages a parent goes through can be misleading. Jennifer Simpson, a former policy associate in the national office of United Cerebral Palsy and the parent of a son with disabilities, states, "The course of your feelings is not like the linear model of this theory. I cycle through denial and anger periodically in new ways when I am confronted with a new aspect of my son's disability" (Simpson, 2000, p. 1). However, knowledge about the various stages can be helpful to the teacher in understanding the parents' feelings associated with having a child with disabilities.

Most parents envision having a perfect child. When a disability is diagnosed, there can be any number of natural reactions such as shock, disbelief, and even grief. The parents may experience an initial phase of numbness and disbelief that their child has a disability. The parents' anticipation of having a perfect child is destroyed, and the encompassing emotions can be overwhelming. These feelings may lead to inner concerns that they may have caused the child's disability. This can lead to feelings of worthlessness and the need to cope with these frustrations by developing defense mechanisms.

To avoid the reality of having a child with a disability, there may be complete denial. During this denial stage, parents attempt to change the reality by searching for professionals and others who will agree with them and offer easy resolutions.

However, if parents demonstrate denial about the disability, they may set goals that put unrealistic pressure on the child to achieve. The parents may enroll their child in extracurricular activities such as dance lessons and karate, in which the child may not be able to perform. Often, it is only when the child is older and is with peers that the disability becomes more obvious to the parents. As long as there is denial of the disabling condition, it is difficult for professionals to guide the parent. Therefore, it is important for educators to demonstrate sensitivity to the parents as well and help them establish attainable academic and social goals for the child with disabilities.

Parents sometimes have strong feelings of guilt, and often there is a manifestation of anger for their circumstance. Instead of outwardly expressing their anger, they use a displacement coping mechanism to shift the blame from themselves to others. This displacement relieves their feelings of guilt. They may blame doctors and other professionals, including teachers. It is important for teachers not to take such blame personally. The teacher needs to communicate to the parents that the teacher cares, is "on their side," and wants their child to reach his or her own individual potential. It is important for the teacher to understand that parents are often just trying to find a reason for their difficult situation. Educators must keep in mind that most parents are simply doing their best to raise their child.

In time, parents come to the stage of resignation that their child has a disability. There may be confusion, anxiety, and possibly hopelessness. Some parents may go into seclusion by avoiding all social encounters, thereby concealing their child with a disability. This is considered an abnormal isolation resulting in damage to the family unit.

During the stage of acceptance, parents finally begin to appreciate and help their child to strengthen that child's ability to cope with the disability. However, there is a tendency to overprotect the child with a disability more than the reality of the situation demands. Parents, as well as teachers, may feel a need to protect the child from any failure or rejection. The child is kept out of any competitive activity in which the disability may become obvious or in which there might be a chance of failure. Overprotection prevents the child from having any opportunity for problem solving and decision making and does not foster the child's independence or social and emotional development. If the child with a disability is to grow socially and emotionally, it is necessary for parents and teachers to understand that the disabled child needs less protection rather than more. Becoming less protective allows the child to become more self-reliant and self-assured. Even though the child with a disability may not always succeed in competitive events, that child often will feel successful in having tried if the focus is on achievement rather than on the disability. The child needs to be allowed to enter the mainstream of life whenever possible.

The final stage relates to the family unit and the ability to decrease the emotionalism when talking about a child with a disability. It is during this stage that parents can realistically discuss the options to provide opportunities for their child. This stage is also critical in the parents' need for social acceptance and understanding to progress and maintain their own social growth. The actions of people and professionals can make this stage of adjustment easy or difficult. If minimal acceptance and negative experiences are in the social climate, parents can regress back into the stage of anger. One must remember the following:

> It may be that many parents do respond in many ways that are well-described by the stage model. But it is dangerous to impose this model on all parents. Those who exhibit different response patterns might be inappropriately judged as deviant. Parents who do not progress through the stages might be considered slow to adjust. And those who exhibit emotions in a

different sequence might be thought of as regressing. (Allen & Affleck, 1985, p. 201)

The other children in the family often reflect the parental attitude toward the child with a disability. When parents show ongoing attention and love to all the children, there is less chance that the nondisabled siblings will feel neglected or resentful of the time the parent takes to care for the child with a disability.

When an older sibling needs to assume the role of caretaker, it often impinges on the time spent with that sibling's friends. Normal daily socialization with peers becomes impossible for that sibling. Having to assume the role as caretaker also causes concern about that sibling's own future adult life if he or she is required to continue the role as a caretaker when the parents may no longer be able to care for the child with a disability.

Siblings of the child with a disability are often concerned about the reaction of their friends. They have a fear of being rejected by their friends and of no longer being part of the peer group. Siblings often worry about how they are going to explain the disability of their brother or sister to their friends. In addition, older siblings are apprehensive about the possibility that any children they may have in the future may have the same disability.

Because of a lack of understanding, some may tease the child with disabilities. This presents another concern for siblings without disabilities as to how to stop the teasing and prevent further disputes. Both parent and teacher have an obligation to help ease the many different problems confronted by the sibling of a child with a disability and help to provide all with an accepting and secure environment.

Having a child with a disability puts stress on marital relationships. Ideally, each partner in a marriage has a specific role and responsibility in providing for the child with a disability. Unfortunately, this does not always occur. Often, one parent has to assume full responsibility, creating additional tensions in the family structure. This can lead to an outpouring of blame and accusations, with each partner blaming the other for being the cause of the disability. Marriages often falter, and tensions increase within the family members. The lifelong financial burden of providing for the child brings about continued stress. The time and energy spent on the child with disabilities puts a strain on marital relations. Sometimes, however, the stress brings families closer together by their mastery of the challenges of having a child with a disability. Many parents of children with disabilities grow to appreciate the special lessons and gifts their children contribute to their lives.

Unfortunately, many parents do not accept the fact that they, too, are entitled to normal lives. Even though their family life may be disrupted, there are many professionals and support groups that can help them to adjust. Parents can be guided throughout the various crises that might occur and learn how to accept the challenges of having a child with a disability. The positive environment of an intervention team of professionals and support groups can help improve their ability to confront and surmount these challenges.

Before teachers can genuinely assist parents through the process of adjustment, it is imperative to address one's own attitude toward children with disabilities. One must discard stereotypes and replace them with a respect for differences. The concern for the child with disabilities should be the primary focus.

It is essential that the teacher listens attentively to the parents. The parents know more about their child than the teacher, and this information will help in understanding the ramifications of a child's problems. The parents' views should be encouraged, as well as their questions. At the same time, teachers should readily admit that they do not have the information to answer a question satisfactorily but that they will attempt to find the information for the parent. Establishing credibility is necessary for any parent discussion.

Teachers should inform the parents of a child with a disability of the many resources and agencies available to help them. Families with a child who has a disability have special concerns, and parent groups can offer a place to share information, give emotional support, and work as a team to address these common concerns.

Every family unit and individual is unique, with individual characteristics and abilities. A positive and caring environment is essential for the family unit. Parents and teachers need to develop self-awareness in all children by focusing on the qualities, strengths, and talents that make them unique. If given the opportunity, every child with a disability can contribute to the family experience.

The National Dissemination Center for Children with Disabilities (NICHCY) is an information clearinghouse that provides information on disabilities and disability-related issues. Their special focus concerns children and youth with disabilities from birth to age 22. NICHCY compiled *A Parent's Guide: Accessing Parent Groups*. This guide helps parents identify the parent groups that exist nationally and in various states and communities. NICHCY also publishes listings of individual state resources that the parent can contact for help. The majority of these publications are free by writing to NICHCY, P.O. Box 1492, Washington, DC 20013-1492 or calling 1-800-695-0285.

Many people benefit from joining support groups. Resource B, pages 209–212, offers many agencies that can assist in providing the names of support groups in a particular location. Support groups can be of inestimable value to parents and guardians of children with disabilities.

For teachers and parents who have access to the Internet, the U.S. Department of Education has published the *Parent's Guide to the Internet* (2001). This booklet is of great value and lists many sites for parents, children, and references. Regardless of one's lack of technological understanding, this guide is written in easy-to-understand language. It can be obtained free from the U.S. Department of Education, Office of Educational Research and Improvement, Office of Educational Technology, Washington, DC 20202.

For Further Information

Books

Anderson, W., Chitwood, S., Hayden, D. *Negotiating the special education maze: A guide for parents and teachers.*

Batshaw, M. L. *When your child has a disability: The complete sourcebook of daily and medical care.*

Dunst, C., Trivette, C., Starnes, A., Hamby, D., & Gordon, N. *Building and evaluating family support initiatives.*

Gartner, A., Lipsky, D. K., & Turnbull, A. I. *Supporting families with a child with a disability.*

Gorman, J. C. *Working with challenging parents of students with special needs.*

Kroth, R., & Edge, D. *Strategies far communicating with parents of exceptional children.*

Lawrence, D., & Cook, L. *Supporting black pupils and parents.*

Paune, R. K. *Working with parents.*

Powell, T., & Gallagher, P. *Brothers and sisters.*

Rudhey, G. *Every teacher's guide to working with parents.*

Organizations and Agencies

Family and Home Network (FAHN)
P.O. Box 545
Merrifield, VA 22116
703-352-1072
E-mail: fahm@familyhome.org
www.familyandhome.org

National Parent Network on Disabilities
1727 King Street, Suite 305
Alexandria, VA 22314
703-684-6763 (V/TTY)

NICHCY
P.O. Box 1492
Washington, DC 20013-1492
800-695-0285 (V/TTY)
E-mail: nichcy@aed.org
www.nichcy.org

Sibling Information Network
A. J. Pappanikou Center
University of Connecticut
249 Glenbrook Road, Box U-64
Storrs, CT 06269
Fax: 860-486-4985

Technical Assistance to Parent Programs Network (TASH)
95 Berkeley Street, Suite 104
Boston, MA 02116
617-482-2915
800-331-0688

4

Disabilities and Health Disorders

Strategies for Educators

It is only through knowledge that the many commonly held misconceptions about disabilities are dispelled and that a better understanding of the needs of students with disabilities is gained. The background and characteristics of specific disabilities are discussed in this chapter. The specific disabilities are arranged alphabetically to provide quick and easy reference.

Many of the characteristics for one type of disability can also be found under other types of disabilities. Given the overlap among different disabilities, many of the suggestions in this chapter for teaching a student with a particular disability can be successfully applied to one with another disability.

Educators have always used many different teaching strategies to meet the needs of their students. The disabilities covered in this chapter are the ones that teachers are most apt to encounter in the general education classroom. Although not specific categories of disabilities, the auditory processing and visual processing disorders have also been included. When students with disabilities are in the general education classroom, additional strategies are needed. Strategies for educators are discussed under each specific disability.

Aphasia

Definition

Aphasia is the total or partial loss of the ability to make sense of spoken or written language, irrespective of intelligence.

Background

Aphasia is not a disease but rather a symptom of brain damage. It can be the result of a stroke, brain tumor, infection, or head injury. Head injury is considered a main cause of aphasia in children, although aphasia can occur in children as either a congenital or an acquired condition. Physicians often mistakenly consider aphasia to be the result of confusion or mental disturbance. As such, it is difficult to determine how many people have aphasia because it may not be reported, and the brain injury is not detected.

Different types of aphasia exist. One type, called *receptive aphasia*, causes problems in comprehension. Even though the speech of the person with aphasia may be fluent, that person's impaired comprehension distorts what is heard or what is seen in print. The person with aphasia hears the voice or sees the print but is unable to make sense of the sounds or the words. When a person with aphasia speaks, irrelevant words often interfere with communication to the extent of being unintelligible. The person with aphasia experiences impaired reading and writing. This type of aphasia is also referred to as *Wernicke's aphasia*, because damage to the Wernicke's area in the brain causes the problem.

Another type of aphasia is *global aphasia*, in which there is total or almost total inability to speak, write, or understand the written word. This is the most severe form of aphasia. All language functions, including expression and comprehension, are lost. Global aphasia is due to extensive damage to the language areas of the brain.

Nominal aphasia, also referred to as *anomic aphasia* or *amnesic aphasia*, is a milder form of aphasia, which manifests when someone has trouble correctly naming objects, people, places, or events. This type of aphasia makes it difficult for persons to find words for things they want to talk about. This obstacle to finding words is also evident in their writing. Although their speech may be fluent, it is often redundant with wordiness and expressions of frustration. According to the American Medical Association (1989), it may be caused by a "generalized cerebral dysfunction or damage to specific language areas" (p. 125).

Expressive aphasia, also called *Broca's aphasia*, causes difficulty in language expression. A person with this type of aphasia is able to use only a few meaningful words and is limited to short utterances of less than four words. The speech is not only nonfluent but also generally very slow and deliberate. Damage to the Broca's area of the brain causes this type of aphasia.

If a brain injury occurs in a child whose speech and language have just begun to develop, that child may have what is called *acquired aphasia*, or the loss of language. This can occur when blood flow to the brain is blocked during surgery or when the child has a severe head trauma or brain infection. A child who has an acquired aphasic condition is better able to recover than an adult who has acquired it. Fortunately, the neurons in a child's brain seem to be capable of compensating for the injury, and the brain will continue to reorganize itself until adolescence.

It is difficult to ascertain how many people have aphasia since the general public knows very little about the disorder. According to the International Dyslexia Association, 1 million Americans suffer from aphasia. The ratio is 1 of every 250 people will acquire the disorder. About two-thirds of these are the result of stroke or head injuries. As awareness of the disorder increases, so will the number of people with aphasia.

Aphasia occurs in persons regardless of their age, sex, or ethnicity. The main cause of aphasia is the result of strokes and accidents that damage neurological connections within the brain.

Although there is no cure for aphasia at this time, research continues. There are new developments in therapy for people with aphasia. Dr. Michael Weinrich, a professor at the University of Maryland in Baltimore, is a pioneer in the field of computer-assisted aphasia therapy. He states that a carefully designed computer treatment program can help severe, nonfluent persons with aphasia retrieve and produce verbs (as cited in Albert & Velez, 2000).

One computer-assisted therapy, the C-ViC (computerized visual communication) has produced modest benefits for some individuals with aphasia. Dr. Marjorie Nicholas of the Aphasia Research Center in Boston has increased the flexibility of the C-ViC program with a computer-assisted aphasia therapy program called C-Speak aphasia (as cited in Albert & Velez, 2000). This augmentative communication is an aid for adults with nonfluent aphasia.

Technology has provided many options for individuals with aphasia. The term *augmented communication devices* describes low-tech and high-tech aids. An example of a low-tech aid is the alphabet board, and the use of a computer that is driven by the eye blinks of its user is considered a high-tech aid. It is important to match the augmented communication devices to the specific needs and abilities of the individual with aphasia. Technological advances show promise for all individuals with aphasia.

Therapy research is also ongoing in the field of cognitive rehabilitation. This approach is an attempt to understand why an individual with aphasia has lost normal language patterns. The research encompasses a study of the brain's interaction between language and cognition that produces normal language. With this knowledge, attempts can be made to try to reestablish normal language. Another approach focuses on attention. It is believed that by improving the attentional function, the language of the person with aphasia will also improve (Albert & Velez, 2000). There have been positive research results for both cognitive rehabilitation and the attentional focus approach.

The focus of many diagnosticians in aphasia has been predominantly on the speech/language approach, which has been a feature of all rehabilitation. Due to advances in research, there is awareness that assessment should also include the functional communication that impacts his or her relationship with family, peers, and social and vocational life. Pharmacological interventions are still in the process of being investigated. At present, the results have been encouraging. The important aspect of treatment is that it now reaches beyond the clinic setting into the real-life setting.

The use of drugs in the treatment of aphasia is still in the beginning of the research phase. At this time, the use of drugs has not produced long-term results (Albert & Velez, 2000). Sometimes surgery is successful if the person has a brain tumor or a hematoma that affects a critical speech center. For many, speech therapy is used to help the person with aphasia to use individual remaining skills and to learn ways to compensate for the lack of communication skills. At school, the speech therapist can be instrumental in helping children with aphasia develop better communication skills.

The American Medical Association (1989) states that there is less chance of complete recovery in severe cases of aphasia, but after a stroke or head injury, some recovery from aphasia can be expected.

Characteristics

The symptoms of aphasia vary greatly, depending on the severity of language loss. In addition to the effects of aphasia, some individuals with aphasia have experienced many of the following characteristics:

- Muscle weakness
- Paralysis on one side of the body
- Frequent headaches
- Seizures
- Loss of peripheral vision
- Hearing impairments
- Articulation problems
- Inability to produce voice
- Making incomplete sentences
- Syntax errors
- Inability to understand symbolic meanings
- Short attention span
- Memory difficulties
- Shifting moods
- Tears and laughter for no apparent reason
- Loss of personal habits
- Compulsive neatness and orderliness
- Feelings of helplessness
- Lethargy
- Fatigue
- Depression
- Feelings of unworthiness
- Memory loss
- Inability to perform simple tasks

If a student exhibits some of the characteristics of aphasia, it does not necessarily mean that the student has aphasia. Many students lack adequate communication skills; a younger student has not acquired a large vocabulary. During communication, these students not only may be hesitant in expressing themselves but also have difficulty finding the word they need to express themselves. It is only over a period of time, when a teacher notices that a student is constantly having difficulty retrieving a word(s) that the student had just used, that the teacher may have cause for concern. Even though the language patterns of the student may appear normal, this inability to retrieve the words is a characteristic that teachers may readily recognize along with the longer time needed to make statements or answer questions. Even though the student has constant ongoing difficulties with communication, it is still not the position of a teacher to ascertain if the student has aphasia. A referral must be made to the school speech therapist to make this determination.

Strategies for Educators

Because most individuals with aphasia are taught in special classes, the general education classroom may have students who have mild aphasia. In this case, the teacher needs to bear in mind that the receptive student with aphasia will not perceive the complete stimuli. The teacher will have to encourage the student to use other cues, such as sight and the olfactory, tactile, and kinesthetic senses, to help the student formulate meaning from the spoken expression or visual symbol. In some cases, the student with aphasia may be unable to distinguish an item by sight, but if other senses are used, the item can be identified. The teacher must make allowances for the deficit and for the communication needs of the student with aphasia. As with many disabilities, the teacher needs to use a multisensory approach.

The student with mild aphasia needs additional time to answer questions posed by the teacher. It is essential that the teacher shows the necessary patience to give the student time to answer. Unfortunately, there is always a tendency to finish the sentence for the student. If the student has difficulty retrieving a word to use, the teacher should allow sufficient time for retrieval and not quickly supply the word(s) that the student cannot produce spontaneously. This should only be done when the teacher senses that the student wants help with the words. Whenever possible, questions that can be answered with *yes* or *no* should be given to the student to allow participation in the class discussion.

It is important for a teacher to successfully communicate with the student with aphasia and all others in the class. This involves having everyone's attention before speaking and is especially true for a student with aphasia. Emphasizing key words is helpful. Using meaningful gestures and visual aids will help not only the student with aphasia but also everyone else in the class.

The physiological and psychological effects of aphasia can be devastating to a child. It is degrading to the student with aphasia if the teacher treats that student as being mentally incompetent. Self-esteem suffers, and recovery is slowed. The frustration and annoyance experienced by the student with aphasia cannot be underestimated. When the ability to communicate is gone, a person feels helpless and isolated.

Results of medical and therapy intervention cannot be accurately predicted, but many students with aphasia do regain their capacity for language. The teacher can expect these students to be in the general education classroom. It is essential for the teacher to have ongoing conferences with the speech and language specialist. Although some students with aphasia may never regain their language skills, they will still be able to participate in family activities and enjoy social gatherings.

The National Aphasia Association provides an identification card to individuals with aphasia that states the following:

> Please Take Time to Communicate
> I have aphasia (uh fay'zhuh), a communication impairment.
> My intelligence is intact.
> I am not drunk, retarded, or mentally unstable.

> How You Can Help
> Give me time to communicate.
> Speak simply and directly to me.
> Do not shout. It does not help.
> Ask yes/no questions.

For Further Information

Books

Byng, S., Duchan, J. F., & Pound, C. *The aphasia therapy file* (Vol. 2).
Davis, G. A. *Aphasiology: Disorders and clinical practice.*
Hinckley, J. J. *What is it like to have trouble communicating?*
Jones, C., & Loman, J. *Aphasia: A guide for parent and family.*
Lapointe, L. L. *Aphasia and related language disorders.*
McCormick, L., Schiefelbusch, R. L., & Loeb, D. J. *Supporting children with communication difficulties in inclusive settings.*
Samo, M. T. *Understanding aphasia: A guide for family and friends.*
Shimberg, E. F. *Strokes: What families should know.*
Sousa, D. E. *How the brain learns.*
Whitworth, A. *A cognitive approach to assessment and intervention in aphasia.*

Organizations and Agencies

American Speech-Language-Hearing Association
10801 Rockville Pike
Rockville, MD 20852
800-638-8255
301-897-5700 TTY ext. 4157
Fax: 301-571-0457
E-mail: actioncenter@asha.org
www.asha.org

National Aphasia Association
350 Seventh Avenue, Suite 902
New York, NY 10001
800-922-4622
212-255-4329
Fax: 212-989-7777
E-mail: responsecenter@aphasia.org
www.aphasia.org

National Association of Special Education Teachers (NASET)
1250 Connecticut Avenue NW, Suite 200
Washington, DC 20036
800-754-4421 (voice/fax)
E-mail: contactus@naset.org
www.naset.org

National Institute on Deafness and Other Communication Disorders
31 Center Drive MSC 2320
Bethesda, MD 20892-2320
301-496-7243
800-241-1044
800-241-1055 TTD/TTY
E-mail: nidcdinfo@nidcd.nih.gov
www.nidcd.nih.gov

National Institutes of Health
9000 Rockville Pike
Bethesda, MD 20892
301-496-4000
301-402-9612 TTY
E-mail: NIHinfo@od.gov
www.nih.gov

The National Aphasia Association can provide listings of aphasia community groups in specific cities and states. Call 800-922-4622.

Asperger Syndrome

Definition

Asperger syndrome encompasses the lack of general interest, the use of nonverbal behavior, and impaired social interactions and activities. It is linked to the autism spectrum.

Background

Asperger syndrome (AS) is a relatively new diagnosed disorder. However, the disorder has been known in Europe since 1940. In 1944, a Viennese pediatrician, Hans Asperger, labeled the disorder as "Autistic Psychopathy." The disorder has only been included in the medical diagnostic manuals and officially recognized in the fourth edition of *Diagnostic and Statistical Manual of Mental Disorders* since 1994.

AS is grouped under the broad heading of Pervasive Developmental Disorder (PDD). The groupings under PDD, as listed by the American Psychiatric Association (APA; 1994), include Asperger syndrome, Childhood Disintegrative Disorder, Rett's Disorder, and PDD–Not Otherwise Specified (PDDNOS). All exhibit abnormalities in socialization skills, use of language for communication, and behavior, but each group differs in the severity of the deficits.

AS refers to the mildest and highest functioning group of PDD and is characterized by higher cognitive abilities, ranging from average to superior intelligence. Like all other categories on the PDD spectrum, AS is a neurological disorder of development. Both AS and autism are subgroups of PDD. Researchers are not certain if AS is just a milder form of autism or is linked to autism by the similarities between the two disorders.

The impairments of AS and autism are similar but differ in the degree and overall ability of the child. Children with AS have a higher verbal IQ than their performance, whereas the opposite is true for children with autism. Individuals with AS have a more normal language ability than children with autism, and it is this language ability that is one of the criteria for diagnosing AS that differentiates it from autism. The onset of AS is generally later than that of autism. Both AS and autism are characterized by deficits in social and communication skills, but in AS, these deficits are less severe and the outlook for children with AS is more positive than for those who have been diagnosed as autistic.

Currently there is a great deal of research about AS. The majority of the research led to the conclusion that a brain abnormality causes AS. By using advanced brain imaging techniques, scientists have discovered structural and functional differences in specific areas of the brain. They hypothesized that during the fetal development, a migration of embryonic cells in the brain structure affects the neural circuits, which control thought and behavior.

Scientists also found reduced brain activity in children with AS when they were asked to respond to tasks requiring them to use their own judgment. Scientists have known that AS tends to run in families and that a genetic link existed between inherited and genetic mutations. A specific gene for AS has not been identified. However, researchers believe that a common group of genes with variations or deletions makes an individual prone to developing AS.

AS is a congenital neurological condition that affects 0.25% of the population. It is estimated that 20 to 25 individuals per 10,000 are diagnosed as having AS (McCroskery, 2000). Studies also indicate that more boys than girls have AS. Boys are three to four times more likely than girls to have AS. There can be students in the general education program who have not been identified or diagnosed as having AS but still have varying degrees of AS.

Preschool children with AS show symptoms much like that of autism (see section on Autism). However, children with AS show a greater social interest in other children and adults than children with autism show. They also have better language and speech skills and demonstrate more age-appropriate conversational speech. Some preschool children with AS have strong skills such as rote memorization and letter and number recognition. Most preschoolers and kindergarten children have not been diagnosed as having AS. It is their immature social skills and ineptness in peer relationships that teachers consider a behavior problem. This lack of social skills results in escalating difficulties in the classroom. At this time, if not before, the teacher generally refers the child to the Student Success Team (SST) for assistance and considers possible referral for special education services.

In middle school, there is constant peer pressure to conform. This creates problems for students with AS, who already have difficulty in social relatedness. Furthermore, middle school children often have less empathy and tolerance for individual differences. Only when the student with AS goes to high school do students have more understanding and tolerance for individual differences. During this period, many students with AS form lasting friendships with students who share the same interests. After finishing high school, a number of students with AS go on to college and graduate school.

As an adult, the individual with AS still has the problems associated with AS. Many are viewed as different or eccentric. Michael McCroskery (2000) states, "My experiences as an adult recently diagnosed with Asperger's, together with my studies in child development, suggest that individuals with AS are like young children—stuck in time . . . never able to advance beyond early stages in social, cognitive, and language development."

Characteristics

Based on the diagnostic criteria set forth in *DSM-IV*, a Swedish physician, Christopher Gillberg, expanded and simplified the list with the following criteria for diagnosing AS:

a. Severe impairment in reciprocal social interaction (at least two of the following):
   - inability to interact with peers
   - lack of desire to interact with peers
   - lack of appreciation of social cues
   - socially and emotionally inappropriate behavior
b. All-absorbing narrow interest (at least one of the following):
   - exclusion of other activities
   - repetitive adherence
   - more rote than meaning
c. Imposition of routines and interests (at least one of the following):
   - on self, in aspects of life
   - on others
d. Speech and language problems (at least three of the following):
   - delayed development
   - superficially perfect expressive language
   - formal, pedantic language
   - odd prosody, peculiar voice characteristics
   - impairment of comprehension including misinterpretations of literal-implied meanings
e. Nonverbal communication problems (at least one of the following):
   - limited use of gestures
   - clumsy/gauche body language
   - limited facial expression
   - inappropriate expression
   - peculiar, stiff gaze
f. Motor clumsiness; poor performance on neurodevelopmental examination (Online Asperger Syndrome Information and Support, 2001a, 2001b)

Strategies for Educators

The teacher has the task of helping the student develop better communication skills. This requires patience and the need to listen to all attempts made by the student with AS. When the teacher asks the student a question, the student needs a longer time for processing. Rephrasing the question or interrupting the student makes it more difficult for the student and may abruptly end further communication attempts. Although the student may leave out necessary words in speaking and may display certain aspects of spoken language that seem unusual, correcting the speech should be avoided. Modeling the correct format may be all that is needed. A student with AS may also have peculiarities in the volume, intonation, and inflection of speech. Again, it is necessary for the teacher to refrain from anything that might be interpreted as criticism. Not all students with AS have the same type of communication difficulties, but the responses of the teacher must be positive to encourage continued communication.

The teacher, too, must consider his or her own communication skills. Remembering that the student with AS takes things literally, the teacher needs to be concise, concrete, and specific. As an example, instead of saying, "Why did you do that?" it is better to say, "Why did you get out of your chair?" Using vague terms such as *later, perhaps,* or *maybe* should be avoided. In the upper grades, language becomes more abstract and the student with AS experiences great difficulty in communication and comprehension.

Students with AS require a well-structured environment. A seating plan should be in place, and the class schedule posted. When classroom rules are posted, the teacher must remember that students with AS take everything literally. Generalities need to be avoided. The rules for the student with AS do not have to be the same as the rules for the rest of the class. These rules can be different from the posted rules to take into account the individual differences of students with AS. Writing the class schedule specifically for the student with AS gives the teacher latitude in providing rules that address the needs of the student, as well as the needs of the teacher. Upper grade students with AS should be given a handout to be kept in their notebooks. Younger students benefit by having the rules taped on their desks. By knowing the class routine and their expectations, students with AS experience less stress and feel more secure in their class environment.

Knowing that any transition or change is difficult for a student with AS, the teacher can give notice in advance to prepare the student for the change. For example, if there is going to be a future change in the seating arrangement or schedule, the teacher needs to inform the student. Prior notification is also necessary for any change in normal school routines, such as special events, vacation dates, and, if possible, days when substitutes will be teaching the class. Although some changes may seem unimportant to the teacher, any change can be stressful for a student with AS.

The socialization process is one of the greatest sources of anxiety for students with AS. The teacher can relieve part of this anxiety by carefully selecting a peer "buddy" for the student and discussing with the buddy the social needs of the student. The peer buddy can help promote acceptance of the student with AS in the peer group and encourage additional friendships. Having a peer buddy is particularly beneficial in the upper grades where much of the social interaction occurs outside the structured classroom. Students with AS want to be involved, but they are unable to understand the nuances of social interaction. As an example, they tend to answer everything truthfully with no thought about the effect their answer may have on the other person. In conjunction with other aspects of the AS personality, peers often consider the student to be peculiar. The peer buddy can be instrumental in promoting the student's social acceptance.

Because most students with AS have strong academic skills, they can be used as a teacher's aide to help other students, thereby promoting self-confidence. Knowing the strengths of the student with AS, the teacher can use cooperative learning situations that highlight the strengths of the student. Making use of the student's talents and strengths helps foster respect among the peer group.

Many of the behaviors of students without AS may require disciplinary action. However, in the case of the student with AS, it is possible that the behavior is just one of the inherent characteristics of AS. As an example, teachers may become upset with a student who only stares at them when they are speaking. In the case of a student with AS, it is only an attempt to gain meaning from the teacher's facial expression. Repeating words or phrases or talking to oneself can be disturbing but should not be considered a behavior problem. Knowing the characteristics of AS will help teachers discern the difference between a behavior problem and one of the outward symptoms of AS.

Assignments for students with AS should be presented both visually and orally with gesturing, modeling, and demonstrating the concept. It is helpful for a secondary student to get copies of the teacher's notes or to tape-record the lecture. Either way, it gives the student an opportunity to review the material as often as needed. During independent work, students with AS are easily disturbed by noise. Permitting the use of headphones or earplugs eliminates this distraction. As in autism, the use of auditory integration training is very beneficial for students with AS. When students with AS miss assignments, they should be allowed to make up the assignment through extra credit work. Students who exhibit handwriting difficulties should be allowed to use laptop computers. Instead of written examinations, the use of tape recorders must also be considered.

After students learn about AS, they are generally interested in famous people who have been diagnosed as having AS. Craig Nicholls, the front man of the band The Vines, was recently diagnosed as having AS. The creator of *Pokemon*, Satoshi Tajiri, was also diagnosed as having AS. Known for creativity, Satoshi had a fascination and interest in insects to the extent that his friends called him "Dr. Bug."

An identifying characteristic of students with AS is their unique areas of specific interests, which are generally in the intellectual area. This singular focus sometimes changes over time and often persists into adulthood where it becomes the focal point in their livelihood and great achievements can be made. Tony Atwood, a well-known expert on AS, referred to individuals with AS as "a bright thread in the rich tapestry of life. Our civilization would be extremely dull and sterile if we did not have and treasure people with Asperger syndrome" (1998, pp. 184–185).

For Further Information

Books

Cumine, V., Leach, J., & Stevenson, G. *Asperger syndrome: A practical guide for teachers.*
Mesibov, G., & Schopler, E. (Eds.). *Asperger syndrome or high functioning autism.*
Myles, B., & Simpson, R. *A guide for educators and parents.*
Smith, B. *Child and youth with Asperger syndrome.*
Volkmar, F., & Sparrow, S. *Asperger syndrome.*
Wiley, L. *Pretending to be normal: Living with Asperger's syndrome.*

Organizations and Agencies

American Statistical Association
732 North Washington Street
Alexandria, VA 22314-1943
703-684-1221
888-231-3473
Fax: 703-684-2037
E-mail: asainfo@instat.org
www.amstat.org

Asperger Association of New England
85 Main Street, Suite 101
Watertown, MA 02472
617-393-3824
Fax: 617-393-3827
E-mail: info@aane.org
www.aane.org

Autism Society of America
7910 Woodmont Avenue, Suite 300
Washington, DC 20814-0881
800-328-8476
Fax: 301-657-0869
www.autism-society.org

Council for Exceptional Children (CEC)
1110 N. Glebe Road
Arlington, VA 22201-5704
800-328-0272
888-232-7733
Fax: 703-264-9494
E-mail: cec@sped.org
www.cec.sped.org

Indiana Institute on Disability and Community
Indiana University
2853 East Tenth Street
Bloomington, IN 47408-2696
812-855-6508
800-825-4733 (Only in Indiana area)
812-855-9396 (TT)
Fax: 812-855-9630
E-mail: prattc@indiana.edu
www.isdd.indiana.edu/~irca

National Institute of Mental Health (NIMH)
Public Inquiries & Dissemination Branch
6001 Executive Boulevard
Room 8184, MSC 9663
Bethesda, MD 20892-9663
301-443-5413
866-615-NIMH (6464) toll-free
301-443-8431 TTY
866-415-8051 TTY
Fax: 301-443-4279
E-mail: nimhinfo@nih.gov
www.nimh.nih.gov

Attention-Deficit/Hyperactivity Disorder

Definition

The essential feature of attention-deficit/hyperactivity disorder is a persistent pattern of inattention, hyperactivity-impulsivity, or both that is more frequent and severe than is typically observed in individuals at a comparable level of development (American Psychiatric Association, 1994, p. 78).

Background

The *Diagnostic and Statistical Manual of Mental Disorders (DSM-IV)* designated the disorder as Attention-Deficit/Hyperactivity Disorder (AD/HD). Many refer to it as ADD, because there are children and adults with the disorder who do not display the "H" (hyperactive) symptom. However, 80% of people with the disorder are hyperactive so it is also referred to as AD/ADHD (University of California Office of the President, 1996). The disorder has been officially designated as AD/HD and, as such, this is the acronym that is used in this section.

Researchers have divided AD/HD into three subtypes according to the main features associated with the disorder. The AD/HD subtypes are predominately considered as a combined type, an inattentive type, and a hyperactive-impulsive type. Some children with AD/HD have no difficulty sitting still or inhibiting impulsive behavior, but they may be predominately inattentive and lose their focus quickly. Others pay attention but lose their focus because they are the hyperactive-impulsive type and are unable to control their impulses and activity. The combined type of AD/HD has symptoms of both the inattentive and hyperactive-impulse type of behavior.

In some cases, AD/HD is caused by a chemical imbalance in which certain neurotransmitters—the chemicals that regulate the efficiency with which the brain controls behavior—are deficient. Other research implicates fetal exposure to lead, alcohol, or cigarette smoke. A study by Alan Zametkin et al. (1990) at the National Institute of Mental Health showed that the rate at which the brain uses glucose is slower in persons with AD/HD than in the rest of the population. Although the exact cause of AD/HD is unknown at this time, the current consensus is that AD/HD is a neurological medical problem and not the result of poor parenting or diet.

Other research has indicated that AD/HD is genetically transmitted. Russell Barkley of the University of Massachusetts stated that almost one-half of children with AD/HD have a parent who also has the disorder and that a third have siblings with AD/HD (as cited in University of California Office of the President, 1996).

According to the American Psychiatric Association (APA), approximately 8 million children in the United States suffer from a mental disorder. Of these, more than 4.4 million children between the ages of 3 and 17 years have been diagnosed as having AD/HD. AD/HD is more common in boys and generally develops between the ages of 4 and 7. Girls are usually diagnosed between the ages of 8 and 10. The Surgeon General of the United States reported that AD/HD affects between 3% and 5% of school-aged children in any six-month period (NIMH, 2005).

P. M. Wender, professor of psychiatry at the University of Utah School of Medicine, states that children with AD/HD "appear in accident [emergency] rooms at five times the expected rate" (as cited in Wolkenberg, 1987, p. 30). Studies show that 50% of adolescents with AD/HD get into trouble with the law (Wolkenberg, 1987). According to Lily Hechtman, a Canadian psychiatrist, AD/HD alone is not responsible for these adolescents' antisocial behavior but "any hardship is a risk factor whether it be from a lower socioeconomic background, IQ . . . ADD is just one more" (as cited in Wolkenberg, 1987, p. 31).

Since 1902, a great deal of medical literature describing AD/HD has been published, and children have been treated for this disorder for the past 50 years. However, it is only recently that standardized criteria have been used in the diagnosis of AD/HD. According to the *DSM-IV-TR* (APA, 2000, p. 53), there are 18 behaviors associated with a person who has AD/HD that indicate the need for further evaluation. These behaviors are listed under Characteristics. Identifying these symptoms before school age is essential to rule out the possibility that the behaviors are just a reaction to school adjustment.

It is important to understand that there is no simple test, such as a blood test or urinalysis, to determine if a person has AD/HD. Accurate diagnosis is not only complicated but also requires assessment by well-trained professionals such as a developmental pediatrician, child psychologist, child psychiatrist, or pediatric neurologist. AD/HD is a disability that requires proper diagnosis and treatment to prevent long-term, serious complications.

Effective treatment for individuals with AD/HD generally requires three basic components: medication, behavior management, and appropriate educational programs.

Medication, although controversial, has been effective with many children diagnosed with AD/HD. Stimulants are the most widely prescribed type of medication, and it is estimated that over 1 million children in the United States are given daily doses of stimulant medications (Singh & Ellis, 1993). These drugs stimulate the brain's neurotransmitters to enable it to better regulate attention, impulsiveness, and motor behavior. For children who are unable to take stimulant medications, antidepressant medication is prescribed.

A commonly prescribed medicine for AD/HD is methylphenidate, an amphetamine known as Ritalin. Amphetamines generally produce anxiety, but in many children with AD/HD, Ritalin reduces their activity level. Sometimes physicians prescribe Dexedrine or Cylert to increase the child's own control over his or her behavior.

In a study of children with AD/HD, Dr. John Ratey and researchers from Stanford University used the functional MRI (fMRI) (Seay, 2001). The MRI visualizes changes in the hemodynamic properties of blood irrigating neuronal tissue that is engaged in the performance of a task. This test is noninvasive and suitable for children. During the research, both children with AD/HD and children without AD/HD performed two "go/no-go" tasks. The children without AD/HD control group showed an improved response inhibition on one task, but the children with AD/HD on Ritalin showed improvement on both tasks. Although the MRI is useful in providing information about how the AD/HD brain functions, it is still too expensive to be used on a routine basis.

The government investigated the medication Ritalin. This study was conducted because of reports that many preschoolers who had been using Ritalin experienced side effects. The study involved children with severe AD/HD symptoms. About 40% of children in the study experienced different side effects. Side effects of Ritalin on the preschool children included a loss of weight and stunted growth (Turner, 2006, p. A9).

A group of scientists conducted a Multimodal Treatment Study of Children with AD/HD. They concluded that drugs like Ritalin or Concerta were effective for a short period of time, but over a three-year period, the drugs brought no improvement in the children's behavior. The drugs also had an impact on the rate of growth for the children. There was a substantial decrease in their height and weight. The scientists could see no beneficial effects of the drugs used for children with AD/HD. Dr. Tim Kendall, of the Royal College of Psychiatrists, is working with the National Institutes of Health (NIH) to develop new guidelines for the treatment of AD/HD. He stated, "I hope we will be able to make recommendations that will give people a comprehensive approach to treatment and that will advise about what teachers might be able to do within the classroom when they're trying to deal with kids who have different problems of this kind" (Stratton, 2007, n.p.).

Brain research at the Massachusetts Institute of Technology showed that it takes one part of the brain to start concentration and another for distraction. Scientists feel that this discovery will help in finding better treatments for children with AD/HD. Earl Wiley, a neuroscientist at the Institute, feels that the ability to focus attention is physically separate in the brain. There are different degrees of focusing. While some are unable to filter out distractions, others may have a harder time focusing. As Dr. Debra Babcock, a neurologist at the NIH, stated, "Once we understand how attention works we'll understand how better to treat disorders of attention. . . . This could in the long term help us devise therapies" (Neergaard, 2007, p. A3).

According to pediatricians Robin L. Hansen and Penelope C. Krener (University of California Office of the President, 1996) at the University of California, Davis, medication is overprescribed for children with AD/HD. The decision to use medication should be made only after a very thorough evaluation by the physician and consultation with the parent.

Some researchers believe that children with "presumed attention or behavior problems" may not always have an attention-deficit/ hyperactivity disorder. Before a diagnosis of AD/HD is made, a comprehensive evaluation is essential (University of California Office of the President, 1996).

Educators often have unrealistic expectations about what constitutes normal behavior in children. For example, it is not realistic to expect children to remain quiet and restricted for 4 to 6 hours. Such expectations go against the normal developmental behavior of children.

Characteristics

The diagnostic criteria for AD/HD as listed in the *DSM-IV* are as follows:

A. Either (1) or (2):

1. six (or more) of the following symptoms of inattention have persisted for at least 6 months to a degree that is maladaptive and inconsistent with developmental level:
   a. often fails to give close attention to details or makes careless mistakes in schoolwork, work, or other activities
   b. often has difficulty sustaining attention in tasks or play activities

    c. often does not seem to listen when spoken to directly

    d. often does not follow through on instructions and fails to finish schoolwork, chores, or duties in the workplace (not due to oppositional behavior or failure to understand instructions)

    e. often has difficulty organizing tasks and activities

    f. often avoids, dislikes, or is reluctant to engage in tasks that require sustained mental effort (such as schoolwork or homework)

    g. often loses things necessary for tasks or activities (e.g., toys, school assignments, pencils, books, or tools)

    h. is often easily distracted by extraneous stimuli

    i. is often forgetful in daily activities

2. six (or more) of the following symptoms of hyperactivity-impulsivity have persisted for at least 6 months to a degree that is maladaptive and inconsistent with developmental level:

    a. often fidgets with hands or feet or squirms in seat

    b. often leaves seat in classroom or in other situations in which remaining seated is expected

    c. often runs about or climbs excessively in situations in which it is inappropriate (in adolescents or adults, may be limited to subjective feelings of restlessness)

    d. often has difficulty playing or engaging in leisure activities quietly

    e. often talks excessively

    f. impulsivity

    g. often blurts out answers before questions have been completed

    h. often has difficulty awaiting turn

    i. often interrupts or intrudes on others (e.g., butts into conversations or games)

B. Some hyperactive-impulse or inattentive symptoms that caused impairment were present before age 7 years.

C. Some impairment from the symptoms is present in two or more settings (e.g., at school or work and at home).

D. There must be clear evidence of clinically significant impairment in social, academic, or occupational functioning. (*DSM-IV*, 1994, pp. 83–85)

Many of the characteristics of AD/HD are similar to those of bipolar disorder. This has created confusion for a diagnostician to determine if the child has AD/HD or bipolar disorder. For your convenience, the differences between the two disorders can be found in Resource E at the end of this book.

This criteria list helps a teacher identify children who may have AD/HD. However, many children exhibit some of the AD/HD characteristics at one time or another. All teachers have noticed students who are inattentive, impulsive, and overly active. When any of these characteristics are observed, whether the student does or does not have AD/HD, a teacher generally attempts to diminish the inappropriate behavior. The major and important difference between a student without AD/HD and that of a student with AD/HD is that the behavior of the student with AD/HD is the rule and not the exception.

The teacher should also note that inattentiveness and distractibility are not synonymous. Distractibility refers to students who have a short attention span when only part of the attention process is disrupted. The impulsivity of a child with AD/HD is different from that of acting without thinking. Those with AD/HD act before thinking since they have difficulty waiting or deferring gratification and there is no thought of the consequences of their act.

Above all, a teacher should remember that it is not the role of the teacher to determine that a student has AD/HD. It is the physician who makes the diagnosis and who often requests the teacher to provide a behavior rating of the student as an adjunct to the diagnosis.

Strategies for Educators

Developing the student with AD/HD's sense of competency and responsibility is necessary. The teacher needs to identify the student's weaknesses and strengths and to provide opportunities to build on the strengths to help such individuals develop a better self-image. Equally important is the need to develop realistic expectations for the child with AD/HD.

Because most children with AD/HD suffer from low self-esteem and are mildly depressed, understanding, encouragement, and praise are essential. These children are continually bombarded with negative feedback and punishment. It is essential that all students who may have AD/HD be properly diagnosed so that corrective measures can be taken.

It can be difficult for students with AD/HD to adapt to the classroom regime because of their low self-esteem, outbursts of temper, and low frustration tolerance. Some, but not all, may have learning disabilities that add to their frustration.

Likewise, it can be difficult for teachers who have students with AD/HD in the classroom. The inattention, impulsiveness, and hyperactivity of a student with AD/HD are not only disruptive but also tend to affect the behaviors and attitudes of the other students in the class. It is important for the teacher to be knowledgeable about the disorder to meet the educational needs of all students and make the appropriate classroom modifications.

A student with AD/HD responds to a well-structured environment. By establishing rules, routines, and expectations ahead of time, the teacher can provide the needed structured environment for the student with AD/HD. All rules and class routines should be clearly and plainly stated in a positive form. These rules, as well as the daily schedule, should be posted. Taping a copy of the daily schedule to a student's desk or giving the secondary student a handout of the schedule is necessary. If there are any schedule changes, this should be brought to the attention of the student with AD/HD. When there is a transition between classes or activities, notifying them a few minutes ahead of time is of value.

The student with AD/HD is often easily distracted, so any stimuli that may distract the student should be avoided. For instance, whenever possible, the student with AD/HD should not be seated near a window, a door, or any unusually high traffic areas. Heaters, air conditioners, fans, and other equipment also divert the attention of the student. Seating the student in a study carrel, however, may also produce a negative effect because the student may create unruly distractions by tapping the feet, hands, pencil, book, or notebook. It is best that the student with AD/HD remains a part of the class and that he or she is possibly seated between other peers who are respected by the class. If the student is seated near the teacher's desk, that student's back should be toward the rest of the class so there will be fewer distracting influences.

The teacher should place a high priority on orderliness and neatness for the student with AD/HD. Depending on the student's age, the teacher may need to teach organization skills. A student with AD/HD generally has a very cluttered desk, so teachers should help organize that student's materials. The student with AD/HD should not only straighten those belongings daily but always clear out any unnecessary material.

Depending on the age of the student, one method of organizing different subject matter is to use color coding. Colored tapes that denote different subjects can be used inside the desk as an organizational tool. The student's notebook can also be maintained in the same manner; for example, a blue divider might be used for math, green for homework, yellow for language, and other colors for different subjects.

Secondary students should have daily, weekly, monthly, or all three assignment sheets that are easily accessible. They benefit by copying their weekly assignments on a spreadsheet and having the teacher initial each one for accuracy. A copy of the spreadsheet should be made available for parents. The student's notebook should have sections for unfinished and finished assignments. The teacher should make frequent checks for work and assignment completion. It is helpful for a secondary student to have "study buddies" with their phone numbers for each subject area.

Methods used for all students to maintain their attention are equally effective for the student with AD/HD. Teachers should always give clear and concise directions to the student with AD/HD. Complex directions only confuse the student and prevent the student from accomplishing the task. When giving oral directions, it is best to give one direction at a time and to maintain eye contact with the student. Because the student with AD/HD often goes from one task to another and completes neither, give only one assignment at a time. Whenever possible, the directions should be both oral and written. Because of the heightened distractibility of a student with AD/HD, it is often helpful to restate the directions to refocus that student's attention. As often as possible, the student should be actively involved in paraphrasing and repeating the directions back to the teacher.

Secondary students with AD/HD will benefit by copying their weekly assignments on a spreadsheet and having the teachers initial each one. This makes it possible for all of the student's teachers to make certain that the assignments are accurate. Teachers should make duplicate texts and a copy of the spreadsheet available to the parent.

There is a need for the teacher to stress quality rather than quantity. By stressing quality, the student will be less pressured by time and be able to accomplish the task to the best of the student's ability. The teacher thereby relieves the student with AD/HD of much of the excessive pressure to complete the work that the student may feel. It may be necessary to decrease the length of the task by breaking it into smaller parts to be completed at different times. This will prevent the student with AD/HD from being overwhelmed by a large task.

The student with AD/HD usually acts on impulse, blurting out answers in a class or becoming physically abusive, with little regard for the consequences of such actions. A behavioral management system can be very successful in controlling this impulsive behavior if the student clearly understands what is expected. The main principle of behavior management is to increase the student's appropriate behavior and to decrease inappropriate behavior with consequences. Rewarding appropriate behavior will generally increase it. If the student has difficulty remaining seated, that student should be given frequent opportunities to get up and move around. Some psychologists believe that planned ignoring of inappropriate behavior helps decrease its frequency.

Making a contract with the student may motivate the student to gradually bring the undesired behavior under control. Providing the student with a checklist of desired behavioral outcomes will give the student a feeling of individual control, develop the student's awareness of the problem, and help improve the student's self-management. The daily checklist for the specified behavior should be positively worded, using terms such as *fair*, *good*, and *better*. The student can then determine personal growth in achieving the established goal. If a token economy system is used, rewards valued by the student for achieving certain targeted goals should be prearranged. As always, give positive reinforcement for various levels of achievement of the targeted goals.

Much of the inappropriate behavior of students with AD/HD evokes negative responses from others, which may have a detrimental effect on the social and emotional growth of students with AD/HD. Praise and a behavior management program that promotes self-discipline are necessary to create an atmosphere in which students with AD/HD feel comfortable and engage in learning activities.

Students should be told that there are many famous people who have been diagnosed or allegedly have AD/HD. They can find lists on the Internet. This makes an interesting language research project for students.

For Further Information

Books

Barkley, R. *Taking charge of AD/HD: The complete, authoritative guide for parents.*
Brown, T. E. *Attention deficit disorder: The unfocused mind in children and adults.*
Dowdy, D. A., Patton, J. R., Smith, T. E. C., & Polloway, E. A. *Attention deficit hyperactivity disorder: A practical guide for teachers.*
DuPaul, G. J., & Stoner, G. *ADHD in the schools: Assessment and intervention strategies.*
Furman, L. *What is attention deficit hyperactivity disorder?*
Goldstein, S., & Goldstein, M. *Hyperactivity—Why won't my child pay attention? A complete guide to ADD for parents, teachers, and community agencies.*

Gordon, S. B., & Asher, M. J. *Meeting the ADD challenge: A practical guide for teachers.*

Greenbaum, J. *Finding your focus.*

Reiff, M. T. *ADHD: A complete and authoritative guide.*

Rief, S. *How to reach and teach ADD/ADHD children.*

Spisa, D. A. *How the special needs brain learns.*

Organizations and Agencies

American Psychological Association
750 First Street NE
Washington, DC 20002-4242
202-336-5500
202-336-6123 (TDD/TTY)
800-374-2721
E-mail: apa@apa.org
www.apa.org

Children and Adults With Attention Deficit/Hyperactivity Disorder (CHADD)
8181 Professional Place, Suite 150
Landover, MD 20785
800-233-4050
301-306-7070
Fax: 301-306-6788
E-mail: national@add.org
www. help4adhd.org

National Attention Deficit Disorder Association (ADDA)
15000 Commerce Parkway, Suite C
Mount Laurel, NJ 08054
Fax: 856-439-0525
E-mail: adda@ahint.com
www.add.org

Auditory Processing Disorder

Definition

H. R. Myklebust, a psychologist and educator recognized for his distinguished service to exceptional children, defined *auditory processing* as the ability to "structure the auditory world and select those sounds that are immediately pertinent to adjustment" (as cited in Chalfant & Scheffelin, 1969, p. 209). The inability to accurately process receptive or expressive auditory stimuli is considered a dysfunction. Auditory processing has also been used to describe many behavioral responses to auditory stimuli.

Background

Auditory processing disorder (APD) is often referred to with different names. The National Institutes of Health states that APD has also been referred to as a "central auditory processing disorder (CAPD), auditory perception problem, auditory comprehension deficit, central auditory dysfunction, and word deafness." Auditory processing refers to the recognition and interpretation of sounds by the brain. Acoustic (sound) energy traveling through the ear is transformed into electrical signals that are interpreted by the brain. If this is dysfunctional, it is considered a disorder.

The auditory channel is one of the most important avenues through which we receive information about our environment. Even though the hearing acuity is within the normal range, someone with an auditory processing disorder has difficulty processing and obtaining meaning from auditory stimuli.

Many theorists attempt to attribute the localization of sensory perception to an isolated area of the brain. Some evidence suggests that the primary receiving strip for auditory stimuli is located in the Sylvian margin of the temporal lobe. It may be here that the complex forms of auditory analysis and integration occur. This region may be largely responsible for the systematic deciphering of sound signals necessary for the perception of speech. Research concerning the function of the secondary divisions of the auditory cortex is less clear.

Many advances in technology make it possible to study the brain. Imaging is one of the ways that allows a study of brain activity without surgery. The great value of imaging is the objectivity it provides. It will help in the understanding of auditory processing and has already given scientists new insights into the processing of language by the brain. Scientists are beginning to identify sources of the difficulties associated with APD. Cognitive neuroscientists are now able to describe the process of recognition and comprehension work in both normal and disordered systems. Continued research is needed to fully understand auditory processing disorders.

Northwestern University conducted a study of the effect of music on the auditory system. The study appeared in *Nature Neuroscience* (Wong, Skoe, Russo, Dees, & Kraus, 2007). Several conclusions were derived from the study. One finding was that playing a musical instrument increased the brain stem's sensitivity to speech sounds. This applies to sound encoding skills involved in both music and language. The study also indicated that music experience at a young age increases the effectiveness of the auditory system. Nina Kraus, the director of Northwestern's Auditory Neuroscience Laboratory, stated, "Increasing music experience appears to benefit all children—whether musically exceptional or not—in a wide range of learning activities."

At this time, the exact cause of APD is unknown. However, it is a neurological problem that may be inherited or caused by a birth defect or injury. In children, auditory processing problems are often associated with other disorders such as dyslexia, attention deficit, autism, autism spectrum disorder, specific language impairment, pervasive developmental disorder, or developmental delay.

Children who have difficulty processing auditory stimuli may have trouble identifying the source of sounds or understanding the meaning of environmental sounds. It is difficult for them to differentiate between significant and insignificant stimuli. There is also evidence that people with an auditory processing disorder have difficulty reproducing pitch, rhythm, and melody.

The rate of processing information is slower for children with an auditory processing disorder. If the information is stored in the short-term memory, it might not get into the long-term memory. Oral presentations require a longer time for processing for children with this disorder. This makes it difficult to understand information presented orally. Some children compensate for this disorder by getting meaning from the context. If the auditory processing disorder is severe, the student may have great difficulty understanding much of what they hear. This can be likened to being in another country and not knowing the spoken language of that country.

Characteristics

Children with an auditory processing disorder often have a deficit in discrimination skills. They have difficulty both hearing vowel sounds or the soft consonant sounds in spoken words and understanding subtle differences in sounds. Words and phrases are misidentified; for example, "blue" might be mistaken for "ball," or "ball" for "bell." If children are unable to recognize auditory differences and similarities, they will have difficulty acquiring and understanding the spoken language.

Children with auditory discrimination disorder have difficulty not only in determining if the language sounds of two words are the same or different but also whether the initial, medial, or final sounds of two words are the same or different. This deficit also carries over to the discrimination of blended sounds.

The analysis and synthesis of a series of speech sounds is essential to learning the phonemic structure of language. A deficit that affects the auditory memory, speech, and reading ability of the individual has far-reaching implications in education. Because many students improve these skills until their eighth year (but they never completely close the gap), the chronological age of the individual should always be taken into consideration in determining the severity of the disability.

A common characteristic of a person with an auditory processing disorder, and one that is often mistaken for inattention, is the inability to isolate a sound from background sounds. The inability to understand when there is background noise is considered an auditory figure-ground difficulty affecting auditory processing. This creates a problem when there is an attempt to retrieve the needed auditory impression from memory. The auditory sequential memory is affected, and it is difficult for the individual to remember oral directions or the sequence of events. The student may habitually ask that questions or directions be repeated. When questions are repeated, the student may be confused, not because of the student's lack of knowledge but for the additional time the student needs to process and answer the questions. The individual's inattention, due to the auditory sequential memory deficit, makes it extremely difficult to attend to auditory stimuli and many environmental and speech sounds. The implications for a person with an auditory processing problem are clear.

A general listing of the characteristics of a child with APD consists of the following:

- Inattention and poor listening skills
- Remembering information presented orally
- Inability to follow multistep directions
- Low academic performance
- Poor expressive or receptive language
- Behavior problems
- Easily distracted
- Delays in responding to questions and instructions
- Often misunderstands directions or instructions

Strategies for Educators

Some students may have an auditory processing disorder that has not been identified. Those who have been identified as having an auditory processing disorder are helped in special education classes and by being included in general education classes.

Students who have an auditory processing disorder learn best when the teacher presents information in a visual mode, so teachers should seat students where eye contact can be made easily. Remember: A student with an auditory processing disorder has difficulty following the verbal directions and explanations, so verbal instructions should be interrelated with visual stimuli and demonstrations. Students with this disability should be asked to repeat back directions to be sure they understand.

All directions and questions should be brief. Using gestures helps reinforce what is being said. However, gestures should only be used to reinforce key points. The same key points can be presented visually, for example, using chalkboard, overhead projector, charts, or illustrations. Students with an auditory processing disorder should be given directions for an assignment in the order it is to be completed. For a secondary student, it is helpful to provide a handout with the key points to be covered in the lesson and always briefly summarize the key points for additional reinforcement.

For students with an auditory processing disorder, it is difficult to listen and take notes at the same time. It is helpful for the student to have a photocopy covering the main points of the lesson. A tape recorder is also useful because the student can listen to the recording as many times as is needed to process the information.

The teacher is obligated to provide instruction that is meaningful for students who may have an auditory processing disorder. It is inappropriate for the teacher to use a phonetically based instruction in reading for students with auditory processing disorders. The use of sight words and the configuration of words are more appropriate when teaching students to read. Teachers should use visual stimuli, such as pictures, whenever possible. Students will enjoy reading descriptive material because of the visualization required. The teacher can expect excellent responses when asking students to relate details that involve visual imagery, and students should be encouraged to apply their visualization skills to creative writing. As with all students, positive feedback encourages the students with auditory processing disorders to continue with their writing endeavors.

For Further Information

Books

Chermak, G. D., & Musiek, F. E. *Central auditory processing disorders: New perspectives.*

Davis, G. A. *Aphasiology: Disorders and clinical practice.*

Friedman, F. G. *Listening processes: Attention, understanding, evaluation.*

Gillet, P. *Auditoria processes.*

Mullen, W. J., Gerace, W. J., Mestre, J. P., & Velleman, S. L. *Fundamentals of sound with applications to speech and hearing.*

Musiek, F. E., & Baran, J. A. *The auditory system: Its anatomy, physiology and clinical correlates.*

Shelton, C. E., & Pollingue, A. B. *The exceptional teacher's handbook: The first year special education teacher's guide to success.*

Velleman, S. L. *Childhood apraxia of speech resource guide.*

Wolvin, A. D., & Coakley, C. G. *Listening.*

Organizations and Agencies

American Academy of Audiology (AAA)
11730 Plaza America Drive, Suite 300
Reston, VA 20190
703-790-8466
800-222-2336 TTY
Fax: 703-790-8631
E-mail: info@audiology.com
www.audiology.com

American Speech-Language-Hearing Association (ASHA)
10801 Rockville Pike
Rockville, MD 20852
301-897-5700
800-638-8255
301-897-0157 TTY
Fax: 301-571-0457
E-mail: actioncenter@asha.org
www.asha.org

Council for Exceptional Children (CEC)
1110 North Glebe Road, Suite 300
Arlington, VA 22201
888-232-7733
Fax: 703-264-9494
E-mail: service@cec.sped.org
www.cec.sped.org

National Attention Deficit Disorder Association
15000 Commerce Parkway, Suite C

Mount Laurel, NJ 08054
Fax: 856-439-0525
E-mail: adda@ahint.com
www.add.org

National Dissemination Center for Children with Disabilities (NICHCY)
P.O. Box 1492
Washington, DC 20013
800-695-0285 (voice/TTY)
202-884-8200 (voice/TTY)
Fax: 202-884-8441
E-mail: nichcy@aed.org
www.nichcy.org

National Institute on Deafness and Other Communication Disorders (NIDCD)
NIDCD Office of Health Communications and Public Liaison
31 Center Drive, MSC 2320
Bethesda, MD 20892-2320
301-496-7243 (voice)
301-402-0252 (TTY)
Fax: 301-402-0018

Autism

Definition

Autism is defined in the Individuals with Disabilities Education Act (1990) as a developmental disability, generally evident before age 3, affecting verbal and nonverbal communication and social interaction that affects a child's performance. Other characteristics often associated with autism are engagement in repetitive activities and stereotyped movements, resistance to environmental change or change in daily routines, and unusual responses to sensory experiences. Autism does not apply if a child's educational performance is adversely affected primarily because the child has a serious emotional disturbance (34 C.F.R., Part 300, 300.7 [b] [11]). The Los Angeles chapter of the Autism Society of America defines autism as a lifelong developmental disability with disturbances in "physical, social, and language skills" (as cited in Gillingham, 1995, p. 208).

Background

Autism is a developmental disability and is often referred to as an autism spectrum disorder. It is one of five disorders in the category of Pervasive Developmental Disorders (PDD). Other disorders under the PDD category are Asperger syndrome, Childhood Disintegrative Disorder, Rett's Disorder, and PDD–Not Otherwise Specified (PDD-NOS). All have symptoms of severe and pervasive impairment in several senses of development as listed and stated in the *DSM-IV-TR* (2000) and reported by the Autism Society of America.

Although autism has had a long past, it was not until 1943 that Leo Kanner, a child psychiatrist at Johns Hopkins University Medical School, named this developmental disorder autism (as cited in Gillingham, 1995). He borrowed the name from Eugene Bleuler, a Swiss psychiatrist, who used the term in 1911 to describe the active withdrawal from social interactions of his schizophrenic patients.

From the 1940s through the 1960s, it was generally believed that people with autism had a conscious desire to withdraw from any social interaction. However, today it is understood that the withdrawal is not a conscious desire but, rather, the result of neurological and biochemical alterations in the brain.

The exact cause of autism is unknown. At one point, it was thought that a lack of warmth from parents caused the disorder. This has been proven to be untrue. Autism is not caused by psychological factors. All evidence indicates that autism has a biological origin resulting in a metabolic dysfunction of the brain. Because about one-fourth of children with autism have signs of a neurological disorder, it is possible that they have a degree of brain damage. Bernard Rimland, the founder of the National Society for Children, former director of the Autism Research Institute in San Diego, and an early advocate in the use of behavior modification, believed that a neurological cause of autism involves a possible dysfunction of the brain stem reticular formation. The reticular formation is the web of nerve cells in the brain stem that is involved in perception. A perceptual malfunction may be the result of impaired reticular functioning.

Autism occurs in all socioeconomic classes, although it seems to be more prevalent in the higher socioeconomic classes. This may be attributed to the fact that better educated families are more apt to recognize autistic-like behavior in their child and to seek help. It is estimated that approximately 5 to 15 of every 10,000 children are diagnosed as having autism. Autism is rarely found to affect more than one child in a family. Boys are affected four to five times more often than girls. According to the U.S. Department of Education (1999), during the school year of 1996–1997, 34,101 students ages 6 to 21 received special education services under the IDEA category of autism. In 2000 the Center for Disease Control and Prevention estimated that 2 of every 1,000 children had autism. In 2007, the Autism

Society of America (ASA) stated that autism occurred in 1 of every 150 births. The ASA estimated that 1 to 1.5 million Americans have autism. The estimated growth of autism since the 1990s is 17%. At this rate, the ASA estimated that the prevalence of autism could reach 4 million Americans in the next decade.

A child with autism appears normal for the first few months of life. The onset of autism at 18 months is more than twice that of the onset at birth. In the past decade, there has been a 50% increase in autism. The symptoms of autism emerge as the child develops and the deficit progresses. According to the American Medical Association (1989), autism usually becomes evident by the age of 30 months. The child fails to develop language skills appropriate for the child's age. Indications that a child has autism become apparent as the child becomes unresponsive to the parents or any stimuli. The child may resist cuddling by the parents and, when picked up, may scream until put down. This may occur even if the child is not hurt or tired. It is a misconception to believe that all children with autism react in this manner. Many children with autism can and do give affection.

Evaluation of autism is based on observation of communication, behavior, and developmental levels. This can be difficult because many of the characteristics of autism are also common in other disabilities. A multidisciplinary team consisting of a neurologist, psychologist, developmental pediatrician, speech/language therapist, learning consultant, or other professionals who are knowledgeable about autism is needed to make the determination.

The current upsurge in autism has given rise to the theory that vaccines may be a mitigating cause. At 18 months old, many children receive a measles-mumps-rubella (MMR) vaccine. The onset of autism at 18 months is a recent development. Children who were autistic from birth outnumbered those diagnosed with autism at 18 months at a ratio of 2:1. The picture reversed in the early 1980s when the MMR triple vaccine was introduced in the United States. Researcher Vijendra Singh of the Autism Research Institute reported new evidence that the MMR vaccine may cause the brain damage that gives rise to autism (Autism Research Review International, 2000). The controversy over vaccines and autism continues. As stated by Dr. Bernard Rimland, a foremost authority on autism, "There is a good deal of evidence, none of it yet conclusive, implicating the MMR as causing the autism epidemic. The evidence includes both clinical research studies and thousands of parent reports linking autism to a vaccine—especially MMR" (as cited in Autism Research Review International, 1999, p. 3).

Research findings suggest that there are abnormalities in the synthesis or usage of the neurotransmitter serotonin in autism. Using positron emission tomography (PET) scanning, nonautistic children's serotonin synthesis capacity was more than 200% of the adult value until the age of 5 years, and then it gradually decreased to an adult level. In children with autism, the serotonin level gradually increased between the ages of 2 years and 25 years to 1.5 times that of adult normal values. This indicated that altered serotonin synthesis in the brain area involved with sensory integration and language development might be one of the underlying pathophysiologies of autism.

The intellect of children with autism is generally well below normal, with 70% being mentally retarded. Thirty percent of people with autism have average or above-average intellect. As in the general population, there is a wide variance in intellectual ability. In addition, there is a basic difference between the person with autism who is also mentally retarded and the person who is mentally retarded. In the child with mental retardation, there is a generalized developmental delay. In the child with autism, delays in development vary over the child's life span.

Researchers at the University of Wisconsin–Madison reported their findings on their research. The researchers documented changes in the brain's emotional center that may explain the social impairment seen in children with autism. The males with autism who were in the study had much smaller amygdalae than the males without autism. The amygdalae are "almond-shaped, danger-detecting regions of the brain." The children with small amygdalae had difficulty discerning any emotion from facial expressions. In April 2007, the University's study was published in the *Archives of General Psychology*. Richard Davidson, professor of psychology and psychiatry at the University of Wisconsin, said, "The findings have opened the door to future studies to clarify the role of the amygdalae in autism" (Newson, 2006, p. A9).

The impairment of language development in children with autism has always presented a challenge to parents and educators. In the early 1960s, Rosalind Oppenheim, founder of the Illinois School for Autistic Children, attempted to meet this challenge. She discovered that her son was able to compose sentences on a typewriter as she touched his hand. This method was originally referred to as a "talking typewriter" and now is known as "facilitated communication."

In facilitated communication, another person "holds and guides the subject's hand over the keyboard" (Shapiro, 1992, p. 63), allowing the subject to express thoughts by way of the keyboard. To date, independent researchers have not objectively or scientifically verified facilitated communication, and many believe it is nothing more than the facilitator expressing the facilitator's own thoughts and feelings. Still, there are parents who are very enthusiastic about facilitated communication and report that they have had excellent results using the method.

There are many various therapies for individuals with autism. Some students with autism benefit from auditory training. This treatment is generally used for those who are oversensitive or hypersensitive to sound. It involves listening to a variety of different sound frequencies, coordinated to the level of impairment in the person with autism. Auditory training is performed by an audiologist trained in this particular method. Music therapy is also used in a structured setting or is included in a child's educational program at school.

Erroneous beliefs about autism often have led to the removal of the child with autism from the home. This has changed because of increasing advances in research about and our understanding of autism. New and innovative techniques are now used in the treatment of children with autism. In addition, greater help is available for parents.

Characteristics

Because autism has many varied symptoms and characteristics, including a wide variety of combinations, autism is considered a spectrum disorder. As such, there are different terms to describe children with autism such as *autistic-like, autistic tendencies, autism spectrum, high-functioning* or *low-functioning autism, more abled, or less abled.* Any one or more of the characteristics may also occur in children with other disabilities. In these cases, *autistic-like* behavior is used. It must be noted that not all people with autism manifest every characteristic, but the following behaviors are typical of autism:

- Difficulty relating to people, objects, and events
- Using toys and objects in an unconventional manner
- Lack of interaction with other children
- Appearing to be unaware of others
- Treating others as inanimate objects
- Avoiding eye contact
- Inability to accept affection
- Dislike of being touched
- Insistence that the environment and routine remain unchanged

- Compulsive and ritualistic behaviors
- Self-stimulatory behavior
- Self-injurious behavior, such as head banging
- Hyper- or hyposensitivity to various sensory stimuli
- Tantrums, often for no apparent reason
- Violent behavior toward others
- Severely impaired verbal and nonverbal communication skills
- Inability to communicate with words or gestures
- Nonspeech vocalizations
- Repetition of others' words (echolalia)
- Repetition of something heard earlier (delayed echolalia)
- Preoccupation with hands
- Fascination with spinning objects
- Obsessive attachment to objects
- May be unresponsive to verbal clues

The prevalence of savant abilities in autism is 10%. Fifty percent of individuals who have the savant syndrome are autistic. The skills of the savant can be very impressive—for example, having a photographic memory, remembering entire train schedules, accurately drawing an object seen only once, or hearing a musical composition once and being able to play it back in its entirety. A few autistic savants include Nadia, a child whose drawings of houses have been compared to Rembrandt, and Richard Weaver, who is also blind, who draws in crayons and sells his works for $10,000. At present, it is unknown why some individuals with autism have savant abilities.

Strategies for Educators

Although many students with autism are enrolled in special classes, others are in the general education program. The teacher has the task of providing instruction to all the students in his or her class, with or without autism. The following strategies are general but can be adapted to meet the needs of the students.

All students with autism have communication problems. It is difficult for them to understand what a teacher is trying to convey. Giving too many directions and explanations at one time becomes confusing. Directions should be given one step at a time, but the teacher should avoid giving many repetitions of a direction. This only encourages a student not to listen. Explanations should also be broken down into smaller chunks. It is essential to confer with the speech and language specialist and the special education teacher who address the concerns of the teacher.

An augmentative alternative system, the Picture Exchange Communication System (PECS), helps children with autism who have communication deficits. Created by educators, resident care providers, and families, it was first used at the Delaware Autistic Program and has received worldwide recognition (Pyramid Educational Consultants, n.d.). The program requires no expensive equipment or materials. Children are taught to exchange a picture for the item they want, which is immediately honored. They are also trained in discrimination skills, such as matching symbols. For the children with visual discrimination deficits, pictures are used instead of symbols. The pictures are then used to form sentences helping them to learn simple sentence structure and better communication action skills.

Effective teaching includes attention to behavior plans, positive behavior management, and clear expectations and rules. The student with autism needs to know the expectations a teacher has and the consequence of failing to meet those expectations. Keep in mind that the child with autism has an increase in unusual or difficult behaviors when stressed or anxious. At times, the misbehavior may be an attempt to cope with the stressful situation. There should be a plan to help the student to either stay in the stressful situation or to go to another place to regain composure. Along with this, there should be a plan for the student's reentry into the class to avoid creating additional stress on the student. One must remember that the misbehavior of the high-functioning student with autism is not a case of manipulation and should never be taken personally.

Many students with autism are visual learners and are less confused when information is presented visually. The use of concrete, tangible visual aids such as pictures or charts in conjunction with verbal instruction is essential. Much of the material used for students with learning disabilities is appropriate for students with autism. Some students with autism are skillful in drawing, music, and mathematics, and they often have normal or advanced competency in these areas. The teacher should encourage such students' talents, provide additional learning opportunities in these areas, and always provide positive reinforcement.

Making generalizations is very difficult for students with autism. They need to practice skills that are functional for real-life situations. For example, it is best to use real foods in the study of nutrition. When teaching money skills, the teacher should use real money rather than play money. Whenever possible, the students should be taken to real places when learning about and practicing acceptable public behavior. Class field trips provide excellent concrete learning experiences for the student with autism.

It is advantageous for general education students to learn about the difficulties a person with autism has to overcome. Temple Grandin, PhD, overcame autism to become a well-known designer of livestock handling facilities and an author. At present, she is a professor of animal science at Colorado State University. In her book *Thinking in Pictures: Autism and Visual Thought,* she wrote, "The more I learn, the more I realize more and more that how I think and feel from a normal person. . . . Details are assembled into concepts like putting a jigsaw puzzle together. The picture on the puzzle can be seen when only 20 percent of the puzzle is put together forming a big picture"(Grandin, 1995, n.p.).

Educators should be aware of the many problems faced by parents of children with autism. These parents may need advice on seeking professional help. Many organizations and support groups will offer help and guidance to them. (Check your local telephone directory for the chapter of the Autism Society of America nearest you.)

Early diagnosis and educational evaluation of autism are very important, although help given at any age can make a significant difference. Some people with autism will need supervision throughout their lives. According to Bernard Rimland, former director of the Autism Research Institute, although autism is a lifelong condition, "a small percentage do recover to the point that they can live independently; and, in several cases, become world-famous" (personal communication, April 12, 1996).

For Further Information

Books

Abrams, P., & Henriques, L. *The autism spectrum parents' daily helper.*
Buten, H. *Through the glass wall: Journeys in the closed off worlds of the autistic.*
Dawson, G., & Sterling, J. Early intervention in autism. In M. J. Guralnick (Ed.), *The effectiveness of early intervention* (pp. 307–326).
Grandin, T. *Thinking in pictures, expanded edition: My life with autism.*
Grandin, T., & Barron, S. *The unwritten rules of social relationships: Decoding social mysteries through unique perspective of autism.*
Koegel, L. K., & Lazebnik, C. *Overcoming autism.*
Koegel, R. L., & Koegel, L. K. *Teaching children with autism: Strategies for initiating positive interactions and improving learning outcomes.*
Mesibov, G. B., Adams, L., & Kilinger, L. *Autism: Understanding the disorder.*
Siegel, B. *World of the autistic child: Understanding and treating autistic spectrum disorders.*
Simpson, R. L. (with coauthors). *Autism spectrum disorders: Interventions and treatments for children and youth.*

Williams, D *Somebody somewhere: Breaking free from the world of autism.*
Zager, D. (2004). *Autism spectrum disorders: Identification, education, and treatment.*
Zysk, V., & Notbohm, E. *1001 great ideas for teaching children with autism spectrum disorders.*

Organizations and Agencies

The American Academy of Pediatrics
Department of Federal Affairs
601 13th Street NW
Suite 400 North
Washington, DC 2005 USA
202-347-8600
Fax: 202-395-6137
www.aap.org
For electronic mail, the AAP has a list of addresses on the Web site. You can select the most appropriate e-mail address for your location.

Autism Research Institute (ARI)
4182 Adams Avenue
San Diego, CA 92116
866-366-3361
Fax: 619-563-6840

Autism Society of America
7910 Woodmont Avenue, Suite 300
Bethesda, MD 20814-3067
800-328-8476
301-657-0881
Fax: 301-657-0869
E-mail: Please choose the appropriate department as listed on the ASA Web site.
www.autism-society.org

Autism Speaks
2 Park Avenue, 11th Floor
New York, NY 10016
212-252-8584
Fax: 212-252-8676
E-mail: webmaster@americaspeaks.org
www.americaspeaks.org

Council for Exceptional Children (CEC)
1110 North Glebe Road, Suite 300
Arlington, VA 22201
888-232-7733
Fax: 703-264-9494
E-mail: service@cec.sped.org
www.cec.sped.org

Indiana Resource Center for Autism
Indiana Institute on Disability and Community
2853 East Tenth Street
Bloomington, IN 47408-2696
812-855-6508
812-855-9396 (TTY)
Fax: 812-855-9630
www.iidc.indiana.edu/irca

National Autism Association
1330 Schatz Lane
Nixa, MO 65714
877-NAA-Autism

National Institute of Mental Health (NIMH)
National Information and Communications Branch
Room 8184, MSC 9663
Bethesda, MD 20892-9663
301-443-5413
800-615-NIMH (6464)
301-443-8431 TTY
866-415-8051 TTY
Fax: 391-443-4279
E-mail: nimhinfo@nih.gov
www.nimh.nih.giv

Bipolar Disorder

Definition

Pediatric bipolar disorder (PBD), previously known as manic depression, is a mood disorder associated with recurrent episodes of mania and depression marked by extreme changes in mood, energy, and behavior in children. The cycles may be continuous and the mania and depression may overlap in time.

Background

Bipolar is one of the oldest known illnesses dating as far back as the second century A.D. The earliest writing linking melancholia and mania was by a medical philosopher, Aretaeus of Cappadocia, between 30 and 150 A.D. He is credited with most of the surviving writings about the unification of mania and melancholia. He believed that excess yellow bile or a mixture of black and yellow bile resulted in mania. Aretaeus theorized that both mania and depression had their origin in black bile, leading to his conclusion that there was a linkage between mania and depression and that it was a manic-depressive illness.

In 1650, scientist Richard Burton used his own findings on the linkage between depression and melancholia to write *The Anatomy of Melancholia*. Burton became known as the father of depression as a mental illness. Two hundred years later, Jules Falret established a link between depression and suicide. His extensive research led to the term *bipolar disorder*.

In 1902, before the use of mood stabilizers, German psychiatrist Emil Kraepelin studied the effects of depression and mania on untreated patients. He noticed that his patients had symptom-free intervals between their episodes of extreme manic-depressive symptoms. Kraepelin used the term *manic-depressive psychosis* in describing his patients.

Kraepelin also spent many hours studying the mentally ill. Ninety percent of his patients with manic depression had a family history of the illness. He concluded that the greatest frequency of manic-depressive attacks occurred between the ages of 15 and 20 (Papolos, 2006). Because of his approach to mental illness, Kraepelin has become known as the father of modern psychiatry.

After World War II, Dr. John Cade, a psychiatrist at Bundoora Repatriation Hospital in Melbourne, Australia, investigated the effect of various compounds on veterans with manic-depressive psychosis. He discovered that lithium carbonate was a successful treatment for psychotic patients with manic-depressive psychosis. This marked the beginning of psychopharmacological treatment.

The term *manic-depressive illness* first appeared in 1958. Although some still use the term *manic-depressive illness*, the National Association of Mental Illness (NAMI) replaced the term *manic-depressive disorder* with *bipolar disorder* in 1980. The term *bipolar disorder* (BP) is now the accepted term.

It is only recently that bipolar disorder has been acknowledged as a medical illness in children and youth. Mental health professionals appear to agree that bipolar disorder is an illness in children and adolescents; however, they seem to disagree as to whether the symptoms seen in children and adolescents relate to the diagnosis of bipolar disorder in adults. Regardless of the disagreements, pediatric bipolar disorder (PBD) is now accepted by the majority of mental health professionals as an illness.

Bipolar disorder is a serious mental illness that not only affects adults but also children and adolescents. BP is also considered a long-term illness with extreme mood changes. The person with BP can go from feeling very sad and helpless to feeling grandiose and great. The moods will alternate between the two opposite poles of hopelessness and hopefulness. These extreme mood changes generally occur in cycles. Between the cycles, some individuals may be able to function normally. However, children often cycle back and forth rapidly and have few periods in between. Others may experience milder symptoms of the moods. Bipolar disorder has this type of alternating mood patterns of depression and mania.

In the manic phase, children and adolescents with bipolar disorder may have feelings of paranoia as well as delusions of grandeur that give them special powers and abilities. They also can become irritable and prone to destructive outbursts rather than being euphoric and elated. In the manic stage, many physical complaints are made, such as headaches, stomachaches, and muscle aches. If the manic episode is mild or moderate, it is referred to as hypomania.

Some of the symptoms in a depressed state include extreme feelings of sadness and hopelessness. Children with bipolar disorder have episodes of feeling worthless and of being a burden to their family and friends. They have decreased energy and either sleep too much or are unable to sleep. Activities that were once enjoyed are no longer important. Their appetite fluctuates between eating too much and not eating enough, causing either weight gain or loss.

Some children or adolescents with bipolar disorder may have thoughts of suicide or may actually attempt to commit suicide. If any child or adolescent thinks or talks about suicide, immediate action is necessary. A mental health professional or doctor should be contacted. According to the National Association for Mental Illness (NAMI), the risk for suicide appears to be higher earlier in the course of the illness. Therefore, recognizing bipolar disorder early and learning how to manage it may decrease the risk of death by suicide.

Diagnosis of bipolar disorder is difficult. The similarity of symptoms in other disabilities, such as attention-deficit/hyperactive disorder (AD/HD), presents difficulties in accurately diagnosing an individual. Examples of similar symptoms in both AD/HD and bipolar disorder include inattentiveness, destructiveness, and aggressiveness Angry outbursts are common to both disorders. These outbursts of anger in a child with AD/HD are of a shorter duration than those of a child with bipolar disorder. Angry outbursts in a child with bipolar disorder can last for hours at a time. Having similar symptoms to those with other disorders adds additional confusion. The probability exists that an underlying bipolar disorder has been undiagnosed. A long-standing question regarding bipolar disorder is whether the bipolar disorder is being underdiagnosed or overdiagnosed. An article by F. Russell Crites, *Characteristics of ADHD and Bipolar Disorder*, compares the differences between the two disorders. The article can be found in Resource E at the back of this book.

There has been a lack of standardized criteria for identifying children and adolescents who might have a bipolar disorder. Currently, psychiatrists use the *DSM-IV*, published by the APA (1994). It has standardized criteria, including the symptoms, periods, and duration of time for episodes for the identification of adults—not children—who may have bipolar disorder. Even without using the specific data for adults, professionals have found the *DSM-IV* to be of great value in their work with children and adolescents.

Three major subtypes of bipolar disorder include BP-I, BP-II, and BP-NOS (Bipolar Disorder–Not Otherwise Specified). According to the guidelines of the manual, BP-I consists of major manic and depression episodes, BP-II consists of an alternating pattern between less pronounced and long-standing episodes of depression (dysthymia) with less severe manic (hypomanic) episodes. BP-NOS includes bipolar features that are mixed and vacillate between moods.

At this time, there are no standardized criteria to identify children with bipolar disorder. As NIMH director Dr. Thomas Insel states, "These aren't children with the occasional bad moods you see in most kids. They're typically very ill with symptoms that interfere with their lives in major ways. Establishing clear diagnostic criteria is an essential step toward making sure they get the help they need" (Cahill, 2007, n.p.).

Bipolar disorder does not have a single cause. Since the illness tends to run in families, heredity appears to be one of the factors, and it appears to be highly genetic. Research scientists have been looking for specific genes as a cause, but they have concluded that many different genes working together combined with environmental and other factors may be a cause of bipolar disorder. Symptoms of bipolar disorder might be caused by chemical imbalances in the brain. The cells release chemicals known as neurotransmitters. Two of the neurotransmitters, serotonin and dopamine, are essential for emotional health. Scientists believe that an imbalance in these two neurotransmitters will cause a bipolar disorder. Too much dopamine may cause symptoms of BP such as delusions, whereas, too little dopamine may cause symptoms such as a lack of emotion and energy. Another neurotransmitter, norepinephrine, may also be involved. When norepinephrine levels are too high, mania might occur, but when norepinphrine drops below a normal level, a state of depression can occur. Other scientists believe that bipolar disorder is the result of a premature death of brain cells.

Researchers are also conducting imaging studies to take pictures of a living brain at work to better understand the brain's structure and activity. These techniques include magnetic resonance imaging (MRI), positron emission tomography (PET), and functional magnetic resonance imaging (fMRI). There is evidence from imaging that the brains of individuals with bipolar disorder may differ from the brains of healthy individuals. The advanced tools that are being used may lead to discovery of the exact cause of BP and may provide the best treatment for an individual with bipolar disorder.

Bipolar disorder has no cure; rather, it is a recurring illness requiring long-term treatment. In most cases, bipolar disorder is better controlled if treatment is continuous. Medications, psychosocial treatment, and psychotherapy are usually used in treating patients with bipolar disorder.

The psychiatrist or doctor who is familiar with bipolar disorder usually prescribes mood stabilizers such as lithium or valproate to control symptoms of mania and to prevent the recurring of both manic and depressive episodes. Both medications have been approved by the U.S. Food and Drug Administration (FDA). However, according to the NIMH, the medication used to treat depression in a person who has bipolar disorder may actually induce manic symptoms as well as worsen the manic symptoms. On October 25, 2004, the FDA issued a public health advisory to warn the public about the increased risk of suicidal thoughts and behaviors in children and adolescents being treated with antidepressant medications.

As an addition to medication, psychosocial treatment includes various types of therapies: cognitive, behavior, psychoeducation, family, interpersonal, and social therapy. These interventions along with medications will assist in providing stabilization of moods, improved functioning, and fewer hospitalizations. NAMI states that even though there currently is no cure for bipolar disorder, staying on treatment can help to keep the disease under control.

Characteristics

The NIMH listed the following characteristics for BP:

Manic characteristics include

- Severe changes in mood, either extremely irritable or overly silly and elated
- Overly inflated self-esteem; grandiosity

- Increased energy
- Decreased need for sleep; ability to go with very little or no sleep for days without tiring
- Increased talking; talking too much or too fast; changing topics too quickly; cannot be interrupted
- Distractibility; attention moves constantly from one thing to the next
- Hypersexuality; increased sexual thoughts, feelings, or behaviors; use of explicit sexual language
- Increased goal-directed activity or physical agitation
- Disregard of risk, excessive involvement in risky behaviors or activities

Depressive characteristics include
- Persistent sad or irritable mood
- Loss of interest in activities once enjoyed
- Significant change in appetite or body weight
- Difficulty sleeping or oversleeping
- Physical agitation or slowing
- Loss of energy
- Feelings of worthlessness or inappropriate guilt
- Difficulty concentrating
- Recurrent thoughts of death or suicide

Characteristics of mania and depression in children and adolescents may manifest themselves through a variety of different behaviors. When manic, children and adolescents, in contrast to adults, are more likely to be irritable and prone to destructive outbursts than to be elated or euphoric. When depressed, there may be many physical complaints such as headaches, muscle aches, stomachaches or tiredness, frequent absences from school or poor performance in school, talk of or efforts to run away from home, irritability, complaining, unexplained crying, social isolation, poor communication, and extreme sensitivity to rejection or failure.

Strategies for Educators

Every teacher has the immense responsibility to manage the students and the classroom environment to provide the best learning possible for all children and adolescents with or without disabilities. Teaching can and should be a satisfying and rewarding experience for the students as well as the teacher.

Having a student on medications requires additional responsibilities. Of utmost importance is establishing an ongoing communication with the parents regarding their child. If the medication is to be administered at school, the parents should be requested to sign a form giving permission for the nurse or other person(s) to medicate the student in case of absences of the dedicated personnel. In all cases, the names of all the designated school personnel who are in charge of the student's medication should be listed on the permission form. This is necessary in order to cover any absences that might occur.

The student's teacher has the responsibility to make certain that the student leaves the room in order to take the medicine at the scheduled time. It is advisable for the teacher to keep a log of the student's medications and the times they should be administered. In addition, the teacher should keep a log stating the time the student left the room to receive his or her medication. The teacher should remind the student when to leave using an unobtrusive prearranged signal.

Some medications may be taken at home and do not require the student to take any medication at school. When this is the case, the parent has the responsibility to inform the school personnel.

As with all medicines, there is always the possibility that side effects from the medication may occur. There are medications that dehydrate a person. In this case, the physician may want the student to have water available at all times. The student should be able to have a water bottle on his or her desk at all times. If the physician wants the student to have juice, the parent should send individual-sized cans of juice to school.

A student with bipolar disorder may experience gastrointestinal or urologic side effects and should be allowed to leave the room at any time. To avoid interruptions of the class, the teacher and student can use a prearranged signal. Giving the student with bipolar disorder a permanent hall pass would relieve the student of possible anxiety about his or her physical condition.

Some medicines or side effects may produce blurring of vision in the student with bipolar disorder. Then it is necessary to reduce the amount of reading required. There are many ways this can be achieved, such as having the reading material recorded on tape so the student can listen to the assigned reading material. It is also beneficial to allow another student to listen to the recording at the same time as the student with bipolar disorder. Both students would benefit and still be able to participate in the oral discussion. Some of the strategies discussed under "Visually Impaired" in this book would also be helpful for the student.

In some cases, when medication starts to wear off, a worsening of symptoms can occur. In this case, it is necessary for the teacher to be less demanding for finished tasks. Many of the strategies discussed under the strategies for AD/HD in this book are equally beneficial for a student with bipolar disorder.

The teacher should make a daily checklist about the student in order to maintain a daily log. In this way, with a minimum of time, a check mark can be used to record certain behaviors/symptoms of the student. Space should be provided in the event that additional information needs to be recorded. Time constraints on a teacher make it prudent to have a simplified checklist in order to eliminate much-needed writing. When contact is made with the parent, guardian, or psychiatrist, this information from the checklist is very necessary.

Informing the rest of the faculty about bipolar disorder is necessary in order to help them understand the difficulties facing a student with bipolar disorder. It is advisable to either speak at one of the many scheduled teacher meetings or to request an inservice to discuss the needs of the student with bipolar disorder. At that time, the medication, side effects, and needs of the student should be covered. Providing a handout about the disorder would be beneficial for all. It is prudent for the teacher to regard certain information as confidential.

The needs of the student with bipolar disorder would also be addressed on the student's IEP. The general education teacher who has the student in class needs the information in order to understand the problems facing the student with bipolar disorder. A positive attitude and patience are needed to help all the students to reach their individual potential.

Many well-known, successful people have surmounted the difficulties inherent to bipolar disorder. All students in the class would enjoy a research project regarding a specific celebrity who has bipolar disorder. Bipolar disorder has crossed over into many professions including music, entertainment, space, art, sports, television and radio, and more. All students, including the student with bipolar disorder, will benefit from this project.

For Further Information

Books

Amador, X. *I am not sick. I don't need your help.*
Birmaher, B. *New hope for children and teens with bipolar disorder.*
Boyd, M., & Nihart, M. *Psychiatric nursing: Contemporary practice.*
Findling, R. L., Kowatch, R. A., & Post, R. M. *Pediatric bipolar disorder.*
Geller, B. *Bipolar disorder in children and early adolescent.*
Greene, R. W. *The explosive child: A new approach for understanding and parenting easily frustrated, clinically inflexible children.*
Jamison, K. R. *An unquiet mind.*
Jensen, E. *Different brains, different learners: How to reach the hard to reach.*
Lederman, J., & Fink, C. *The ups and downs of raising a bipolar child: A survival guide for parents.*
Papolos, D., & Papolos, J. *The bipolar child.*

Organizations and Associations

American Psychiatric Association (APA)
1000 Wilson Boulevard, Suite 1825
Arlington, VA 22209
703-907-7300
888-357-7924 toll-free
E-mail: apa@psych.org
www.apa.org

Child & Adolescent Bipolar Foundation (CABF)
1000 Skokie Boulevard, Suite 425
Wilmette, IL 60091
847-256-8525
www.bpkids.org

International Society for Bipolar Disorder
P.O. Box 7168
Pittsburgh, PA 15213-0168
412-802-6940
Fax: 412-802-6941
E-mail: chadd@isbd.org
www.isbd.org

The Juvenile Bipolar Research Foundation (JBRF)
550 Ridgewood Road
Maplewood, NJ 07040
973-275-0400
E-mail: info@jbrf.org
www.jbrf.org

Lithium Information Center
c/o Madison Institute of Medicine
P.O. Box 628365
Middleton, WI 53562-8365
608-827-2470
Fax: 608-827-2479

National Alliance for the Mentally Ill (NAMI)
Colonial Place Three
2107 Wilson Blvd., Suite 300
Arlington, VA 22201-3042
703-524-7600
www.nami.org

National Institute of Mental Health (NIMH)
Public Information and Communications Branch
6001 Executive Boulevard, Room 8184 MSC 9663
Bethesda, MD 20892-9663
301-443-5413
866-615-NIMH (6461) toll-free
301-443-8051 (TTY)
866-514-8051 (TTY)
Fax: 301-443-4279
E-mail: nimhinfo@nih.gov
www.nimh.nih.gov

S.T.E.P. Up for Kids, Inc.
P.O. Box 65
Scituate, MA 02066
866-922-KIDS
www.stepup4kids.com

Cerebral Palsy

Definition

Cerebral palsy (CP) is a group of disorders characterized by nerve and muscle dysfunctions that affect body movement and muscle control. *Cerebral* refers to the brain, and *palsy* refers to a disorder of movement or posture.

Background

In 1862, William Little summarized 20 years of research by stating that spasticity and deformity associated with cerebral palsy were due to cerebral hemorrhage resulting from trauma during the birth process. During the latter part of the nineteenth century, Sigmund Freud made a distinction between congenital and acquired palsy and placed greater emphasis on "intrauterine development" than on actual birth trauma (Sternfeld, 1988).

Even though researchers in Europe had shown great interest in CP, little interest was shown in the United States from 1900 to 1925. Leon Sternfeld (1988) stated in a discussion on the history of research in CP that it was not until after World War II that interest in CP was rekindled. The American Academy for Cerebral Palsy was organized in 1947, and the United Cerebral Palsy Association, a national organization, was formed in 1949–1950. Congress then authorized the establishment of the National Institute of Neurological and Communicative Disorders, which is very instrumental in providing information to the public.

According to the United Cerebral Palsy Research and Educational Foundation, there are between 1.5 and 2 million children and adults in the United States who have cerebral palsy. Annually 1,200 to 1,500 preschool children are recognized as having CP. Six out of 10 people with CP will have normal intelligence. Deafness occurs in 1 out of 50 children. One out of 11 children is legally blind. One in three children is unable to walk, and one in four children is unable to feed or dress themselves. One in three children is mentally retarded.

According to the American Medical Association (1989), 90% of the cases of CP occur before or at birth. Any damage to the brain may result in CP. The causes include infection of the mother with German measles or other viral diseases during pregnancy, premature delivery, lack of oxygen supply to the infant due to premature separation of the placenta, an awkward birth position, labor that goes on too long or is too abrupt, or interference with the umbilical cord. CP may be associated with Rh or ABO blood type incompatibility between parents, microorganisms that attack the newborn's central nervous system, or the lack of good prenatal care.

When the brain is under development, CP also develops. Eighty percent of all cases of CP occur before the baby reaches 1 month old, although CP can and does occur within the first five years of growth. Once the damage in the brain occurs, it is nonprogressive. CP does not improve or get worse. Although the symptoms may seem to increase, this is more than likely due to the aging process of the individual.

It is also possible to have an acquired type of CP resulting from head injuries. Motor vehicle accidents, falls, or child abuse that results in a head injury to the child can also cause CP. Brain infection can be another cause.

There are three main types of CP: *spastic, athetoid,* and *ataxic.*

Spastic CP is the most common form. In this type of CP, the muscles are tense, contracted, and resistant to movement. The lower legs may turn in and cross at the ankles, and movement is slow. Sometimes, the leg muscles are so contracted that the child's heels do not touch the floor and the child has to tiptoe. The use of physical therapy, plaster casts, orthopedic surgery, or all three may help alleviate the problems.

Athetoid CP is characterized by involuntary movements of parts of the body that are affected, such as facial grimaces, hand twisting, or tonguing and drooling. The person's body may make jerking and flailing motions. Because of these characteristics, many who have athetoid CP are mistakenly considered to be mentally or emotionally unstable.

Ataxic CP involves disturbances such as a lack of balance, coordination, and depth perception. With ataxic CP, there may be swaying when standing and difficulty in maintaining balance. Persons with this type of CP may walk with their feet wide apart in order to avoid falling. This disability, as with other disabilities, varies from mild to severe and, in some cases of ataxic cerebral palsy, there may be a complete loss of mobility.

If several motor centers are affected, the symptoms of CP may be mixed, with a combination of the characteristics of all three main types of CP affecting the same or different parts of the body. Although individuals may have a combination of these types of CP, it is believed that most children with CP have either spastic or athetoid cerebral palsy.

Terms used to describe other areas of the body that can be affected by CP include the following:

Diplegia: This means that only the legs are affected.
Hemiplegia: This means that one-half of the body (such as the right arm and leg) is affected.
Quadriplegia: This means that both arms and legs are affected, sometimes including the facial muscles and torso. (NICHCY)

According to the American Medical Association (1989), about 75% of individuals with CP have mental retardation, with an IQ below 70. The exceptions are important, because some people who have spastic or athetoid CP are highly intelligent.

With early intervention, the effects of CP can be greatly reduced. Children with CP need different kinds of therapy. Physical therapy helps them to develop stronger muscles. During this therapy, work on walking, sitting, and keeping balanced is of value. A child with CP will also be given speech and language therapy. This therapy helps the child with CP to improve his or her speaking voice due to the possible lack of muscular control of the tongue and throat. Therapy also consists of adapting to the use of special equipment. This assistive equipment makes it possible for the child to enjoy activities such as horseback riding, swimming, and other activities that are of interest to the particular child with CP.

In addition to therapy, there are new medical treatments for CP. Some of the available treatments are regenerative techniques, functional neuromuscular stimulation, biofeedback, and robotics. Biomedical engineers at the New Jersey Institute of Technology are investigating robots and a wide variety of augmented reality and virtual reality technologies to help children with CP improve their movements, which will give them more independence. Researchers have been working with a robotic arm called the Haptic Master. Children with CP will hold the robot's arm, which is programmed to use repetitive arm and fingers to perform motions. Children will also wear a computerized cable glove that helps to move the paralyzed fingers. Researchers at the Institute are working on ways to improve spasticity and to help children control their movements.

CP is not contagious and is only rarely associated with a hereditary condition. Because brain damage does not worsen over time, CP is non-progressive and is not a primary cause of a person's death. Fortunately, researchers are now finding ways to prevent and treat cases of CP.

Characteristics

Depending on which part of the brain has been damaged and the degree of involvement of the central nervous system, one or more of the following may occur:

- Spasms
- Muscle tone problems
- Involuntary movements
- Disturbances in gait and mobility
- Seizures
- Abnormal sensation and perception
- Impairment of sight
- Impairment of hearing
- Impairment of speech
- Mental retardation

Not all of these characteristics are necessarily present in all cases of CP. In some instances, there may be only a slight disturbance that is unnoticed by the teacher or students.

Strategies for Educators

The general education teacher of a student with CP must make certain that the individual educational needs of the student are addressed. Due to the physical appearance of some children with CP, mistaken impressions about the child's intelligence are sometimes made. CP can give the child mannerisms that lead a teacher to believe that the child is incapable of learning as much as other students. This is unfortunate because they have the same range of intelligence as children without CP. There is no correlation between physical characteristics and cognitive abilities. Previously held misconceptions need to be abandoned, and the focus should always be on the person and not the disability.

Many assistive devices are available to help students with disabilities. Depending on the severity of the CP, there are many academic aids that are used by students with CP, such as book holders; page turners; adaptive keyboards; mobility, orthopedic, and communication aids; and interactive computer programs. Generally, the assistive technology needs of the student are addressed and determined during the development of an IEP. The assistive technology specialist then arranges for the student to have the specific devices needed to help the individual student with CP. The teacher should always have ongoing communication with the assistive technology specialist who provides necessary information about the type of CP the student has and shows the teacher how the equipment is to be used by the student.

If possible, the student with CP should be given the opportunity to explain and to demonstrate to the class how a particular piece of equipment is used, and, when feasible, other students in the class should have an opportunity to use the aid. By trying some of the various types of devices, students can better appreciate some of the difficulties faced by students who are dependent on specialized equipment for their daily existence.

It is difficult for teachers not to be concerned about their students. In the case of a student with CP, this tendency can be especially strong. A teacher may feel that the student may get hurt in various sports, but if medically approved, the student should be allowed to participate. The impulse to protect the student needs to be avoided. Too often, students with CP feel isolated and need this involvement. The student with CP needs to experience failures and successes like all the other students.

It is important for the teacher to stress the fact that CP is neither contagious nor is it a disease. With knowledge, the students will forgo any previous misconceptions they may have held about CP.

In some cases, it may be necessary to schedule restroom breaks for the student, with a paraprofessional to provide assistance. It is best to schedule the break time to occur before the general education class breaks to allow the student with CP additional time.

Another consideration concerns the difficulty some students with CP have in carrying books and materials. In this case, all teachers of these students should lend another set of texts to be kept at home. In secondary school, where there are class changes during the day, a peer buddy can be assigned to help the student.

The handling of students with CP, such as moving them from one position to another, depends on the nature of the various characteristics displayed by each individual. If the student has another coexisting disability, suggestions for strategies to use with the student can be found in this book under that disability. The one thing that needs to remain constant is that the teacher be thoughtful and sensitive to the needs of the student.

Many advances have taken place in the past 15 years that have had an enormous positive effect on the long-term well-being of children born with CP. Technological innovations have made it possible for many persons with CP to be employed and have lives as near to normal as possible.

For Further Information

Books

Aaseng, N. *Cerebral palsy (for grades 9–12).*
Geralis, E. *Children with cerebral palsy: A parents' guide.*
Keller, R. A., & Holt, R. *Family guide to assistive technology.*
Miller, F., & Bachrach, S. J. *Cerebral palsy: A complete guide for caregiving.*
Nolan, C. *Under the eye of the clock.*
Schleichkorn, J. *Coping with cerebral palsy: Answers to questions parents often ask.*

Organizations and Agencies

Children's Neurological Solutions (CNS)
1826 State Street
Santa Barbara, CA 93101
866-267-5580
805-898-4442
E-mail: info@cnsfoundation.org
www.cnsfoundation.org

Children's Hemiplegia and Stroke Association (CHASA)
44101 Green Oaks Boulevard, Suite 305
PMB 149
Arlington, TX 76016
817-492-4325
E-mail: info437@chasa.org
www.hemi-kids.org

National Easter Seal Society
230 West Monroe Street, Suite 1800
Chicago, IL 60606-4802
800-221-6827
312-726-6200
Fax: 312-726-1494
E-mail: info@easter-seals.org
www.seals.org

National Institute of Mental Health (NIMH)
Office of Communications
6001 Executive Boulevard, Room 8184, MSC 9693
Bethesda, MD 20892-9663
301-443-8431
866-615-6464
301-443-8431 TTY
Fax: 301-443-4279
E-mail: nimhinfo@nih.gov
www.nimh.nih.gov

United Cerebral Palsy Association, Inc.
1660 L Street NW, Suite 700
Washington, DC 20036
800-872-5827
202-776-0406
202-973-7196 (TTY)
Fax: 202-776-0414
E-mail:webmaster@ucp.org
www.ucp.org

National Dissemination Center for Children with Disabilities (NICHCY)
P.O. Box 1492
Washington, DC 20013
800-695-0285 (voice/TTY)
Fax: 202-884-8441
E-mail: nichcy@aed.org
www.nichcy.org

Down Syndrome

Definition

Down syndrome is a chromosomal disorder resulting in a delay in physical, intellectual, and language development. It is the most commonly recognizable chromosomal disorder associated with mental retardation. People with Down syndrome have a characteristic physical appearance.

Background

For centuries, people with Down syndrome were depicted in art, science, and literature. In 1866, John Langdon Down, an English physician, published a report describing the condition as a distinct and separate entity. He described the characteristics of mental retardation. In his report, he used the terms *Mongolian* and *Mongolian idiocy*. At that time, *idiocy* was used in reference to a severe degree of intellectual retrogression. He became recognized as the father of research on the syndrome.

The term *Mongolian* was used until 1959, when a group of scientists felt that the term should not be used since it had misleading connotations. Some refer to the syndrome as *Down's syndrome*. However, it was only recently that the Down Syndrome Society determined that the possessive form for the syndrome, Down's syndrome, carried an incorrect meaning. It was determined that there should be no apostrophe and that the syndrome should be referred to as Down syndrome.

In 1959, a French physician, Jerome Lejeune, identified Down syndrome as a chromosomal anomaly. Through advances in molecular biology, it was discovered that people with Down syndrome have 47 chromosomes in each cell instead of the usual 46. This extra chromosome, partial or complete 21st chromosome, results in the characteristics associated with Down syndrome (National Down Syndrome Society, 2001).

Two other types of chromosomal abnormalities are also implicated in Down syndrome. Nondisjunction is a faulty cell division in which there are three number 21 chromosomes instead of two. This occurs in 95% of all cases of Down syndrome. Mosaicism is the nondisjunction of the 21st chromosome in which there is a mixture of two types of cells, some containing 46 chromosomes and others 47. This occurs in only 1% to 2% of all cases of Down syndrome. Translocation, in which the 21st chromosome breaks off during cell division and attaches to another chromosome, occurs in only 3% to 4%. Although the number of chromosomes remains at 46, the extra part attached to another chromosome causes the features of Down syndrome. Because 95% of all cases of Down syndrome occur because there are three copies of the 21st chromosome, it is referred to as trisomy 21.

At the present time, researchers do not know what causes the chromosomal abnormality of the development of 47 chromosomes instead of the usual 46 chromosomes. This extra chromosome in the fetus prevents a normal development of the body and brain. Generally, the diagnosis of Down syndrome is made from a chromosome test administered shortly after birth.

Of all the chromosome-related disorders, Down syndrome is the most prevalent. A diagnosis of Down syndrome is often suspected after birth due to the physical appearance of the baby, although these same physical characteristics are also seen in the general population. Therefore, if Down syndrome is suspected, a chromosome test is administered shortly after birth. It is estimated that 1 in every 800 to 1,100 live births results in a child with Down syndrome (National Down Syndrome Congress, 1988a, 1988b). In the United States, approximately 5,000 children annually are born with Down syndrome. Research has indicated that significantly more males than females are born with this chromosomal disorder.

Either the father or the mother may carry the extra chromosome. However, in 70% to 80% of the cases, the extra chromosome originates with the mother.

Eighty percent of children with Down syndrome are born to women under 35 years of age, but the rate of incidence is higher for women over age 35. At age 40, the chance of having a baby with Down syndrome is 1 in 110 births. At age 45, the risk increases to approximately 1 in 35 births. Women who have Down syndrome can and do have children, and there is a 50% chance that their children will also have Down syndrome.

The mortality rate of children with Down syndrome is decreasing. Around 1910, the life expectancy for children with Down syndrome was 9 years. The National Down Syndrome Society (1993a, 1993b) states that with the recent advances in medical treatment, around 80% of adults with Down syndrome now reach age 55 and beyond. In addition, many individuals now postpone having a family until later in life, when the incidence rate of Down syndrome is higher. Thus, the number of Down syndrome cases is expected to increase and possibly double in the next 10 years (National Down Syndrome Society, 1993a, 1993b).

Unfortunately, children with Down syndrome often have other health-related problems. Their lowered resistance causes them to have more respiratory problems. Hearing and speech problems also are possible. Many infants born with Down syndrome have defective hearts and gastrointestinal defects. Most of the defects are correctable by surgery or other means by a medical doctor. At this time, most of the defects are correctable.

Some may have what is called *atlantoaxial instability*, which is a misalignment of the top two vertebrae of the neck. This condition makes them prone to injury during certain activities. It makes it difficult for a child with Down syndrome to participate in sports that place undue strain on the neck. There is also a tendency for these children to be obese. This puts more strain on the body, causing additional physical ailments.

Scientific and medical research on Down syndrome is gaining momentum. Research is continuing on identifying the genes in chromosome 21 that cause the characteristics of Down syndrome. According to the National Down Syndrome Society, it will be possible, eventually, to improve, correct, and prevent many of the problems associated with Down syndrome. There is hope that in the future the ongoing research on Down syndrome will lead to development of an intervention and cure.

Characteristics

Individuals with Down syndrome are usually smaller in stature than their peers without Down syndrome. Not only is their physical development slower but their intellectual development is also delayed. According to the American Medical Association (1989), the IQ of a child with Down syndrome may range anywhere from 30 to 80, although in some cases it may be as high as 120. The mental retardation of individuals with Down syndrome falls within the range of minimal to severe, with many who are mildly to moderately disabled.

Approximately one-third of babies born with Down syndrome have heart defects, most of which can now be surgically corrected. Adults with Down syndrome are prone to atherosclerosis, which can lead to heart disease.

Gastrointestinal problems are also common. Many who have Down syndrome have a higher-than-average incidence of a narrowing at some point in the intestines.

Visual problems, such as crossed eyes, far- or nearsightedness, and cataract formation, are higher in those with Down syndrome.

Persons with Down syndrome are prone to repeated ear infections, and they often have mild to moderate hearing loss generally caused by retention of fluid in the inner ear (see Auditory Processing Disorder). They often have speech impediments due to enlargement of the tongue.

Many individuals with Down syndrome have the same changes in the brain as those who have Alzheimer's disease. This does not necessarily mean that all show clinical signs of Alzheimer's disease. There is a 25% chance that individuals with Down syndrome who are over the age of 35 will develop Alzheimer's-type dementia.

They also have a 5 to 20 times greater risk than the general population of developing leukemia. According to Charles Epstein, who studies genes related to Down syndrome, someone with Down syndrome has a 1% chance of developing leukemia.

The National Dissemination Center for Children with Disabilities states that there are more than 50 clinical signs of Down syndrome, but it is rare to find all, or even most, of the signs in one person. Some common characteristics include the following:

- Speech problems
- Poor muscle tone
- Upward slanting of the eyes with folds of skin at the inner corners
- White spots in the iris of the eye
- Short, broad hands with a single crease across the palm of one or both hands
- Broad feet with short toes
- Flat bridge of the nose
- Short, low-set ears
- Short neck and small head
- Flattened back of the head
- Small oral cavity
- Short, high-pitched cries in infancy

- Large protruding tongue
- Excessive ability for flexing extremities
- Only one flexion furrow on the fifth finger instead of two

As previously mentioned, some people with Down syndrome also may have atlantoaxial instability. This is a misalignment of the top two vertebrae of the neck. This condition makes these individuals more prone to injury if they participate in activities that overextend or flex the neck.

Strategies for Educators

Students with Down syndrome are often placed in special education classes. Some of these students are mainstreamed for special classes and activities in the general education class. Others are sometimes fully included in the general education class. Whether it is mainstreaming or inclusion, the teacher needs to have communication with the parents, special education teacher, and all in the support system of the student with Down syndrome.

Students need to realize that all students have feelings. Teachers can encourage students to discuss how they feel when someone teases them versus how they feel when they are given positive feedback. Only with positive feedback will the disabled student develop a feeling of self-worth. A student who is well liked by peers and has leadership qualities may be selected to act as a "buddy" for the student. The buddy needs to be made aware that he or she can be instrumental in promoting the acceptance of a student with Down syndrome by the other students. Encourage all students to include the student with Down syndrome in their activities.

Students in the general education classroom need to have an understanding of the student with Down syndrome. To help eliminate the stereotyping of people with Down syndrome, teachers can inform students about well-known people with Down syndrome who have attained success. Many students who are television viewers have seen Chris Burke in the ABC series *Life Goes On*, as well as in other shows. Born with Down syndrome, Burke always wanted to be an actor. His own determination and faith helped him achieve his goal. He also coauthored a book with Jo Beth McDaniel, *A Special Kind of Hero: Chris Burke's Own Story* (1991).

Jason Kingsley and Mitchell Levitz, who both have Down syndrome, wrote the book *Count Us In: Growing Up With Down Syndrome* (1994a), which challenges the misconceptions and stereotypes surrounding Down syndrome. This book provides students and teachers with insights into the difficulties facing a person with Down syndrome. As Mitchell Levitz stated, "We are trying to erase all the negative attitudes that people had about Down syndrome" (Kingsley & Levitz, 1994b, p. 19).

The student with Down syndrome must be given every opportunity to succeed. Various techniques may be used to reinforce a concept. These include having the student listen to audiotapes and adjusting the length and type of assignment. Teachers should keep in mind that there is a wide variance in the degree of mental retardation in students with Down syndrome, and they should not only set attainable individual goals but encourage students to reach those goals.

The student with Down syndrome has a difficult time attending to relevant stimuli. The teacher needs to use techniques that help the student attend to tasks. This might include teacher prompts, cues, or a secret signal known only to the student. Placing the work on different colored paper or textures often enhances attention. Putting too many problems on a page confuses a student with Down syndrome. Extraneous stimuli can also be minimized by seating the student away from windows, doors, and high traffic areas.

Due to language delays, the student with Down syndrome has inadequate short-term memory. There is need for much repetition and review using a multisensory approach. For example, the use of visual aids, audiotapes, computer programs, and manipulatives, as well as other concrete materials help maintain the attention and interest of the student. The teacher should use meaningful materials relevant to the lesson being taught. The use of novel items should be avoided because this only confuses the student. Students with Down syndrome learn by active participation and should be provided with hands-on activities as much as possible.

A student with Down syndrome often learns something one day but forgets it the next day. Visual cues help to prompt the memory. In teaching mathematics, the student can use manipulatives for computation. Physically performing the operation aids in the retention of a mathematics concept. Primary students can be used as counting pieces to physically perform the computation problems of addition and subtraction. Word problems are particularly difficult for students with Down syndrome. The teacher should first teach the language or vocabulary of the problem, allowing sufficient time for processing. Showing and labeling the common words that help determine the operation needed to solve the problem is necessary. Examples of cue words for addition and subtraction might be "in all," "altogether," "fewer than," and "more than." Word cues can be charted for the entire class as well as printed on 3×5 cards for each student in the class.

Evidence exists that poor reading performance coincides with slower social development that is characteristic of children with Down syndrome. In the general education class, this can be a challenge for the teacher. For additional assistance, the paraeducator and special education teacher can aid and provide support for both the teacher and the student. Arrangements can also be made for the student to go to another class where the reading approximates the level of the student. When feasible, the selection of reading materials should incorporate previous experiences of a student with Down syndrome. In general, all their reading selections should be broken down into smaller units to check the comprehension and help the student maintain focus. Keeping in mind that the learning characteristics of students with Down syndrome are more similar than different from their general education peers, good reading techniques benefit both.

A common behavior of children with Down syndrome is that of wandering. Medical literature calls this behavior elopement. The child just leaves an area and wanders away. This wandering is impulsive, and the child has no thought that wandering might be dangerous. The teacher needs to be aware of this propensity and take every precaution necessary to prevent wandering from happening. There is a need to establish certain boundaries for the student as well as simple rules that need to be followed. These should be charted and posted for easy referral. Role-playing helps the student understand what is expected. It is important to have an incentive program that rewards adherence to the rules. Giving the student a desk near the teacher makes it easier to watch for any indications that the child may impulsively wander away. If this happens, the school office personnel need to be immediately alerted. The outside area, restrooms, and any room where a teacher may not be present should be checked. Students in the class quickly become aware of the tendency for the student to wander and can be very useful in preventing this from happening. In this case, the buddy system provides an excellent check on the wandering tendencies of a student with Down syndrome. Fortunately, the child outgrows this wandering tendency as he or she matures.

The teacher should expect a level of work that is commensurate with the student's ability. It is helpful to provide the student with a notebook to organize the class assignments. Having a notebook prevents the student from losing important information and avoids calling attention to the fact that the student may have difficulty with regular assignments. Everything possible must be done to maintain and increase feelings of well-being in the student.

Early intervention is important for children with Down syndrome. Research has shown that stimulation during early childhood is necessary for a child with Down syndrome to reach his or her full potential. It is equally important that parents and all school personnel not place limitations on or underestimate the potential capabilities of a child with Down syndrome. Educators should base all intervention strategies on the principles of child development and focus on functional life skills.

Many community support groups can aid parents and teachers. For additional information, free directories are available in each state through the National Down Syndrome Society.

For Further Information

Books

Bruni, M. *Fine motor skills in children with Down syndrome: A guide for parents and professionals.*
Burke, C. (with McDaniel, J. B.). *A special kind of hero: Chris Burke's own story.*
Cohen, W. I. *Down syndrome: Visions for the 21st century.*
Denholm, C. (Ed.). *Adolescents syndrome: International perspectives on research and programme development.*
Kumin, L. *Communication skills in children with Down syndrome.*
Oelwein, P. (Ed.). *Teaching reading to children with Down syndrome: A guide for parents and teachers.*
Pueschel, S., & Sustrova, M. (Eds.). *Adolescents with Down syndrome: Toward a more fulfilling life.*
Winders, P. *Gross motor skills in children with Down syndrome: A guide for parents and professionals.*

Organizations and Agencies

Council for Exceptional Children (CEC)
1110 North Glebe Road, Suite 300
Arlington, VA 22201
888-232-7733
866-915-5000 (TTY)
Fax: 703-264-9494
E-mail: service@cec.sped.org
www.cec.sped.org

Down Syndrome Resource and Treatment Foundation (DSRTF)
753 Page Mill Road
Palo Alto, CA 94304-1003
650-468-1668
Fax: 650-851-7258
E-mail: dsrtf@dsrtf.org
www.dsrtf.org

National Dissemination Center for Children with Disabilities (NICHCY)
P.O. Box 1492
Washington, DC 20013
800-695-0285 (voice/TTY)
Fax: 202-884-8441
E-mail: nichcy@aed.org
www.nichcy.org

National Down Syndrome Congress
1370 Center Drive, Suite 102
Atlanta, GA 30338
800-232-6372
770-604-5502
Fax: 770-604-5898
E-mail: info@ndsccenter.org
www.ndsccenter.org

National Down Syndrome Society
666 Broadway, 8th Floor
New York, NY 10012
800-221-4602
212-460-9330
Fax: 212-979-2873
E-mail: info@ndss.org
www.nds.org

The Arc (formerly the Association for Retarded Citizens of the United States)
1010 Wayne Avenue, Suite 650
Silver Spring, MD 20910
302-565-3842
800-433-5255
Fax: 301-565-3843 / 301-565-5342
E-mail: info@thearc.org
www.thearc.org

Dyslexia

Definition

Dyslexia is a term that applies to a specific reading disability. Medically, it is defined as a condition resulting from neurological, maturational, or genetic causes. The World Federation of Neurology defines dyslexia as "a disorder manifested by difficulty in learning to read despite conventional instruction, adequate intelligence and sociocultural opportunity" (National Institute of Health and Human Development, 1996, n.p.). The International Dyslexia Association (IDA) adds that dyslexia "is referred to as a learning disability because students with dyslexia may experience difficulties in other language skills such as spelling, writing, and speaking. It is often referred to as a learning disability because dyslexia can make it very difficult for a student to succeed academically in the typical instructional environment" (International Dyslexia Association, 2000a).

Background

A great deal of research has been done, and numerous theories have been developed, on the cause of dyslexia. In 1925, Samuel Torrey Orton, a U.S. neuropsychiatrist, was one of the first scientists to investigate dyslexia. He thought the deficiency originated in the visual system (Reynolds & Fletcher-Janzen, 1999). He had been impressed with the kinesthetic method used by Grace Fernald and Helen Keller. Dr. Orton began to believe in a kinesthetic–tactile reinforcement of visual auditory associations. He began using multisensory methods at the Mobile Medical Health Clinic in Iowa, which he directed.

Dr. Orton's associate, Anna Gillingham, continued with the multisensory approach for teaching. It was known as the Orton-Gillingham approach, which included "teaching the structure of written English including the sounds (phonemes), meaning units (morphemes such as prefixes, suffixes, and roots) and common spelling rules" (IDA, 2000b). Dr. Orton concluded from his research that dyslexia was the result of a failure of one of the two hemispheres of the brain to dominate language development.

Albert Galaburda, a neuroscientist at Harvard Medical School and a world authority on brain anatomy, considers dyslexia to be a problem that results from mistakes in brain development ("New Clue," 1994). Several areas in the higher cortex that over time specialize in language development may be abnormal. His research involved perceptual and cognitive problems in written language and temporal processing of rapidly changing sounds. These problems were not easily observed in oral language but only in writing and reading.

Originally, researchers looked for one single cause of dyslexia, but they now believe many factors may be involved. Some believe that dyslexia is caused by either motor defects or visual defects, such as difficulties in eye tracking, directional scanning, or eye movement. Both visual problems and a lack of cerebral dominance are still considered by many to be valid causes of dyslexia.

Others researchers believe dyslexia is caused by alterations in specific parts of the brain. Recent evidence shows that there is a lag in the brain's maturation and a high degree of left-handedness in people with dyslexia, which may indicate differences in brain function (National Institute of Health and Human Development, 1993).

Still other researchers have theorized that disorders in the structure of the brain may be a factor. This was not an accepted theory until recently when postmortem examinations showed characteristic disorders of the brain. Although there is an ongoing debate about this theory, some researchers believe it may have some validity.

Research by Paula Tallal and colleagues at the Center for Molecular and Behavioral Neuroscience at Rutgers University suggests that the cause of dyslexia may be the mishearing of fast sounds (Suplee, 1998). Michael Merzenich, a neuroscientist at the University of California, San Francisco, and Tallal are devising new computerized techniques for drawing out or prolonging the sounds of stop consonants (for example, the sound of the letter *b*) to give children with dyslexia time to hear the consonant (Suplee, 1998). Once they are able to hear the sounds, it is hoped that the child with dyslexia will gradually develop alternative ways to perceive them.

Some experts believe that dyslexia can be attributed to methods of teaching. For example, they criticize the method of teaching reading by using the whole language approach and claim that students with dyslexia can learn to read by using the phonetic approach. Other experts believe that reading should be taught using a combination of phonics and the whole language approach (National Institute of Health and Human Development, 1993).

Frank R. Vellutino, working at the Child Research and Study Center of the State University of New York at Albany, believes that dyslexia is a language deficiency. Because dyslexic readers can perceive and reproduce letters at the same level as normal readers, the problem may be not the visual coding system but, rather, one of linguistics. He states, "Far from being a visual problem, dyslexia appears to be the consequence of limited facility in using language to code other types of information" (Vellutino, 1987, p. 34).

Advanced imaging technology has made it possible to identify specific patterns of brain activity. Scientists are now able to identify brain malfunctions involved in dyslexia (Manzo, 1998). Using magnetic resonance imaging, researchers were able to observe computer-generated images of the brain while the individual did various reading tasks. This imaging showed the person with dyslexia to have less brain activity in the areas of the brain that link the written form of words to the phonic components. This dysfunction in brain timing makes it difficult to accurately process speech sounds. The lack of phonemic awareness is what distinguishes the student with dyslexia from those without dyslexia.

Some studies have found that people with dyslexia have no greater incidence of eye problems than those without dyslexia (U.S. Department of Education, 1984). Their visual acuity, stereo acuity, ocular alignment, motility fusion status, and refractive errors do not differ from those of the general population.

Because approximately 86% of individuals identified as having dyslexia have an auditory language deficit, which prevents the linking of the spoken word with its written equivalent, Mattis (1978) believes the primary factor causing dyslexia is an auditory language deficit.

In contrast to language problems, only 5% of people diagnosed with dyslexia have visual-spatial-motor problems that interfere with sequential organization, scanning, and the perception of temporal and spatial cues. Such problems are common in young children who are just beginning to read and are self-correcting. However, a child with dyslexia whose deficits are undiagnosed and ongoing will miss out on basic instruction in reading.

Studies suggest that 15% to 20% of the population have dyslexia (International Dyslexia Association, 2000a). It occurs among all groups regardless of age, race, gender, or income. Dyslexia occurs in people of all backgrounds and intellectual levels. Studies also show that one of the most important risk factors is the family history (International Dyslexia Association, 2000a). If the child has a parent who has dyslexia, there can be as much as a 65% chance that this dysfunction is inherited. Previously, it was believed that dyslexia primarily affected boys. However, recent studies indicate that the numbers of girls with dyslexia is similar to that of boys (International Dyslexia Association, 2000a). Many are gifted and talented in areas that do not require strong language skills, such as art, music, and sports.

Diagnosis is extremely important to isolate the person with dyslexia's specific difficulties. Generally, a physician is the first diagnostician to investigate the problem. If indicated, a neurological exam may be given, along with a battery of assessment instruments to find how the specific reading problems are related to the intellectual, achievement, perceptual, motor, linguistic, and adaptive capabilities of the individual. Only after an accurate diagnosis has been made can proper intervention techniques be applied.

In 2003, a study was conducted to examine the effects of reading on children with dyslexia at the Academy of Neurology. The fMRI was used to detect the differences in brain activity of children with dyslexia and those without dyslexia. After the children with dyslexia received treatment, the fMRI again was used to discern the difference in the brain's activity. The findings from this study showed that reading treatment in children with dyslexia resulted in improvement of language skills and brain activity, which approximated the brain activity of children without dyslexia.

Persons with dyslexia have the same wide range of intelligence as the general population. Although a student with dyslexia may lag behind in reading and language skills, with individualized instruction, reading, writing, and spelling can usually be mastered at least at a functional level.

Characteristics

Students with dyslexia may exhibit one or more of the following characteristics:

- Inability to learn and remember words by sight
- Difficulty in decoding skills
- Difficulty in spelling
- Lack of organization of materials
- Difficulty in finding the right words for oral and written communication
- No enjoyment of reading independently
- Difficulty writing from dictation
- Reversal of letters and words
- Difficulty in storing and retrieving names of printed words
- Poor visual memory for language symbols
- Erratic eye movements while reading
- Auditory processing disorders

- Difficulty in applying what has been read to social or learning situations
- Illegible handwriting
- Confusing vowels or substituting one consonant (as in *playnate* for *playmate*)
- Inadequate fine motor skills

Dyslexia affects 80% of those labeled "learning disabled," and many of the characteristics are similar. The same strategies used to teach students with learning disabilities are equally applicable for the student with dyslexia who also has learning disabilities.

Strategies for Educators

As with other disabilities, the general education classroom students should be given background information about dyslexia. Too often, students believe that individuals with dyslexia are mentally slow because of the academic difficulties they have. To dispel this erroneous belief, teachers can tell students about famous people who had trouble learning to read and write.

Famous people who have been diagnosed as having dyslexia include George Herbert Walker Bush, former president of the United States; Jackie Stewart, racecar driver; Duncan Goodhew, Olympic swimmer; Tom Cruise, actor; George Burns, actor; Whoopi Goldberg, actress; Susan Hampshire, actress; Danny Glover, actor; Cher, actress and singer; and Valerie Delahaye, a key graphics artist on the feature film *Titanic* (National Institute of Health and Human Development, 1996).

Dyslexia is a language-based learning disability. One of the greatest difficulties that individuals with dyslexia have is processing the sounds of speech. This phonological deficit makes it difficult to develop an awareness that both written and spoken words can be broken down into smaller units of sounds. Without the ability to segment written words into the phonological sections, decoding and identifying words is extremely difficult. In helping students with dyslexia learn to read, training in phonemic awareness is necessary.

Oral blending and segmentation are two basic skills taught in developing phonemic awareness. Oral blending guides students in hearing how sounds are put together to make words. Teachers can devise many activities to accomplish this. One method is to say a word by breaking it into parts and pausing between each part, as an example, "dino....saur." Then the students put the parts of the word together and say the complete word. As proficiency increases, the same technique can be applied to initial consonants by sounding the initial consonant in a word, as an example, "t....iger." The same method can be applied to ending consonants. Initial sound replacement is a procedure that helps a student with dyslexia focus on particular sounds. Many teachers already use this strategy. A common word is written on the chalkboard or overhead transparency. After the word is read, the initial consonant is erased to be replaced by another consonant and then read. This method helps the student with dyslexia focus on the letter and its corresponding sound. Oral blending involves listening and reproducing the sounds into words. Segmentation focuses on separating words into sounds. Both segmentation and oral blending provide support for decoding.

Students with dyslexia have language deficiencies and miss the subtle differences in speech sounds that distinguish one word from another, as an example, *pacific* for *specific*. The older student still needs the phonemic awareness skills missed during their earlier grades. They need to be taught the blending of sounds into words and be able to recognize letter sequences accurately and quickly. Many students with dyslexia have only experienced failure in reading and have avoided reading because it is too slow and frustrating. Ultimately, as reading fluency improves, so does their attitude toward reading. Research indicates that regardless of age, there is a need for teaching phonological awareness to overcome their reading and language challenges.

Using a multisensory approach in language teaching is essential for students with dyslexia. Multisensory techniques are those which use more than one sensory channel to input information. The teacher should employ visual, auditory, and kinesthetic-tactile techniques to provide the student an opportunity to become an active participant in the process. As early as 1920, Dr. Samuel Torrey Orton began using multisensory approaches to teach children with dyslexia (International Dyslexia Association, 2000b). Current research cited by the National Institute of Health and Human Development (1996) states that a multisensory approach in structured language teaching is an effective method to teach students with dyslexia.

Always take into consideration the seating arrangements for students with dyslexia. Seating a student with dyslexia at the front of the class allows the teacher to make sure the student is paying attention and understands what is being taught. With this arrangement, the teacher can provide appropriate work for the student without the rest of the students being made aware of the difference.

Teachers can give students without dyslexia reading selections that demonstrate mirror writing and the halo effect as seen by a student who has dyslexia. When students attempt to read the selections, they immediately understand the difficulties some students with dyslexia have in reading written material.

When students experience difficulty with reading and math, they should never be told by the teacher to try harder or that they are just lazy. Students with dyslexia are already trying to do their best, and the teacher's comments only lead to more frustration and an eventual abandonment of the task.

The teacher should never force a student with dyslexia to read aloud to the class. It is better to let the student follow along silently as others read aloud or to let the student tape-record the reading selection. Follow-up activities that are primarily verbal can eliminate a great deal of stress for the student.

The student with dyslexia often has great difficulty producing written work. Educators should not compare this work with the work of the rest of the class. Offer praise for any written accomplishment, regardless of how slight it might be. The teacher should be flexible and allow the student to tape-record reports or use a word-processing program. On occasion, arrangements may also be made for the other students in the class to do the same. This helps the student with dyslexia feel less "different."

Secondary students with dyslexia are unable to take good notes that require listening and writing at the same time. It is better for the teacher to give the student summary notes at the end of the period. By giving the summary notes to the student after the lesson, the student spends the time concentrating on what is being said and not on trying to read the notes. When it is necessary to copy from the chalkboard, using different colored chalks to highlight different sections makes copying easier. The teacher should write the main points covered in a lesson on the chalkboard and leave them on the chalkboard as long as possible. In so doing, the student has time to copy the notes for the lesson, eliminating the unwanted pressure of time. Having a laptop computer facilitates recording the notes. If this was not in the initial IEP, another meeting can be requested to pursue the possibility of receiving a laptop computer to use at school.

Although students have a deficit in processing written language, many students are creative and talented. The teacher should identify these strengths and provide opportunities to the student to pursue that student's special interests. A mentoring program can be established in which mentors in the community with similar interests provide enriching experiences for the student. This is equally valuable for both elementary and secondary students. Depending on the interests of the students, there is generally a person in the community who shares the same interest. Suggested mentors might include artists, engineers, businesspersons, architects, engineers, or scientists.

As stated by Margaret Byrd Rawson of the Orton Dyslexia Association, "Dyslexic students need a different approach to learning language from that employed by most classrooms. They need to be taught slowly and thoroughly, the basic elements of their language—the sounds and letters which represent them—and how to put these together and take them apart. They have to have lots of practice in having their writing hands, eyes, ears, and voices working together for the conscious organization and retention of their learning" (International Dyslexia Association, 2000b).

The teacher should concentrate on the strengths of the student with dyslexia and give continued encouragement to succeed. The teacher should think of the student with dyslexia not as one with a disability but as one with ability.

For Further Information

Books

Albramont, G., & Brescher, A. *Test smart: Ready to use strategies and activities for grades 5–12.*
Broomfield, H. *Overcoming dyslexia: Resource book 1.*
Clark, D., & Uhry, J. *Dyslexia: Theory and practice of remedial instruction.*
Davis, R. *The gift of dyslexia: Why some of the smartest people can't read and how they learn.*
Henry, M., & Brickley, S. *Dyslexia: Samuel T. Orton and his legacy.*
Rawson, M. *Dyslexia over the lifespan: A fifty-five year longitudinal study.*
Sagmiller, G. J. *Dyslexia my life: One man's story of his life with a learning disability.*
Shaywitz, S. *Overcoming dyslexia: A new and complete science based program for reading problems at any level.*
Sousa, D. *How the brain learns: A classroom teacher's guide.*
Sousa, D. S. *How the brain learns to read.*

Organizations and Agencies

Council for Exceptional Children (CEC)
1110 North Glebe Road, Suite 300
Arlington, VA 22201
888-232-7733

866-915-5000 (TTY)
Fax: 703-264-9494
E-mail: service@cec.sped.org
www.cec.sped.org

International Dyslexia Association
40 York Road, 4th floor
Baltimore, MD 51204-5202
800-ABC-D123
410-296-0232
Fax: 410-321-5069
E-mail: info@interdys.org
www.interdys.org

Psych Central
55 Pleasant Street, Suite 207
Newburyport, MA 01950
978-992-0008
E-mail: talkback@psychcentral.com
www.psychcentral.com

Emotional Disturbance

Definition

Currently, emotional disturbance is defined under the Individuals with Disabilities Act (IDEA) as follows:

> A. condition exhibiting one or more of the following characteristics over a long period of time and to a marked degree that adversely affects a child's educational performance . . .
>
> a. An inability to learn that cannot be explained by intellectual, sensory, or health factors.
> b. An inability to build or maintain satisfactory interpersonal relationships with peers and teachers.
> c. Inappropriate types of behavior or feelings under normal circumstances.
> d. A general pervasive mood of unhappiness or depression.
> e. A tendency to develop physical symptoms or fears associated with personal or school problems. (C.F.R., Title 34. § 300.7(c)(4)(ii))

As defined by the IDEA, emotional disturbance includes schizo-phrenia but does not apply to children who are socially maladjusted, unless it is determined that they have an emotional disturbance (C.F.R., Title 34, § 300.7(c)(4)(ii)).

Background

Many terms are used to describe emotional and behavioral disorders. At present, students who have these disorders are categorized as having an emotional disturbance, which is defined in the IDEA. During the developmental period in a child's life, there may be many displays of emotional disturbance. However, the duration and intensity of these disturbances must be taken into consideration as to whether it is disruptive to the child's educational progress. The term *emotional disturbance* is used in this book as referred to in IDEA.

Estimates vary as to the number of identified children with emotional disturbance. The 24th Annual Report to Congress listed the incidence of children with emotional disturbance to be 473,663 in the 2000–2001 school year. The same number of children with emotional disturbance was in the 34th Report to Congress. In 2006 the National Center for Health Statistics reported that 9% to 13% of American children and adolescents are affected by emotional disturbances.

After leaving school, 75% of those identified with the disturbance are males. Females are 20% more likely to become mothers within 3 to 5 years after finishing school. Of youth with emotional disturbance, 10% were living in correctional facilities, in halfway houses, in drug treatment centers, or on the street.

Various factors have been suggested as possible causes of emotional disturbances, such as genetic deficiency, neurological impairment, brain injury, a chemical imbalance, nutritional deficiencies, and the use of alcohol or drugs by the parents.

Divorce, death or birth of siblings, moving, changing schools, and peer pressure are but a few of the many external events that may lead to an emotional disturbance in a child. Sometimes children grow up in unpredictable, stressful surroundings; inappropriate behavior is not only learned but also constantly reinforced. Such children may either act out or repress their feelings. Both types of behavior if they continue for a long time or form part of a larger pattern of behavior can be considered those of individuals who have emotional disturbance.

When one suspects that a child has an emotional problem, it is important to consider one's personal perception of the child. The teacher's tolerance for misbehavior should be examined. To accurately identify children with an emotional disturbance, testing and observation by trained medical professionals or psychologists is required.

When students have been identified as having serious emotional disturbances, their IEP may include psychological therapy or counseling as a related service. This service is provided by a qualified social worker, psychologist, guidance counselor, or other qualified personnel. The families, as well as children with an emotional disturbance, also need support. This is important for a family to provide them with strategies to help their child and create a nurturing home environment for the child. Many parent groups, agencies, and organizations provide information and support services to the family. The National Alliance for the Mentally Ill (NAMI) and the Federation of Families for Children's Mental Health have parent representatives and groups in each state. Both are listed at the end of this section under "Organizations and Agencies."

Characteristics

The following are some basic characteristics and behaviors seen in children who have emotional disturbances:

- Hyperactivity
- Short attention span
- Impulsiveness
- Inconsistencies of behavior
- Low frustration tolerance
- Aggression (acting out, fighting)
- Self-injurious behavior
- Withdrawal from interaction with others
- Inappropriate social skills
- Immaturity (inappropriate crying, temper tantrums)
- Poor coping skills
- Learning problems
- Unfocused
- Unexplainable mood shifts

Children with the most serious emotional disturbances exhibit distorted thinking, excessive anxiety, bizarre motor acts, and abnormal mood swings and are sometimes identified as having a severe psychosis or schizophrenia.

Strategies for Educators

Most children in the class misbehave at some time, but students with an emotional disturbance have a continuous pattern of misbehavior that disrupts the classroom environment. Consequently, the disruption causes the teacher to devote much time in attempts to restore order to the learning environment. The use of behavior modifications can be used to improve the student's attitudes and behaviors to meet classroom expectations and attaining adequate self-management skills.

Structure in a classroom is of primary importance for an emotionally disturbed student. The teacher must define clear and explicit limits and consequences for unacceptable behaviors. A crucial point to remember is who is in charge, and it is not the student. The student must understand the consequences of undesirable behaviors; teachers should always and consistently carry out the expected consequences.

Teachers should work at developing a good rapport with an emotionally disturbed student. The teacher can take advantage of many opportunities throughout the day to reinforce feelings of self-worth in a student. Simple things such as eye contact, smiling, praise for good work, and close proximity can help nurture the relationship.

Too often attention is focused on the misbehavior, and the desired behavior is ignored. Praise should be given even when there is an approximation of the desired behavior. Reinforcing positive behavior is essential for emotionally disturbed students. Rewarding positive behavior is very motivational and can lead to a change in behavior. If a token system is used, the selection of a specific reward should take into account the age and interests of the student. In selecting a particular tangible reward, the teacher should keep in mind the need to be discrete to avoid problems with other students in the classroom. Having a reward system for good behavior makes it possible to withhold the reward from the student for misbehavior. When the student is reminded of the potential loss of a particular reward, the inappropriate behavior often ceases. In time, tangible reinforcements should gradually be eliminated and replaced with social reinforcements. Suggestions for various rewards can be found in the chapter on behavior including various types of behavior management techniques.

At times, an emotionally disturbed student may become abusive and physically aggressive. In this case, removal from the classroom may be necessary. For elementary students, it is advisable to make previous arrangements with a teacher in another classroom to accept the student for a short period or to send the student to the office. This often helps the student regain composure. Secondary students may display aggression that is more violent. This requires assistance from the proper personnel, such as security, to remove the student from the classroom for the protection of other students in the class.

The teacher should also be alert to any sign that the student may be experiencing an emotional difficulty or crisis and may be on the verge of losing control. The teacher should provide a preestablished time-out area or place where the student can go. This helps the student regain individual composure and to sidetrack an episode. The student should not be required to ask permission; instead, the student can be alerted by a preestablished sign from the teacher.

Not all emotionally disturbed students externalize their behavior. Some students cause little disturbance in class, socially withdraw from groups, have fewer friends, act immature, and tend to daydream and fantasize. This type of nondisruptive student may have a serious emotional disturbance that needs to be identified. This student, having little social interaction with other students, needs help from the teacher to provide situations that involve the student with other peers. Cooperative learning groups are excellent and nonthreatening for the student. The teacher needs to help the student become involved in all class activities. Being a teacher's aide builds the confidence and self-esteem of the student. When feasible, the student can also be allowed to help students in lower grades with their academics. A referral should be made to the SST for assistance and possible referral for assessment.

The teacher can sometimes prevent problems simply by diverting the student's attention. Without alerting the other students to the situation, the teacher can quietly remind an emotionally disturbed student of the consequences of certain misbehaviors. This helps prevent the unwanted behavior from taking place. Many of the suggestions for helping an AD/HD student are also applicable for an emotionally disturbed student.

A student whose behavior is disruptive and who is apt to cause physical harm to other students may need to be removed from the classroom. This may require the assistance of other school personnel.

If a student tries to or is expected to change too many types of behavior at one time, the student will likely experience feelings of frustration and failure. Teachers must go slowly when attempting any type of behavioral change. For the teacher, dealing with an emotionally disturbed student also often requires a change in one's own behavior patterns. Difficult as it may be, when possible, it may be best to ignore the undesirable behavior. Annoying behavior that gets attention tends to be repeated, whereas praising and rewarding provides the kind of attention that leads to improvement.

All persons dealing with an emotionally disturbed child should keep in mind what Mark Twain (as cited in Phillips, 1993) said: "Habit is habit, and not to be flung out of the window by any man, but coaxed downstairs a step at a time" (p. 153).

For Further Information

Books

Algozzine, B., & Kay, P. *Preventing problem behavior.*
Doyle, T. *Why is everybody picking on me? A guide to handling bullies.*
Evertson, C., Emmer, E., Clements, B., & Worsham, M. *Classroom management for elementary teachers.*
Kerr, M., & Nelson, C. *Strategies for managing behavior problems in the classroom.*
Koplewicz, H. *It's nobody's fault: New hope and help for difficult children.*
Kranowitz, M. A., & Stock, C. *The out of sync child.*
Penn, M. *Psychiatric medications for children: Medication treatment for children and youth with emotional and behavioral challenges.*
Pepler, D., & Rubin, K. (Eds.). *The development and treatment of childhood aggression.*
Rockwell, S. *You can't make me: From chaos to cooperation in the elementary classroom.*
Sprick, R. *Discipline in the secondary classroom: A problem-by-problem survival guide.*

Organizations and Agencies

Federation of Families for Children's Mental Health
9605 Medical Center Drive, Suite 280
Rockville, MD 20850
240-403-1901
Fax: 240-403-1909
E-mail: ffcmh@ffcmh.org
http://www.ffcmh.org

National Alliance for the Mentally Ill
Colonial Place Three
2107 Wilson Blvd., Suite 300
Arlington, VA 22201-3042
888-999-6264 toll-free
703-516-7227 (TTY)
703-524-7600
Fax: 703-524-9093
E-mail: info@nami.org
http://www.nami.org

National Institute of Mental Health
Public Information and Communications Branch
6001 Executive Boulevard, Room 8184
Bethesda, MD 20894-9663
301-443-4513
301-443-8431 (TTY)
866-415-8051 (TTY)
866-615-6464 toll-free
Fax: 301-443-4279
E-mail: nimhinfo@nimh.gov
http://www.nimh.nih.gov

Epilepsy

Definition

Epilepsy is a chronic condition that is a sign or symptom of an underlying neurological disorder. It consists of recurrent seizures of varying degrees of intensity and duration. These seizures are the result of a temporary alteration in one or more brain functions. According to the Epilepsy Foundation of America (1985a, 1985b, 1987, 1988), a person's consciousness, movement, or actions may be altered for a short time when the brain cells are not working properly. Although epilepsy is sometimes called a seizure disorder, the two terms are not synonymous. A person can suffer a seizure without being epileptic. Isolated and provoked seizures, as might occur with the use of alcohol or drugs, are not epilepsy. Persons with epilepsy have recurring, unprovoked seizures.

Background

Epilepsy is one of the oldest known brain disorders. Reference was made to epilepsy in 2000 B.C.E. and in ancient Greek writings. However, it was not until the middle of the nineteenth century that epilepsy began to be studied scientifically.

Throughout history, society has regarded people with epilepsy in different ways. Ignorance of its causes gave way to many erroneous beliefs. In some cultures, individuals with epilepsy were thought to have divine or demonic power. Epilepsy also was thought to be contagious and the cause of mental retardation or mental illness. Unfortunately, some believe these myths to this day. Such erroneous beliefs have created a social stigma surrounding epilepsy that has plagued both individuals with epilepsy and their families.

Estimates are that 1% to 2% of the population have or have had some form of epilepsy. It is possible that there is an inherited tendency to have epilepsy. According to the Epilepsy Research Foundation, more than 2.7 million people in the United States and an estimated 50 million people worldwide have epilepsy. Of the 125,000 new cases that develop each year, 50% involve children and adolescents. Generally, epileptic seizures start before the age of 21 (National Dissemination Center for Children with Disabilities, 2000a).

According to the Comprehensive Epilepsy Program of the University of Minnesota (1980), more than 50% of all people with epilepsy can control their seizures with medicine, and another 20% to 30% have improved control of seizures with medication. A small number of children are not helped by medication or may become worse by using medication, but medication controls seizure attacks in the majority of children with epilepsy. Fortunately, children may outgrow epilepsy and require no medication for the disorder later in life.

The causes of epilepsy are numerous: birth trauma, brain infection, head injury, brain tumor, stroke, drug intoxication, interruption of blood flow to the brain, or a metabolic imbalance in the body. Environmental factors can also bring on an epileptic seizure. In some cases, they can be triggered by sudden changes from light to dark or vice versa, flashing lights, loud noises, or monotonous sounds. Withdrawal from alcohol and illicit drugs can also bring out an underlying epileptic disorder. Seizures are unpredictable, and nonhuman animals as well as people can have them.

Sometimes, for no apparent reason, seizures develop that are unrelated to epilepsy. Pseudoepileptic seizures can occur in people who do not have diagnosed epilepsy, and the symptoms may be much like those of an epileptic seizure. These attacks may be brought on by a conscious or unconscious desire for attention and care. When seizures occur so frequently that they interfere with academic learning, they are considered a health impairment that makes the student eligible for special education placement.

Seizures may affect intelligence because a prolonged seizure reduces the oxygen in the brain during the episode. However, impaired intellectual functioning in a person with epilepsy who is developmentally delayed is usually not caused by the epilepsy but is rather a result of the developmental delay. Generally, people with epilepsy have normal intelligence.

Researchers believe that faulty wiring in the brain is a cause of epilepsy. This abnormality causes an imbalance of nerve signaling chemicals called neurotransmitters. Scientists believe that an abnormally high level of excitatory neurotransmitters in the brain increases neuronal activity in some people who are epileptic. Others with epilepsy may have an abnormally low level of inhibitory neurotransmitters, which decrease neuronal activity in the brain. Either situation can cause too much neuronal activity and cause epilepsy.

Genetic abnormalities may be another cause of epilepsy. Researchers believe that 100 genes may play a role in epilepsy. However, some types of epilepsy have been traced to an abnormality in a specific gene. Researchers have discovered that the abnormal gene can influence epilepsy in other ways such as increase a resistance to drugs. Scientists also believe that the genes may also control the body's response to medications.

The Epilepsy Foundation of America conducted studies of the behavior of children with unrecognized new onset of epilepsy. This study was done before the children had medication. It was found that the children were already at risk for behavior problems. This study concluded that even before the teacher rating of behavior problems, these children's underlying neurological problems caused both behavior problems and seizures (Dunn, 2002). One of the studies was to investigate teachers' perception of children with epilepsy compared to those with asthma. They showed more consideration for the aggressive behavior of children with epilepsy than for those with chronic illnesses (Hsieh, 2001). Teachers did not encourage preschool children with epilepsy to play with others, which may account for their lower performance. Conclusions reflected the need for children with epilepsy to participate "in all physical education and school event based on individual considerations." Teachers, on the other hand, expressed the need for correct information about epilepsy and the need for close communication between teachers and physicians (Kankirawatana, 2002).

Because there are more than 30 different types of seizures, the International League Against Epilepsy has replaced the outdated classifications of the different types with two main categories: partial and generalized. A seizure is considered partial if the electrical activity involves only a limited area of the brain. If the electrical discharge involves the entire brain, the seizure is considered generalized. Each of these classifications is further divided into different subdivisions. The partial and generalized categories are now generally accepted by the medical community.

Characteristics

The National Information Center for Children and Youth With Disabilities (1990b) states that the signs of epilepsy generally include episodes of staring or unexplained periods of unresponsiveness, involuntary movement of arms and legs, fainting spells with incontinence, odd sounds, distorted perceptions, and episodic feelings of fear that cannot be explained. Blackouts or confused memory can also be signs of epilepsy.

Generalized Seizures

Characteristics can vary, depending on the nature of the epilepsy. A prolonged seizure can last for many hours. A *tonic-clonic* seizure, formerly called *grand mal,* is a generalized seizure that usually lasts 30 seconds to several minutes. (If a person has multiple seizures of this type or a seizure that lasts longer than 5 minutes, medical attention is definitely indicated.) A tonic-clonic seizure can be very unnerving to the onlooker. There is a cry and an ensuing loss of consciousness. The body becomes rigid and the person falls unconscious to the ground. This is followed by jerky muscle contractions. There may be a loss of bladder and bowel control. The breathing becomes shallow and very irregular or temporarily ceases. After regaining consciousness, the person may not recall the events of the seizure but is usually very fatigued and requires rest.

Another form of generalized seizure is an *absence seizure,* often referred to as *petit mal.* During the seizure, the person is out of touch with reality but returns to normal when the seizure is over. Petit mal seizures start with a blank stare and end abruptly. There can be chewing movements of the mouth and rapid blinking, but it is not accompanied by abnormal movements of the body. The episode can last a few seconds to half a minute or so. It is sometimes accompanied by a momentary loss of consciousness, but it can also go completely unnoticed by bystanders. This type of seizure can occur hundreds of times daily, and the teacher often mistakes it for daydreaming or lack of attention.

Partial Seizures

Partial seizures are categorized as simple or complex. Simple partial seizures are also called *sensory* or *Jacksonian seizures.* Simple partial seizures can occur without warning and may last several minutes. There may be abnormal tingling sensations and twitching. If the twitching spreads slowly from one part of the body to another, it eventually may involve the whole body and lead to a convulsive seizure. The person may have unexplained feelings of anger, joy, and fear, as well as a distinct feeling of nausea. Although there is no loss of consciousness and the person retains all awareness, the person may hear and see nonexistent things.

In complex partial seizures, also known as *psychomotor* or *temporal lobe seizures,* the person becomes dazed and may not respond to others. This person's actions are inappropriate, out of character, or uncoordinated. Some individuals may pick at their clothing or take their clothes off, and others may fumble with buttons or smack their lips. They may experience sudden fear, try to run, and struggle against any kind of restraint. As with the simple partial seizure, there may be distortions of hearing or seeing. After the seizure, the person does not recall the events that occurred during the attack. Although partial seizures may begin in a limited area of the brain, the disturbance may spread and affect the entire brain, thus leading to a generalized seizure (Epilepsy Foundation of America, 1988).

Strategies for Educators

All educators should be made aware of students who have a history of epilepsy. Vital information can be obtained by checking students' cumulative and health records. Parents can also provide additional information about the type of seizure their child has and its frequency. Even if seizures are controlled by medication, school personnel should be aware that there might be side effects from the medication. Document any changes in physical or intellectual functioning, and keep the child's parents and doctor informed of such changes.

The teacher can be instrumental in helping students without disabilities understand what epilepsy is and in alleviating their misconceptions and fears. It is sufficient for younger students to know that seizures do not hurt and are generally of short duration; older students should be taught the nature of epilepsy and the effect it has on the student who has seizures.

Students may wonder why the teacher does not try to stop a student's seizure. They need to understand that once a seizure has started, it should not be interrupted. The seizure must be allowed to run its course.

When someone has a seizure (with the exception of the absence and petit mal forms), take the following actions:

- Keep calm and do not try to revive the student.
- Ease the student to the floor and put something soft under his or her head.

- Turn the student on one side to keep the airway open.
- Allow fluid in the mouth to drain.
- Remove any hard, sharp, or hot objects from the immediate area.
- Do not attempt to restrain any movements of the student.
- Loosen the student's clothing.
- Do not give the student anything to drink or swallow during the seizure.
- Do not force the mouth open or put anything in the student's mouth.
- Do not hold the student's tongue. The student will not swallow it.
- If the student walks aimlessly during the seizure, clear the area of potentially dangerous objects.

During the seizure attack, the student's breathing may be shallow. Because of the lack of oxygen, the lips and skin may have a bluish tinge. There is no cause for alarm unless the breathing ceases. It is then necessary to immediately check to see if something is blocking the student's airway and remove it. Artificial respiration also may be needed.

After the seizure is over, the person may be extremely tired and should be allowed to rest.

Many people with epilepsy have led very successful lives, and the teacher should provide students with information about them. This also gives students an opportunity for research and language activities. The following is a partial list of famous people who had or who have epilepsy: Alexander the Great, military leader and king of Macedonia; Julius Caesar, Roman statesman and general; Charles Dickens, English novelist; George Handel, German composer; Hector Berlioz, French composer; Paganini, Italian violinist and composer; Ludwig van Beethoven, German composer; Vincent van Gogh, Dutch painter; Sir Isaac Newton, English mathematician and natural philosopher; Marion Clignet, champion cyclist; Deborah McFadden, Commissioner, Administration on Developmental Disabilities; Margaux Hemingway, actress; Patty Wilson, long-distance runner; Richard Burton, actor; Gary Howatt, professional hockey player; John Considine, actor; and Buddy Bell, professional baseball player.

A student's epileptic seizures may interfere with the ability to learn. A student whose seizures are characterized by a brief period of fixed staring may miss out on what is being said. Teachers must consider this.

Individuals with epilepsy should not be overprotected, as this hinders their psychological and social growth. For people with epilepsy to feel more confident about themselves and to accept their condition, they need to be treated with respect and acceptance.

For Further Information

Books

Bigge, J. L. *Teaching individuals with physical and multiple disabilities.*
David, J. B. *Epileptic.*
Day, R., Brown, S., Chappell, B., & Crawford, P. *Epilepsy—The at your fingertips guide.*
Fletcher, S. *The challenge of epilepsy.*
Freeman, J. M., Vining, E., & Pillas, D. J. *Seizures and epilepsy in childhood.*
Gummit, R. *Living well with epilepsy.*
Karten, J. *Inclusion strategies that work: Research based methods for the classroom.*
Michael, R. J. *The educator's guide to students with epilepsy.*
Reisner, H. *Children with epilepsy.*

Organizations and Agencies

Centers for Disease Control and Prevention
1600 Clifton Road
Atlanta, GA 30333
404-659-3311
404-659-5534 Public Inquiries
800-311-3435
http://www.cdc.gov

Epilepsy Foundation, National Office
8301 Professional Place, East
Landover, MD 20785
800-332-1000
301-459-3700
301-918-3773 for publications
E-mail: postmaster@efa.org
http://www.epilepsyfoundation.org

Epilepsy Institute
287 Park Avenue South, Suite 302
New York, NY 10010
212-677-8550
Fax: 212-677-5825
http://www.epilepsyinstitute.org

National Institute of Neurological Disorders and Strokes
National Institutes of Health
Building 31, Room 8A06
31 Center Drive, MSC 2540
Bethesda, MD 20892
800-352-9424
301-496-5751
E-mail: braininfo@ninds.nih.gov
http://www.ninds.nih.gov

Fetal Alcohol Syndrome

Definition

Fetal alcohol syndrome (FAS) refers to fetal developmental defects that result from a woman's consumption of alcohol during pregnancy. In cases in which these defects are not severe enough to meet all the criteria for an FAS diagnosis, the term *fetal alcohol effects* (FAE) is used.

Background

Since the beginning of the eighteenth century, physicians and researchers in England and France have reported the harmful effects of maternal alcohol consumption on the fetus (Cook, Petersen, & Moore, 1990). In 1973 a group of scientists at the University of Washington, Seattle, coined the term *fetal alcohol syndrome* to describe the characteristic birth defects of the affected infants (Cook et al., 1990). In 1980 the Fetal Alcohol Study Group of the Research Society on Alcoholism outlined standards for an FAS diagnosis. As stated in *Alcohol, Tobacco, and Other Drugs May Harm the Unborn* (Cook et al., 1990, p. 17), these standards require that an infant have at least one feature from each of the following categories to be classified as having FAS:

1. Pre- and postnatal growth retardation, with abnormally small-for-age weight, length, and/or head circumference

2. Central nervous systems disorders, with signs of abnormal brain functioning and delays in behavioral development or intellectual development, or both

3. At least two of the following abnormal craniofacial features: small head, small eyes or short eye openings, or a poorly developed groove above the upper lip, thin upper lip, or flattened midfacial area.

The severe end of a spectrum of effects may occur when a woman drinks during pregnancy. The most extreme outcome is fetal death. Abnormalities in facial features, growth, and the central nervous system are effects of FAS. If not all symptoms of FAS are in evidence, there is possibly another alcohol-related neurodevelopmental disorder.

Later, many learning and behavioral problems may also be caused by prenatal exposure to alcohol. Fetal alcohol exposure may also increase the risk of future dependency on alcohol, tobacco, and other drugs during adulthood.

Exposure to alcohol as a fetus can cause lifelong physical and mental problems. This is unfortunate since FAS is completely preventable. According to the Center for Disease Control, research suggests that all pregnant women should be screened for alcohol use during prenatal visits. If in testing a woman tests positive, she should be referred by the physician for counseling and treatment.

The standards for an FAS diagnosis do not include other abnormalities that sometimes occur. Babies who had been prenatally exposed to alcohol and have other birth defects, but who have only a few of the official accepted signs of FAS, may be categorized as having suspected FAE.

The report of SAMHSA's National Survey on Drug Use and Health (NSDUH), authorized by the government, conducted a survey from 2004 to 2006 in the United States. The survey indicated that an annual average of 6.3 million women (9.4%) aged 18 to 49 needed treatment for substance abuse. Of those needing treatment, only 5.5% thought it was necessary and received treatment. Some 36.1% of the women did not want to stop drinking or using illicit drugs. Another 28.9% did not seek treatment because of the cost, insufficient funds, or inadequate or lack of health insurance. Another 28.9% did not seek substance abuse treatment because of perceived social stigma. Prenatal drinking adversely affects 1 in 100 infants.

According to the U.S. Department of Health and Human Services (as cited in Cook et al., 1990), risk factors for having a baby with FAS include "the mother's persistent drinking throughout pregnancy, a greater number of alcohol-related problems, and a larger number of previous births" (p. 18). In addition, women who had previous babies with FAS had an increased risk of having another baby with FAS.

Studies also have been conducted on the effects on the fetus of paternal drinking. Cicero (1994) states that paternal alcohol consumption may have a direct effect on fetal development. In addition, there are indications that paternal drinking may contribute to cognitive and biochemical disturbances in the fetus.

It is difficult to ascertain the exact amount of alcohol that can safely be consumed by a woman during pregnancy. Even very small amounts of alcohol may be harmful and increase the risk of a miscarriage or congenital birth defects. Infants with neurobehavioral deficits and intrauterine growth retardation have been born to women who stated that they were only moderate drinkers. In evaluating this statement, it is important to take into account that individuals may underreport their alcohol consumption. In some cases, women who drank heavily during pregnancy have borne babies with no signs of FAS. However, these babies are the exception rather than the rule. Many times, women bear infants who have FAE with no apparent outward symptoms, and it is only later that symptoms become evident. The American Medical Association (1989) states that there is no safe level of alcohol consumption for women during pregnancy. Most authorities and the medical profession advise abstinence from consuming alcohol during pregnancy.

High doses of alcohol interfere with the passage of amino acids across the placenta and the conversion of amino acids into proteins. It appears that the breakdown products in alcohol of ethanol and its metabolite, acetaldehyde, alter fetal development by "disrupting cell differentiation and cell growth." The American Medical Association (1989, as cited in Cook et al., 1990) also states that the immature and underdeveloped fetus's organs break down alcohol much more slowly than the pregnant woman's, causing a higher level of toxins in the fetus.

Michael Dorris (1989) writes, "There have been babies born whose skin, the whole baby, smells like wine. It's like they're pickled and the amniotic fluid is saturated with alcohol" (p. 158).

The BBC reported on February 21, 2006, that researchers from Cornell University injected pregnant rats with alcohol equal to a binge-drinking episode by a human mother. It caused cell death and behavioral abnormalities in a fetus. The researchers followed the alcohol dose with an injection of nicotinomide. This injection stopped the cell death and behavioral changes. However, Mukherjee, an FAS expert at St. George's Hospital Medical School in London, said, "Surely the safest way, as the piece (research) suggests, is not take anything in the first place."

Any drug taken during pregnancy crosses the placenta (DeVane, 1991). Alcohol consumption not only increases the chances of producing a baby with FAS or FAE but also contributes to stress, lack of stability, and a dysfunctional family.

Characteristics

Almost one-fifth of FAS infants die during their first few weeks of life. Those who survive usually are physically and mentally impaired in varying degrees. The following are some of the characteristics commonly found in FAS infants and children. Not all of the characteristics listed are found in every FAS case.

Physical Abnormalities
Small infant size
Small head circumference
Low, narrow forehead
Small midface
Thin and long upper lip
Brain damage
Heart defects
Delayed dental development
Joint and limb irregularities
Abnormal central nervous system
Hearing impairment
Slow growth after birth
Mental retardation
Fine motor dysfunction
Seizures

Behavioral Deficits
Hyperactivity
Short- and long-term memory
    problems
Learning disabilities
Extreme nervousness
Impulsiveness
Inability to understand outcomes
    of behavior
Slow academic progress

Strategies for Educators

The many disorders exhibited by students with FAS and FAE (e.g., AD/HD, emotional disturbances, and other impairments) require teachers to make various educational modifications. Suggestions for teaching students with FAS or FAE with multiple disabilities can be found under specific disabilities in this book (see, e.g., AD/HD and emotional disturbances).

Because the child's future total environment is unpredictable, it is difficult to determine what the long-term developmental effects of the drug use will be on the infant. However, the importance of family, school, peers, and community cannot be underestimated. It is only with support and understanding that the potential of a child with FAS and FAE can be tapped.

With the use of alcohol increasing, one can expect that an increasing number of babies will be born with FAS or FAE. The importance of educating teachers, students, and parents about the dangers is clear.

For Further Information

Books

Dorris, M. *The broken cord.*

Kleinfield, J. *Fantastic Antone grows up: Adolescents and adults with fetal alcohol syndrome.*

Lasser, P. *Challenges and opportunities: A handbook for teachers of students with special needs.*

Malbin, D. *Fetal alcohol syndrome/fetal alcohol effects: Strategies for professionals.*

McCuen, E. *Born hooked.*

Morse, B. A., & Weiner, L. *FAS: Parent and child. A handbook.*

Soby, J. M. *Prenatal exposure to drugs/alcohol: Characteristics and educational implications of fetal alcohol syndrome cocaine polydrug effects.*

Streissguth, A. P. *Fetal alcohol syndrome: A guide for families and community.*

Organizations and Agencies

The Centers for Disease Control
FAS Prevention Branch
1600 Clifton Road
Atlanta, GA 30333
404-639-3311
404-639-3534 Public Inquiries
800-311-3435
http://www.cdc.gov

Council for Exceptional Children (CEC)
1110 North Glebe Road, Suite 300
Arlington, VA 22201
888-232-7733
Fax: 703-264-9494
E-mail: service@cec.sped.org
http://www.cec.sped.org

National Alliance for the Mentally Ill (NAMI)
Colonial Place Three
2107 Wilson Blvd., Suite 300
Arlington, VA 22201-30422
703-524-7600
Fax: 703-524-9094
http://www.nami.org

National Clearinghouse for Alcohol and Drug Information
P.O. Box 2345
Rockville, MD 20847-2345
800-729-6686
240-221-4019

877-767-9432 (Spanish speaking)
800-487-4889 (TDD)
Fax: 240-221-4292
E-mail: info@health.org
http://www.health.org

National Institute of Mental Health (NIMH)
National Information and Communications Branch, Room 8184, MSC 9663
Bethesda, MD 20892-0663
301-443-5413
800-615-NIMH (6464)
301-443-8431 (TTY)
800-415-8051 (TTY)
Fax: 391-443-4279
E-mail: nimhinfo@nih.gov
www.nimh.nih.gov

National Organization on Fetal Alcohol Syndrome
900 17th Street NW
Washington, DC 20006
800-666-6327
202-785-4585
Fax: 202-466-6456
E-mail: healthfinder@nhic.org
http://www.nofas.org

Gifted Students With Learning Disabilities

Definition

The Gifted and Talented Children's Act of 1978 defines gifted and talented children as

> possessing demonstrated or potential abilities that give evidence of high performance capability in such areas as intellectual, creative, specific academic or leadership ability, or in the performing or visual arts, and who by reason thereof require services or activities not ordinarily provided by the school. (PL 95-561, Title IX, § 902)

The federal definition has been widely used to identify and serve children who are gifted and talented. Students with high abilities and learning difficulties meet not only the description of gifted but also that of being learning disabled as defined in IDEA. Refer to the section on learning disabilities.

Background

Little attention was given to gifted students until it became compulsory to attend school. Then, as early as 1870, some schools began tracking gifted and slow learners. However, it was not until the 1920s that schools such as Los Angeles, Cincinnati, Manhattan, and Cleveland began classes for the gifted. Although gifted education continued through the 1950s, there was little difference in the approach to teaching gifted students than that of teaching the other students who were not gifted. The event of Sputnik in 1957 spurred action to address the needs of gifted students. Nonetheless, gifted education was still largely ignored. This is no longer the case. Gifted education is now being implemented in school systems across the nation. The individual needs of gifted students are being addressed as required by the federal law IDEA.

In reference to identification of giftedness, the U.S. Department of Education (1993) asserted, "[O]utstanding talents are present in children and youth from all cultural groups, across all economic strata, and in all areas of human endeavor" (p. 26). Research in gifted education has also changed the focus from reliance on intelligence tests for identification of giftedness to consideration of other factors such as high levels of commitment, creativity, and above-average general ability.

Most definitions of giftedness imply that a child has to be exceptional at everything. This is a parody because it excludes students who are gifted and who have a learning disability (LD). Students who have an LD and who are gifted often go unrecognized because they seldom show consistently high achievement. This is compounded because there are so many possible learning disabilities as well as types of giftedness. Problematic is the contradictory belief that a student who is gifted might also have an LD. The child's disability may override the child's ability, which makes it difficult to determine if the ability is outstanding enough to indicate giftedness. Many children with high abilities and learning difficulties are rarely identified as being gifted until middle school, high school, or college.

Another obstacle to identification is the misconception that gifted children are always mature, self-directed, and well behaved in the classroom. Many of the traits and characteristics associated with learning disabilities are exhibited by the student who is gifted and has a learning disability. As an example, this student may not achieve the same academic gains as their peers do if their own behavior is disruptive. Attention becomes focused on the particular manifestation of the disability rather than the strengths or talents of the student. This impedes the identification of the student as being gifted. The student who is gifted and has an LD rarely qualifies for multiple services.

Some students with high achievement or high IQ scores are gifted and learning disabled. It is only when they become older that the discrepancy widens between the expected achievement for gifted students and the performance. Other factors may be involved as to why the student who is gifted is underachieving, such as setting too high and unrealistic expectations. To address the problem, screening procedures are necessary to identify a possible learning disability that should be addressed.

Students who are gifted and have an LD must deal with most of the same stereotyping as other students with disabilities when emphasis is placed on their LD and not their strengths or talents. Inherent is the notion that the LD categorization indicates there is something wrong with the student and needs to be addressed before anything else can be accomplished. Expectations are unrealistically lower for students with an LD. For the student who is gifted and has an LD, this can result in a loss of self-worth, lack of motivation, depression, and feelings of inadequacy. Emphasis being placed on remediating a particular academic weakness ignores the interests and strengths of the giftedness of the student. Unable to pursue or explore individual particular talents or strengths at school, the student is unstimulated and frustrated with the school experience.

Students who are gifted and have an LD are aware of their problem but are given little opportunities to demonstrate their gifted behaviors. The greatest loss among students who are gifted and have an LD is their latent talent that goes by the wayside being masked by their disability.

Characteristics

Listing typical characteristics of students who are gifted and have an LD is difficult because there are so many varying degrees of learning disabilities. The following are generalizations of the basic characteristics exhibited by students who are gifted and have an LD:

- Noticeable discrepant scores between verbal and nonverbal parts of ability tests
- Extremely uneven academic skills
- Auditory and visual processing problems
- Extreme frustration with school
- Lack of organizational and study skills

- Unusual and sometimes bizarre sense of humor
- Superior vocabulary
- Sophisticated ideas and opinions
- High abstract reasoning ability
- Good mathematical reasoning ability
- Advanced vocabulary
- Imagination and creativity
- Insight
- Exceptional ability in geometry, science, arts, and music
- Good problem-finding and problem-solving skills
- Difficulty with memorization, computation, phonics, and/or spelling
- Distractibility
- Supersensitivity
- Perfectionism
- Grasp of metaphors, analogies, and satire
- Comprehension of complex systems
- Unreasonable self-expectations
- Frequent failure to complete assignments
- Difficulties with sequential tasks
- Wide range of knowledge and interests

Strategies for Educators

The special talents and strengths of the student who is gifted and has an LD are often overlooked. The teacher can be instrumental in encouraging and developing these strengths. By using the special skills of the student who has an LD, there is less focus on the disability. The student's self-esteem improves, and the productivity level increases.

As the productivity level increases, so does the need for time management, helping the student to analyze each day and each week to maximize the use of time. The teacher can help provide a management plan in which tasks are listed sequentially along with a target date for completion. Secondary students should keep the management log in their notebook for handy reference. The objective is for the student to self-monitor individual time.

Students who are gifted and have an LD need to advance in their areas of strength. Some students have difficulty in math computation but are extremely capable of high-level mathematical problem solving. Unfortunately, many are never able to use this skill because the time is spent on developing satisfactory math computation skills as well as memorizing arithmetic facts. Most students who are gifted and have an LD have difficulty with any memorizing. The student who is gifted and has an LD might not be held back if a calculator were to be used for computation. The time is better spent developing higher-order thinking skills.

Students who have difficulty with handwriting may be helped by the use of a microcomputer with a word-processing program. A microcomputer eliminates the need for extensive handwriting practice and makes it possible to produce written work that is acceptable. It also makes it easier to take notes and complete research papers or any creative endeavor that requires writing.

Writing is not the only method of communicating. All learning can be expressed in a variety of ways, such as the use of slides, speeches, models, and film production. The method used for communication should take into consideration the strengths of the student who is gifted to help nurture and build on those strengths. When other modes of communication are presented, the entire class should also be given the opportunity to select a different method of presentation.

Some students who are gifted and have an LD have difficulty reading. In this case, the teacher can find suitable sources of information that are appropriate for the student. Some examples might include pictorial histories, photographs, tape-recorded books, visitations by outside professionals, or computer software designed for reading.

Many students who are gifted and have an LD are never identified and as such are not provided with specialized education. It is imperative, as it is with all students, that a teacher identifies the potential ability of all the students.

For Further Information

Books

Baum, S., Owen, S. V., & Dixon, J. *To be gifted and learning disabled: From definition to practical intervention strategies.*
Clark, B. *Growing up gifted: Developing the potential of children at home and at school.*
Daniels, P. R. *Teaching the learning-disabled gifted child.*
Fox, L. H., Brody, L., & Tobin, D. *Learning disabled/gifted children: Identification and programming.*
Maker, C. J., & Nelson, A. B. *Teaching models in education of the gifted.*
Sousa, D. A. *How the gifted brain learns.*
Thurlow, M. L., Elliott, J. L., & Ysseldyke, J. E. *Testing students with disabilities.*
Whitmore, J. R., & Maker, C. J. *Intellectual giftedness in disabled persons.*
Winebrenner, S. *Teaching gifted kids in the regular classroom.*

Organizations and Agencies

Council for Exceptional Children (CEC)
1110 North Glebe Road, Suite 300
Arlington, VA 22201
888-232-7733
866-915-5000 (TTY)
Fax: 703-264-9494
E-mail: service@cec.sped.org
http://www.cec.sped.org

National Dissemination Center for Children with Disabilities (NICHCY)
P.O. Box 1492
Washington, DC 20013
800-695-0285 (TTY)
Fax: 202-884-8441
E-mail: nichcy@aed.org
http://www.nichcy.org

National Institute of Mental Health (NIMH)
Public Inquiries and Dissemination Branch
6001 Executive Boulevard
Room 8184, MSC 9693
Bethesda, MD 20892-9663
866-615-NIMH (6464) toll-free
301-443-8431 (TTY)
866-415-9051 (TTY)
Fax: 301-443-4279
E-mail: nimhinfo@nih.gov
http://www.nami.org

National Research Center on the Gifted and Talented
University of Connecticut
2131 Hillside Road, Unit 3007
Storrs, CT 06269
860-486-0283
800-486-4826
Fax: 860-486-2900
E-mail: adnub@gifted.org
http://www.gifted.uconn.edu

Head Injury

Definition

The Individuals with Disabilities Education Act (IDEA, 1990) defines
traumatic brain injury (TBI) as an acquired injury to the brain caused

by an external force resulting in total or partial functional disability or psychosocial impairment that adversely affects a child's educational performance. This term does not apply to brain injuries that are congenital or degenerative or to brain injuries induced by birth trauma (34 C.F.R. § 300.7[12]). The IDEA now includes TBI as a separate disability category (National Dissemination Center for Children with Disabilities, 1995).

Background

A closed head injury is generally the result of a sharp acceleration and deceleration of the head that results in the brain being shaken. This stress pulls apart the nerve fibers and damages the neurofibers that send messages to all parts of the body. This type of injury puts stress on the brain stem, which is the lowest section of the brain where 10 of the 12 pairs of cranial nerves connect. These nerves automatically control basic functions of the body, such as eye reflexes, breathing, facial movements, and heartbeat. All messages going to the brain pass through the brain stem first.

In contrast to a closed head injury, an open head injury is the result of a head trauma that damages a focal point in the brain, which in turn causes specific problems for the individual. For example, an individual may have difficulty producing speech but have no difficulty putting thoughts on paper. In any open head injury, there is always the potential for serious infection because of dirt or a foreign object being implanted in the brain. If the skull is fractured, bone fragments may be driven into the brain. A severe blow to the head may bruise brain tissue, resulting in brain cell death, or cause the blood vessels to tear, causing a brain hemorrhage.

Although many people sustain some type of head injury at least once in their lifetime, they seldom require treatment by a neurosurgeon. According to the National Head Injury Foundation (now known as the Brian Injury Association), however, more than 2 million people sustain traumatic brain injuries each year, with 500,000 requiring hospital admission. It is also estimated that every 15 seconds someone receives a head injury in the United States. Estimates are that each year 75,000 to 100,000 die either at the time of the injury or within several hours of the injury. It is also estimated that 70,000 to 90,000 survivors of traumatic head injuries sustain lifelong loss of function and that 2,000 remain in a persistent vegetative state (National Head Injury Foundation, 1989). Government statistics indicate that in the

United States, brain injury annually leaves 80,000 people with the onset of a long-term disability. More than 1 million children receive brain injuries every year and of these children, 30,000 have lifelong disabilities as a result of their injuries.

TBI is one of the leading causes of death or disability in children and young adults. Between the ages of 15 and 24, twice as many males than females suffer serious head injuries. Child abuse causes 64% of infant head injuries. In the United States, 50,000 children sustain bicycle-related head injuries every year (National Head Injury Foundation, 1989). Overall, motor vehicle accidents cause one-half of all traumatic head injuries, falls make up 21%, assaults and violence lead to 12%, and sports and recreation cause 10% (National Institute of Neurological Disorders and Stroke, 1989).

Brain injury can also be acquired. This is the result of an internal disturbance of the brain. The physiological changes can be caused by various factors including anoxia, a growth, certain diseases, or the removal of part of the brain. The University of Michigan Health System states that approximately 1 to 2 in 1,000 newborn babies either die or are at risk for brain damage. This is due to an interruption of oxygen to the brain during labor or delivery. Those who do survive this lack of oxygen or blood flow will have long-lasting physical disabilities (University of Michigan Health System, 2004).

An international study analyzed brain damage during the birth of babies who had an interrupted blood and oxygen supply. The research involved a head-cooling device that was developed in New Zealand and the United Kingdom. This treatment, CoolCap, had 28 participating institutions. The University of Michigan Health System's C.S. Mott Children's Hospital was one of the 28 institutions that participated in the study.

Babies were fitted with the CoolCap, and they wore it for 72 hours. Results showed that covering the head reduced brain damage in babies who had experienced a lack of blood flow and oxygen. The same babies were thoroughly examined after 18 months. The doctors found that there was a significant reduction of disability and of death. One of the investigators in the study at University of Michigan Health System, John Barks, M.D., stated, "Previously we had no therapy to offer to reverse this damage once it had occurred" (University of Michigan Health System, 2004).

Generally, an individual who suffers a severe head injury has to undergo intensive treatment for 5 to 10 years, sometimes for a lifetime. The effects of a head injury are both physical and psychological, and they can change the individual's present and future life dramatically.

Characteristics

The characteristics of TBIs are as wide and varied as the individuals who sustain the injuries. The impairments may be temporary or permanent and may include the following:

- Speech, vision, and other sensory disadvantages
- Fine motor coordination impairment
- Muscle spasticity
- Paralysis on one or both sides of the body
- Seizure disorders
- Short- and long-term memory impairment
- Short attention span
- Poor reading and writing skills
- Impairment of judgment
- Mood swings and depression
- Emotion- and impulse-control impairment
- Difficulties in relating to others
- Lowered self-esteem

Children who have suffered a TBI often remember what they were like before the brain injury, which may cause many emotional and psychosocial difficulties. Although the rates of emotional and social development vary from individual to individual, all people with TBI must deal with both physical and social problems. One factor remains constant: These individuals have to completely restructure their lives.

Strategies for Educators

Many education professionals are unaware of the consequences of childhood head injury. Often, students with TBI are inappropriately classified as having learning disabilities, emotional disturbances, or mental retardation. Although children with TBI have always been eligible for special education services, the designation of TBI as a separate category of disability requires schools to provide needed and related special services for the student with TBI. A thorough evaluation is necessary to develop an appropriate individualized education program to meet the special needs of the student with TBI. When the student has a current IEP, the plan is flexible and can be amended to reflect the changing needs of the student.

Teachers usually become aware of students in the general education class who may exhibit many of the characteristics associated with

TBI but have not been identified as a student with TBI. Often, a head injury occurring during the child's early years may have been forgotten. It is only when the behaviors continue over a period of time that the earlier head injury is recalled because it may be the causative factor in the difficulties experienced by the student. The teacher should then make a referral for assessment and evaluation.

Background information on TBI should be given to all students, including the fact that head injury is the leading cause of death and disability in the United States. Students should also be aware of the many dangers of sustaining a head injury and learn the importance of taking preventive safety measures. To reinforce the importance of safety measures, students should be actively involved in many varied activities, for example, making murals and posters for the school, writing safety slogans, and role-playing.

To maximize the comfort and productivity of a student with a head injury, educators can apply the same suggestions given earlier in the book for creating an environment that is as free from distraction as possible for the student with AD/HD, making the necessary adjustments based on the severity of the injury.

TBI is considered a "silent epidemic" because the physical signs of it may not always be visible. However, TBI generally results in various disabilities. Depending on the particular disability, other factors need to be considered.

A student with TBI may, for example, have difficulty with orientation and require supervision walking between the classroom and restroom. A buddy system can be advantageous in such cases. Students with TBI may also exhibit other physical disabilities or impairments, and specific suggestions for handling them may be found under those disabilities in this book.

To meet the special needs of a student with TBI, the teacher should readjust the goals and expectations for the student. If the student's long-term memory is impaired, that student often needs to review previously learned material. If there is short-term memory impairment, what was learned the day before may be forgotten and need to be taught again. In addition, teachers must assess whether the student with TBI can only follow one-step instructions or is capable of understanding a sequence of two or more directions.

Educators find that using a multisensory approach is advantageous for the brain-injured student as well as for other students. Educators should demonstrate new tasks and give examples to illustrate ideas and concepts. Reinforce by repetition, and when giving instructions, avoid the use of figurative language.

The teacher of a student with TBI should never focus on the student's disabling injury. This only diminishes the student's self-esteem and could lead to a demeaning attitude on the part of other classmates. Instead, the teacher must focus on the student's strengths to maximize that student's learning potential.

Because children with TBI have varying degrees of impairment, it is essential to have ongoing communication with the parents who can provide much needed information about their child and that child's particular injury. Teachers need to be well informed about the injury to work constructively with the student. In teaching students with TBI, consideration should be given to the following, as listed by the National Dissemination Center for Children with Disabilities (1995):

- Provide repetition and consistency
- Demonstrate new tasks, state instructions, and provide examples to illustrate ideas and concepts
- Avoid figurative language
- Reinforce lengthening periods of attention to appropriate tasks
- Probe skill acquisition frequently and provide repeated practice
- Teach compensatory strategies for increasing memory
- Be prepared for students' reduced stamina and provide rest breaks as needed
- Keep the environment as distraction free as possible

For Further Information

Books

Bigali, V. *Head injury in children and adolescents: A resource and review for school and allied professionals.*

Bigler, E. D., Clark, E., & Farmer, J. E. (Eds.). *Childhood traumatic brain injury: Diagnosis, assessment, and intervention.*

Feinstein, S. G. *Secrets of the teenage brain: Research-based strategies for reading and teaching today's adolescents.*

Gerring, P. J., & Carney, J. M. *Head trauma: Strategies for educational reintegration.*

Glang, A., Singer, G. H. S., & Todis, B. *Students with acquired brain injury: The school's response.*

Hibbard, M., Gordon, W., Martin, T., Rashkin, P. B., & Brown, M. *Students with traumatic brain injury: Identification, assessment, and classroom accommodations.*

Lash, M., Wolcott, G., & Pearson, S. *Signs and strategies for educating students with brain injuries: A practical guide for teachers and schools.*

Savage, R. C., & Wolcott, G. F. (Eds.). *Educational dimensions of acquired brain injury.*

Schoenorodt, L. (Ed.). *Children with traumatic brain injury: A parents' guide.*
Senelick, R. C., & Dougherty, K. *Living with brain injury: A guide for families.*
Ylvisaker, M. *Collaborative brain injury intervention: Positive everyday routines.*

Organizations and Agencies

Brain Injury Association of America
1608 Spring Hill Road, Suite 1110
Vienna, VA 22182
703-761-0750
800-444-6443
Fax: 703-761-0755
E-mail: Check the Web site for a particular state's e-mail address.
www.biausa.org

Epilepsy Foundation, National Office
4351 Garden City Drive, Suite 500
Landover, MD 20785
800-332-1000
301-459-3700
E-mail: postmaster@efa.org
www.efa.org

Southwest Educational Development Laboratory (SEDL)
211 East 7th Street, Suite 200
Austin, TX 78701-3253
800-266-1832
512-476-6861 (TTY)
Fax: 512-476-2286
E-mail: info@sedl.org
www.sedl.org

Hearing Impairment

Definition

A person with a hearing impairment is considered to be deaf if the sense of hearing is nonfunctional for the ordinary purposes of life, or hard of hearing when the sense of hearing is defective but functional, with or without a hearing aid. A hearing impairment should not be confused with auditory processing, which is the inability to interpret auditory stimuli and is not the result of a hearing loss.

Background

Statistics regarding hearing clearly indicate the need for teachers to be aware of the needs of students with hearing impairments. According to the National Institute on Deafness and Other Communication Disorders (NIDCD), approximately 28 million Americans have a hearing impairment. Of these, approximately 17 in 1,000 children under the age of 18 have a hearing loss. Out of 1,000 children, 2 to 3 are born deaf or hard of hearing and 9 of every 10 children are born to parents who do not have a hearing impairment. As stated by the NIDCD (2000), in the United States, nearly 10,000 children have received cochlear implants Approximately 4 babies in every 100,000 births have Usher Syndrome (USH).

USH1 affects individuals who are profoundly deaf. They receive no benefit from hearing aids and use sign language as their primary language. They rarely learn to walk before they are 18 months old and later need support in order to sit. Vision problems begin by the time these children are 10 years old and progress rapidly until they are blind.

If the infant is born with moderate to severe hearing loss, the syndrome is classified as USH2. The hearing loss varies, but most of these children can perform well in school. These children use speech for communication. The vision problems consist of blind spots which tend to appear in the teenage years. The vision deteriorates until blindness occurs. Then these children can no longer read.

Children born with USH3 have normal hearing. Their hearing worsens over time. They develop noticeable hearing loss by the time they are teenagers. They develop night blindness during puberty and blind spots during their late teenage years. They usually become deaf by middle or late adulthood.

Both hereditary and environmental factors play a role in deafness. Total deafness, which is rare, is usually congenital. In about 50% of all cases of deafness, genetic factors are a probable cause. Partial deafness, ranging from moderate to severe, is generally the result of an ear disease, injury, or degeneration of the hearing mechanism with age (National Information Center on Deafness, 1989).

All hearing impairments fall into the categories of *sensorineural*, *conductive*, or *mixed*. Each category has different problems and different possibilities for medical and nonmedical remediation.

Sensorineural hearing loss is the result of damage to the delicate sensory hair cells or the nerves of the inner ear. This type of loss can be due to an inherited fault in a chromosome, as well as to birth injury or damage to the developing fetus, such as when a pregnant woman contracts rubella. Subjection to loud noise for prolonged periods increases the pressure in the labyrinth of the ear, which can result in a sensorineural hearing loss. The loss can range from mild to profound. Even with amplification to increase the sound level, there can be distortion. In some cases, the distortion is so great that the use of a hearing aid is not beneficial.

Conductive hearing loss usually affects all frequencies of hearing but generally does not result in a severe loss of hearing. It can be caused by diseases or obstructions in the outer or middle ear. Conductive deafness can also be caused by damage to the eardrum or middle ear due to pressure, injury, a middle-ear infection, or surgery on the ear. Conductive hearing loss due to earwax blocking the outer ear canal is common in adults. In children, otitis media, a middle-ear infection, is the most common cause of this type of deafness. Most people with this type of hearing loss can be helped medically, surgically, or by the use of a hearing aid.

Hearing tests measure how well a person can hear across the entire range of sound frequencies. Both hertz and decibels are used in hearing tests to find out the degree of loss. A sound's intensity or loudness is measured in decibels (dB), and its frequency or pitch is measured in hertz (Hz). The threshold of hearing is 0 dB. The larger the number, the louder the sound it represents. For example, 18 dB represents the loudness of a soft whisper at 18 feet away, in contrast to 108 dB, which represents the sound of a jet taking off 200 feet away.

The following number system classifies the degree of hearing impairment in decibels:

25–40 dB = mild
41–55 dB = moderate
56–70 dB = moderately severe
71–90 dB = severe
91+ dB = profound

A hertz is a unit of frequency equal to one cycle per second. High-pitched sounds have a higher number of cycles per second, and low-pitched sounds have a lower number of cycles per second.

The majority of children with impaired hearing have already acquired some basic sentence patterns and verbal information when they enter school. They need a symbol and communication system that allows them to be effective and efficient in their social interactions.

American Sign Language (ASL) is one of a variety of communication systems used by people with hearing impairments in the United States. It uses the visual medium rather than the aural. Handshakes, facial expressions, and the orientation of the body's movements convey meaning. ASL is different from English in that it is a universal language with its own vocabulary, grammar, and language patterns.

Signed English, also known as *Pidgin Signed English*, uses both finger spelling and ASL. *Finger spelling* is a manual alphabet. It is similar to writing in the air rather than on paper. Finger spelling is generally used in conjunction with ASL. Finger spelling used in combination with spoken English is referred to as the Rochester method. It is presented in the exact word order as in English as a direct translation.

In *speech reading*, sometimes referred to as *lip reading*, the deaf person watches the speaker's lips, facial expression, and gestures. However, there are difficulties with this form of communication because many English words are not visible on the lips and half of them look like something else. However, some individuals with a degree of hearing impairment have developed great skill in lip reading.

Cued speech uses eight hand shapes in four possible positions to supplement the information that is visible on the lips of the speaker. Hand cues signal the difference between sounds that look alike on the lips. For example, the letters p and b look the same. Using cued speech when communicating with someone whose hearing is impaired helps the person identify the correct word.

Oral communication refers to the use of speech, residual hearing, and lip reading. Some researchers believe that all deaf children may have functional residual hearing. Oral communication relies heavily on an auditory and visual approach to help people acquire and develop language through their residual hearing.

Simultaneous communication uses both spoken words and finger spelling. The person who has a hearing impairment reads lips along with the signs and finger spelling of the speaker.

Total communication uses all possible methods of communication. Many now believe that the approach that works best for an individual with a hearing impairment should be used.

Characteristics

People with a mild degree of hearing loss may have normal speech patterns, and their hearing impairment often may go undetected. A student with a mild degree of hearing loss may have difficulty hearing faint speech as well as speech at a distance. Often, the student with a mild hearing loss is inattentive and therefore is considered disobedient. If language development is lacking, the student may have difficulty understanding abstract ideas and concepts.

If there is a moderate loss of hearing and no hearing aid is used, a student may miss much of what is spoken and be unable to participate in class discussions. If conditions are favorable, such students may be able to understand conversational speech within a distance of 3 to 5 feet. Often, they are able to hear vowels in conversational speech, but some of the consonants may be heard imperfectly or not at all.

A child who has a moderately severe hearing loss and does not use a hearing aid hears very little conversational speech. Because speech develops as the direct result of hearing, a child with a moderately severe hearing loss may have defective speech, minimal expressive vocabulary, and inadequate language structure.

When there is a severe loss of hearing, most ordinary environmental sounds are not heard, but the person may sense loud noises and respond to loud voices. Some who are profoundly deaf may be able to hear loud sounds and loud voices very close to the ear. However, the person's speech is meaningless. In the early developmental years, a child may be entirely without words. That child may have vocalizations, but few sounds are recognizable as words.

Technological advances and telecommunications devices for the deaf, such as teletypewriter machines, have made it possible for persons with hearing impairments to increase their independence. TTY is a teletypewriter-printer device that enables individuals with hearing impairments to communicate by using a typewriter that transforms typed messages into electrical signals and retranslates them into print at the other end of a telephone connector. Telecaption adapters enable a person to read dialogue and captions on the TV screen and can now be added to television sets or purchased with TVs.

Signaling devices or vibrating signals may be added to the already existing auditory signal. When the doorbell rings, these devices flash to alert the person who is hearing impaired. Some alarm clocks have a flashing light or vibrating signal. These devices are also used to alert the person with a hearing impairment when a telephone rings, a baby cries, or a smoke alarm goes off. These are just a few of the devices available to help people who are hearing impaired. Technology is steadily advancing and innovative designs are continually being created to improve the quality of life for people with hearing impairments.

Strategies for Educators

For peers to appreciate what it is like to be hearing impaired, the teacher can purchase inexpensive earplugs for the students, ask the students to place these plugs in their ears, and then proceed with the lessons. Students quickly realize the difficulties encountered by the hearing impaired. In addition, most special education departments have tape recordings available that demonstrate what persons with hearing impairments hear at the different levels of hearing loss.

Many educators mistakenly believe that they must speak very loudly to a student who is hearing impaired. It is best to speak in a normal conversational voice. Speaking slowly and distinctly is indispensable in helping the student with a hearing impairment to understand what you say. Of course, this does not pertain to the person who is profoundly deaf.

Often, teachers have a tendency to overexaggerate mouth movements when speaking to a student with a hearing impairment. This only confuses the student and makes it impossible to lip read. When speaking, the teacher should always face the student. It is helpful to write assignments on the chalkboard, but the teacher should remember to turn around to face the student before explaining the assignment.

Educators should consider the seating arrangement for a student with a hearing impairment. The student should be seated within 10 feet of the teacher; this allows the student to lip read and also interpret visual clues. Minimizing noise sources is necessary, so the student should not be seated near heaters, air conditioners, doorways, or other high traffic areas. Because sound bounces off walls or other hard surfaces, these seating areas should be avoided.

Because the student with impaired hearing may not hear all sounds and may misunderstand certain words, it is important to restate the same thing in a different way to avoid repeating the original misunderstood words. In an unobtrusive way, the teacher should check to make certain the student understands.

The lighting in the room should not fall directly on the face of the student, as this may make it difficult for the student to observe the teacher. It is also harder for the student to lip-read or interpret the teacher's visual clues if the teacher stands in front of a window or light.

Provide handouts on key points to a student with a hearing impairment. This helps that student to follow instructions. When possible, this material should be given to the support person who is also responsible for the education of the student and who, in turn, can provide the reinforcement the student needs to gain a sense of confidence when included in the regular class. Provisions can be made to have an interpreter in the classroom for the student with a hearing impairment. An interpreter gives additional assistance to the student who is hearing impaired and is of great help to the regular teacher.

The possibility that a student may have a hearing loss is often readily observed by the classroom teacher. The student tries to avoid any oral activities that involve verbal interactions. When a direction or request is made, the student always asks for it to be repeated. Another indication that the student may have a hearing impairment is when the student has a practice of cupping the ears or cocking the head to hear better. Generally, the student always turns in the direction of the person talking. Continuous complaining of earaches or buzzing noises in the ear may indicate a hearing loss. If a hearing loss is suspected, the teacher should make a referral to the school audiologist for further evaluation.

It is beneficial for all students to study prominent people who were hearing impaired yet successful, such as Thomas Edison and Helen Keller. (Keller was also blind.)

Our society is composed of many people who have been deaf since birth or who have lost their hearing later in life. They are found in many occupations. Unfortunately, as a group, they are underemployed. The situation is changing as understanding and compassion for people with hearing impairments grows. Educators and society as a whole can do much to increase opportunities for them.

The Captioned Media Program (CMP), funded by the U.S. Department of Education, provides free loan of open-captioned educational, special interest, and theatrical videos to people with hearing impairments and deafness, as well as professionals working with the deaf community. These videos can be obtained by writing or calling the National Association for the Deaf (NAD)/CMP. A catalog of the videos and films can be obtained by calling or writing CMP. Their address and telephone numbers are listed under Organizations and Agencies.

For Further Information

Books

Easterbrooks, S. R., & Estes, E. R. *Helping deaf and hard of hearing to use spoken language.*
Maxon, A. *The hearing-impaired child: Walley through high school years.*
Medwid, D. J. *Kid-friendly parenting with deaf and hard-of-hearing children.*

Moores, D. F. *Educating the deaf: Psychology, principles, and practices.*
Ross, M. (Ed.). *Hearing-impaired children in the mainstream.*
Schark, M. *Educating deaf students: From research to practice.*
Shirmer, B. R. *Teaching language and literacy development in children who are deaf.*
Stewart, D. A., & Kluwin, T. N. *Teaching deaf and hard of hearing students: Content, strategies, and curriculum.*
Wilson, J. J. *The classroom notetaker: How to organize a program serving students with hearing impairments.*

Organizations and Agencies

Alexander Graham Bell Association
3417 Volta Place NW
Washington, DC 20007
202-337-5220 (voice/TTY)
Fax: 202-337-5220
E-mail: info@agbell.org
www.agbell.org

American Speech-Language-Hearing Association (ASHA)
2200 Research Blvd.
Rockville, MD 20850-3289
800-638-8255 (voice/TTY)
Fax: 301-571-0457
E-mail: actioncenter@asha.org
www.asha.org

Described and Captioned Media Program (DCMP)
Mailing address:
Captioned Media Program
National Association of the Deaf
1447 E. Main Street
Spartanburg, SC 29307
864-585-1778
864-585-2617 (TTY)
800-237-6213
800-237-6819 (TTY)
Fax: 800-538-5636
E-mail: info@dcmp.org
www.dcmp.org

National Institute on Deafness and Other Communication Disorders
    Information Clearinghouse
National Institute on Health
31 Center Drive, MSC 2320
Bethesda, MD 20892-3456
301-496-7243
301-402-0252 (TTY)

Fax: 301-402-0018
E-mail: nidcdinfo@nidcd.gov
www.nidcd.nih.gov

Learning Disabilities

Definition

The term learning disability (LD) is currently used to describe a dysfunction that interferes with someone's ability to store, process, or produce information. The IDEA defines a learning disability:

> A disorder in one or more of the basic psychological processes involved in understanding or in using spoken or written language, which may manifest itself in an imperfect ability to listen, think, speak, read, write, spell, or do mathematical calculations. The federal definition further states that learning disabilities include "such conditions as perceptual disabilities, brain injury, minimal brain dysfunction, dyslexia, and developmental aphasia." (National Dissemination Center for Children with Disabilities, 2005)

Learning disability is a general term that describes a specific kind of learning problem. A learning disability can cause a person to have trouble learning and using certain skills. The skills most often affected are: reading, writing, listening, speaking, reasoning, and doing math (LDOnline: http://www.ldonline.org/ldbasics/whatisld).

Background

A review of the literature reveals a number of different terms that are being used to refer to learning disabilities. This is not surprising, because the problem spans many disciplines, including special education, psychology, speech correction, child development, neurology, and medicine.

The many different estimates of the number of children with learning disabilities—ranging from 1% to 30% of the general population—reflect the variation in the definition of learning disabilities. In 1987, the Interagency Committee on Learning Disabilities (NICHCY, 2000b) concluded that 5% to 10% was a reasonable estimate. The U.S. Department of Education reported in 1991 that nearly 5% of all school-age children were receiving special education (NICHCY, 2000b). In the 1997–1998 school year, more than 2.7 million children with learning disabilities were being served (NICHCY, 2000b). Over half of the children being served in special education have learning disabilities. In the United States, 1 out of 5 people have a learning disability (*Twenty-fourth Annual Report to Congress*, U.S. Department of Education, http://www.ed.gov/about/reports/annual/osep/2002/index.html).

Learning disabilities embrace different disabilities. Many aspects of a learning disability affect a child's academic performance in school by not only causing problems in academic performance but also in his or her relationships with others. A learning disability cannot be considered as being only one disability but rather a disability concurrent with other disabilities. For example, a child who has a learning problem might also be identified as being dyslexic or AD/HD. The need for an extensive and accurate diagnosis is of extreme importance. Only then can the correct service be provided.

A child who is doing poorly in school may appear to be lazy or emotionally disturbed, but the problems may be the result of a learning disability and require intervention. It is essential to identify students with learning disabilities as early as possible to prevent or alleviate the frustration and failure these students experience. A collaborative team approach helps facilitate the child's overall development.

The federal education law, IDEA 2004, provides extensive regulations for identification of a learning disability. A few of the changes in the law regarding identification of a learning disability increase the accuracy in identification. It is no longer necessary to have a "severe discrepancy" between the student's intellectual ability and academic performance. Instead, insufficient progress is based on expectations for the student's age or on the grade-level standards set by the individual's state.

Achievement progress needs to be based on scientific research-based interventions (RTI). Evidence of a pattern of strengths and weaknesses in performance as well as the student's intellectual development is also needed. These are just a few of the changes in IDEA 2004 that reflect the need to improve the identification process for learning disabilities.

Characteristics

Individuals with learning disabilities may have problems with reading comprehension, speech, writing, or reasoning abilities. The following characteristics may be exhibited by students with learning disabilities:

- Inappropriate behavior for varied situations
- Excessive variation in mood

- Poor organizational skills
- Failure to see consequence of actions
- Awkward use of pencil and scissors
- Distractibility
- Hyperactivity
- Perceptual coordination problems
- Impulsiveness
- Lack of organizational skills
- Low tolerance for frustrations and problems
- Difficulty in reasoning
- Difficulty in one or more academic areas
- Low self-esteem
- Problems with social relationships
- Difficulty beginning or completing tasks
- Uneven and unpredictable test performance
- Aural sequential memory deficit
- Visual sequential memory deficit
- Auditory processing disorder
- Visual-motor coordination problems

Characteristics of those who have learning disabilities may vary from individual to individual, but one common aspect is that a person with an LD has an average to above-average IQ. There is also a demonstrated discrepancy between intellectual ability and achievement in one or more academic areas. Because 80% of students with LD receive special education services because of their reading difficulties, possibly more focus should be placed on reading deficiencies as an eligibility criteria for services. Depending on the nature of the LD, the student may be quick to learn some skills and slower at other skills.

Unfortunately, students who are learning disabled are sometimes mistakenly considered to be slow learners and to show little academic growth. It is important to check the academic records of a student to ascertain what the academic profile reveals. A slow learner depicts a low, flat profile of growth, whereas the profile of a student with an LD shows a markedly uneven pattern of progress and regression in the acquisition of skills. The language skills of the slow learner are not age appropriate, but the language skills of the student with an LD often are.

Even with intervention, the slow learner's progress is very slow. When intervention techniques are used with a student who has an LD, there may be steady and near-normal progression in academics.

Strategies for Educators

The student with an LD may exhibit one or more of the other disabilities covered in this book. The teacher needs to know what the student's specific disabilities are. Only then can the educational needs of the student be met. For example, if the student has a visual processing dysfunction, it is counterproductive to teach in the visual mode. The teacher should know the student's learning modality in order to capitalize on the student's strengths. However, a multisensory approach is best if the needs of all students in the class are to be met.

The student with an LD requires a well-structured environment. Students generally are able to accomplish more when the teacher routinely outlines the day's activities on the chalkboard and sets goals for the day. Reviewing the schedule and the rules before a new activity also helps the student with an LD bridge the transition from one activity to another.

Some students with LDs are easily overstimulated by certain classroom activities or excessive talking. This often leads to misbehavior by the student that may be disruptive to the class. It is the teacher's responsibility to help the student regain composure. A teacher can provide a time-out place in the classroom where the student can be away from the ongoing activity. Conversely, a teacher can send the student on an errand or to the school library. At no time should this be used as a punitive action but merely as an opportunity to provide a quiet time for the student.

The learning modality of many students with LDs is kinesthetic. These students learn best when they can see and touch concrete objects relating to the subject being taught. They also get a kinesthetic image if they form the letters or numbers with their fingers in the air. Depending on the age of the student, the use of sand and sandpaper to form letters or numbers produces the same effect. However, in the regular class, this type of kinesthetic mode sets the student apart from the rest of the class unless all are using the same method. The use of manipulatives for the entire class or a small group of students is less intimidating, and everyone in the class benefits.

The teacher needs to be flexible in assignment requirements. When a student has difficulty writing a report, the teacher should consider accepting oral or taped reports. Computers are extremely helpful to students who have difficulty writing reports, and many types of software are available to help make writing easier. It may be necessary to reduce the length of the written assignments so that the student with an LD can successfully complete the task.

Above all, the teacher should recognize the successes—no matter how small—of students who are learning disabled. As with all students, there should be immediate and positive feedback. Behavior modification techniques may also foster the student's desire to achieve.

It is essential to diagnose learning disabilities and related problems as early as possible. Without recognition and help, students become increasingly frustrated and distressed by persistent failure. By the time they reach high school, they may quit trying. However, children whose problems are recognized early and treated appropriately can develop strategies to compensate for their disabilities and lead successful and rewarding lives. Many famous people have had to cope with learning disabilities to achieve success.

For Further Information

Books

Bender, W. (Ed.). *Professional issues in learning disabilities: Practical strategies and relevant research findings.*

Bley, N., & Thornton, C. A. *Teaching mathematics to students with learning disabilities.*

Deschler, D., Ellis, E., & Lenz, K. *Teaching adolescents with learning disabilities: Strategies and methods.*

Hallahan, D. P., Kauffman, J. M., & Lloyd, J. W. *Introduction to learning disabilities.*

Harwell, J. M. *Complete learning disabilities handbook: Ready-to-use strategies and activities for teaching students with learning disabilities.*

Lerner, J. W. *Learning disabilities: Theories, diagnosis, and teaching strategies.*

Mather, N., & Goldstein, S. *Learning disabilities and challenging behaviors: A guide to intervention and management.*

Mercer, C. D. *Students with learning disabilities.*

Minskoff, E., & Allsopp, D. *Academic success for adolescents with learning disabilities and ADHD.*

Sousa, D. A. *How the special needs brain learns.*

Strichart, S. S., Iannuzi, P., & Magrum, C. T., II. *Teaching study skills and strategies to students with learning disabilities, attention deficit disorders, or special needs.*

Organizations and Agencies

Division for Learning Disabilities (DLD)
Council for Exceptional Children
110 North Glebe Road, Suite 300
Arlington, VA 2201-5704
703-620-3660
703-264-9446 (TTY; text only)

888-CEC-SPED
Fax: 703-284-9494
E-mail: cec@cec.sped.org
www.dldcec.org

Learning Disabilities Association of America (LDA)
4156 Library Road
Pittsburgh, PA 15234
888-300-6710
412-341-1515
E-mail: info@ldanatl.org
www.ldanatl.org

National Center for Learning Disabilities
381 Park Avenue South, Suite 1401
New York, NY 10016
888-575-7373
212-545-7510
Fax: 212-545-9665
www.ncld.org

Mental Retardation

Definition

The following is the definition for mental retardation as stated in the Education for All Handicapped Children Act (PL 94-142, 1975): "Mentally retarded means significantly subaverage general intellectual functioning existing concurrently with deficits in adaptive behavior and manifested during the developmental period, which adversely affects a child's educational performance." In 1992, the American Association on Mental Retardation (AAMR) defined mental retardation according to three criteria: intellectual functioning level below a 70 to 75 IQ, significant limitations existing in two or more adaptive skill areas, and the presence of these conditions since childhood (as cited in Luckasson et al., 1992).

Background

As many as 3 out of every 100 people in the United States have mental retardation. Nearly 613,000 children ages 6 to 21 have some form of mental retardation and need special education in school. (*Twenty-fourth Annual Report to Congress*, U.S. Department of Education, http://www .ed.gov/about/reports/annual/osep/2002/index.html). Some form of mental retardation affects 1 out of every 10 children and requires them to need special education services. The number has been declining during the past 25 years due to a perceived stigma attached to the term *mentally retarded*. Other disabilities overshadow the retardation, such as AD/HD. The President's Committee on Mental Retardation (2001) stated that "more than seven and a half million Americans of all ages experience mental retardation or significant developmental delay, affecting one in ten families" (p. 1) and that 75% of the population that has mental retardation comes from urban and rural poverty areas (President's Committee on Mental Retardation, 2001). Causative factors may be the result of malnutrition, disease, lead poisoning, and inadequate medical care in those areas. An additional cause may be understimulation of the child after birth. A child has a basic need for everyday, enriching experiences, and a lack of them can curtail that child's mental development. Mental retardation can occur in any family, regardless of racial, educational, or social background.

Mental retardation can be classified as mild, moderate, severe, or profound. The American Association on Mental Retardation, however, no longer labels individuals according to these categories but looks instead at the intensity and pattern of changing supports needed by the individual during the individual's lifetime.

Of those people with mental retardation, 89% are mildly affected and only a little slower than average in learning new information, whereas 13% have serious limitations in functioning (ARC, 1987).

Persons who are mildly affected differ primarily in their rate and degree of mental development. In some of those cases, retardation may not become apparent until the child enters school. In others, it may become obvious well before the child is of school age.

People who are severely and profoundly retarded account for 5% of those with mental retardation (ARC, 1987). In addition to intellectual impairment, they frequently have other disabilities, such as cerebral palsy, epilepsy, or a similar seizure disorder, or visual or hearing impairments. Although they receive special training, they may be dependent on others for the rest of their lives. The educator's primary goal for students who are profoundly retarded is to help them develop skills that enable them to care for their own personal needs and work in a sheltered workplace or home environment.

Most cases of severe retardation can be attributed to genetic irregularities or chromosomal abnormalities. Down syndrome and other inherited or congenital conditions account for many cases of children with mental retardation. Mental retardation may also result from birth trauma or infection at birth or in early childhood. Biological factors may include asphyxia, blood incompatibilities between the pregnant woman and fetus, and maternal infections. Certain drugs have also been linked to problems in fetal development that result in mental retardation.

Although mental retardation is permanent and irreversible, some authorities believe that 50% of the cases could be prevented (ARC, 1987). Routine screening and immunization of the pregnant woman before transfusions, pregnancy, and childbirth helps prevent the type of mental retardation caused by Rh hemolytic blood disease. An infant affected during gestation by Rh factor incompatibility should have a blood exchange at the time of birth.

Children between the ages of 18 months and 24 months should be immunized for *Hemophilus influenza* to prevent mental retardation caused by bacterial meningitis. In addition, all preschool children should be tested for the presence of lead in their bodies. If the level is dangerously high, treatment should follow, and sources of lead poisoning should be identified and removed from the child's environment.

Because the developmental rate may be much slower for children who are mentally retarded, it is important to begin appropriate educational services in infancy and to continue throughout the developmental period.

Characteristics

Short-term memory impairment is common among children with mental retardation. Because of this deficit, it takes much longer for those children to learn a skill. Continuous repetition is needed because they may have difficulty remembering what they learned the previous day. Children with mental retardation are often unable to form generalizations from their learning experiences and thus may have trouble applying what they learn to life situations.

Most children who are mentally retarded exhibit the social behavior of a younger child and prefer playing with younger children. Their emotions are usually inappropriate for a particular situation and generally are expressed in a childlike manner. Their language and speech skills may be well below those of their peers, and they may have difficulty using complex language and following complex directions.

Individuals with mental retardation develop their academic, social, and vocational skills differently, depending on whether the impairment is mild, moderate, severe, or profound. Their less-developed intellectual ability and social skills may lead to rejection by others and a lowering of their self-esteem. However, it is possible for many with mental retardation to have normal life patterns.

Strategies for Educators

Many general education classrooms have students with mental retardation—generally mild to moderate retardation. The teacher should set realistic and age-appropriate goals for students with mental retardation because it is paramount that they feel successful in their endeavors.

Tasks that many people learn to do without instruction are difficult for the student who is mentally retarded. The use of manipulatives and concrete objects is necessary. The student who is mentally retarded is better able to understand a concept with a hands-on approach. The student needs to be able to touch and manipulate materials. Whenever possible, familiar items should be used and related to real-life situations. Cuisenaire Rods, or integer bars, help the student understand math relationships. Counters can be used for teaching basic math skills and reinforced with educational games. A concept needs more than a teacher's explanation and demonstration; it needs actual physical involvement of the student.

Teachers also need to break down tasks into smaller steps or segments, with each step being carefully taught and retaught. As the student gains understanding, the student also gains confidence. The teacher should always adjust the assignment to fit the capabilities of the student who has mild retardation. Shorter assignments than those given to the rest of the class make it possible for the student to complete the task and aids in building the student's confidence.

When testing students in the general education class, modify the test for students who have mild retardation. Alternative measures can be used to avoid the stress of taking a test. Providing different questions that are within the student's capabilities is necessary. Multiple-choice questions should be simplified with language the student understands. It is also less threatening if an assistant can orally give the test to the student in the library or another room out of range of the other students. The student can answer the questions directly to the assistant, or, if preferred, tape the answers. All grading should be based on the individual's growth in a particular area and not be based on the class norm.

A learning center with high-interest activities in a designated area of the room can also be very helpful for the student. The learning center can be designed to focus on a particular need for all students and as a place where students can complete assignments at their own pace.

The teacher should require less written work from a student with mental retardation. If beneficial, the student should be allowed to tape-record the "written" assignment for replay when needed.

Students with mental retardation need to be taught tasks that help them develop working skills they can use in real-life situations. Students who are mentally retarded should be given checklists to account for homework or for completed, turned-in assignments. Many tasks in the school library as well as the office can be successfully handled by students who are mentally retarded.

Elementary students should be taught functional skills relating to the classroom and the playground. It also is advantageous for the student with mild mental retardation to be able to read and understand the meaning of survival signs, such as walk, stop, and all other pertinent signs. In secondary school, the focus is on skills related to work and living in the community. An example of this is teaching the student the value of money in making purchases and receiving change. Many living skills can be adapted to the academic curriculum and to the individual needs of the student who is mildly retarded.

In today's society, the trend is for persons who are mentally retarded to work in a supportive environment in the general sector. Many jobs in the workplace, such as restaurant work and assembly production lines, consist of repetitive tasks. Being able to enter the mainstream gives those who are mentally retarded feelings of success and accomplishment and allows them to become productive and full participants in our society.

For Further Information

Books

American Association on Intellectual and Developmental Disabilities. *Mental retardation: Definition, classification, and systems of supports.*

American Association on Intellectual and Developmental Disabilities. *Definition of mental retardation.*

Baker, B., & Brightman, et al. *Steps to independence: Teaching everyday skills to children with special needs.*

Gable, R. A., & Warren, S. F. (Eds.). *Strategies for teaching students with mild to severe mental retardation.*

Hickson, I., Blackman, L. S., & Reis, E. M. *Mental retardation: Foundations of educational programming.*

Kaufman, S. *Retarded isn't stupid, mom!*

Lovitt, T. C. *Tactics for teaching.*

Robinson, G. A., Patton, J. R., Polloway, E. A., & Sargent, L. R. (Eds.). *Best practices in mild mental disabilities.*

Smith, R. (Ed.). *Children with mental retardation: A parents' guide.*

Trainer, M. *Differences in common: Straight talk on mental retardation, Down syndrome, and life.*

Ysseldyke, J. *Teaching students with mental retardation: A practical guide for every teacher.*

Organizations and Agencies

American Association on Intellectual and Developmental Disabilities
444 North Capitol Street NW, Suite 846
Washington, DC 20001-1512
800-424-3688
202-387-2193
Fax: 202-387-2193
E-mail: info@aaidd.org
www.aaidd.org

The Arc of the United States
1010 Wayne Avenue, Suite 650
Silver Springs, MD 20910
301-565-3842
800-433-5255
Fax: 301-565-3843 / 301-565-5342
E-mail: info@thearc.org
www.thearc.org

Division on Developmental Disabilities
The Council for Exceptional Children
110 North Glebe Road, Suite 300
Arlington, VA 22201-5704
888-232-7733
703-620-3660
866-915-5000 (TTY)
E-mail: service@cec.sped.org
www.addcec.org

NICHCY
P.O. Box 1492
Washington, DC 20013
800-695-0285
202-884-8441 Fax
E-mail: nichcy@aed.org
Web: www.nichcy.org

Muscular Dystrophy

Definition

Muscular dystrophy (MD) consists of a group of more than 30 generic diseases characterized by progressive weakness and degeneration of the skeletal muscles that control movement. Some forms of MD are seen in infancy or childhood while others might not appear until middle age or later. The disorders differ in terms of the distribution and extent of muscle weakness depending on the age of onset, rate of progression, and pattern of inheritance. Some forms also affect cardiac muscles.

Background

Muscular dystrophy should not be confused with multiple sclerosis, which is an acquired disease and usually starts in early adult life. Unlike multiple sclerosis, muscular dystrophy is an inherited muscular disorder affecting children.

It is estimated that 200,000 Americans of all ages are affected by muscular dystrophy (National Institute of Health and Human Development, 1996). There are several types of muscular dystrophy: facioscapulohumeral muscular dystrophy, limb-girdle muscular dystrophy, myotonic dystrophy, ocular dystrophy, Duchenne muscular dystrophy, and Becker's muscular dystrophy.

Facioscapulohumeral muscular dystrophy, which usually appears between the ages of 10 and 40, affects the muscles of the upper arms, shoulder girdle, and face. Progression is slow and rarely leads to complete disability.

Limb-girdle muscular dystrophy differs from facioscapulohumeral muscular dystrophy in its lack of involvement of the facial muscles; it mainly affects the muscles of the hips and shoulders. Limb-girdle dystrophy usually starts in late childhood or in the early 20s. As in facioscapulohumeral muscular dystrophy, the progression of this form of dystrophy is slow.

Myotonic dystrophy is a relatively rare form of dystrophy that affects the hands and feet. Muscles are unable to relax for several seconds after a forceful contraction. Infants show a pronounced floppiness and are slow to develop.

Ocular dystrophy is another rare form. This type affects the eyes and throat. It can result in double vision, drooping eyelids, and difficulty swallowing because of degeneration of the throat muscles.

Duchenne muscular dystrophy is the most common form, and it appears only in males. About 1 to 2 in 10,000 boys are affected, and approximately one-third of those are mentally retarded. This type of dystrophy is genetic, inherited through a recessive sex-linked gene affecting boys, but it may also be passed on to a female, who then becomes a carrier. A female carrier has a 50% chance of passing on this disease to her infant son, and her daughter has a 50% chance of becoming a carrier.

The symptoms of Duchenne muscular dystrophy appear within the first 3 years of life. The first muscles to weaken are the hip-girdle muscles followed by a weakening of the shoulder muscles. There can be an uncertain gait, frequent falling, and difficulty getting up from the floor or climbing stairs. By the time a boy reaches age 12, he usually must use a wheelchair. A steady weakening of the respiratory muscles makes it hard to breathe. The heart muscle is also weakened, and this often leads to heart failure. Duchenne muscular dystrophy progresses steadily, and most who have this disease do not live beyond age 20.

The symptoms of *Becker's muscular dystrophy* are similar to those of Duchenne muscular dystrophy. There may also be curvature of the spine, and the muscles may appear bulky because when the muscles waste away they are replaced with fat. This type of dystrophy starts later in childhood and progression is slow.

At present, medical intervention can neither cure nor halt the disease. Fortunately much research is continuing. The cure has not been found, but a press release in 2003 reported that researchers had developed an affordable blood test that could detect Duchenne muscular dystrophy. This test has been successful in detecting Duchenne muscular dystrophy in more than 95% of the cases. Prior to this blood test, detection had to be accomplished with a muscle biopsy, which was invasive. Continuing research provides hope for solutions for the many problems connected with muscular dystrophy.

Characteristics

The physical characteristics of individuals with muscular dystrophy have been briefly stated under the various types of dystrophy. These individuals require assistance with their personal hygiene, eating, and dressing. This dependence on others understandably affects the individual with muscular dystrophy, and, as with any other severe physical disability, there can be many psychological and social problems as well.

Strategies for Educators

Although many students with muscular dystrophy have learned to adapt to their environment, the teacher can help create a classroom environment to meet their specific educational and physical needs. Although technological aids are available that are useful to students with muscular dystrophy, these devices may create conditions of which teachers need to be aware.

If a student is in a wheelchair or is using other assistance devices, physical movement can be very burdensome. Extra time should be allowed for the student when that student has to move from one place to another. Depending on the particular situation, another student can provide help in the transition. It must be remembered, however, that many do not want or need this additional help, and the student's wishes should be respected. Students wish to achieve but also wish to be as independent as possible.

Cooperative learning is an excellent experience for most students with muscular dystrophy. Teaming together with peers provides an opportunity to interact with others, make new friends, be accepted by others, and work cooperatively. Establishing a network of friends is important to the student with a disability, and this network may continue to grow and extend beyond the school environment.

Students with muscular dystrophy should remain active as long as possible to keep their healthy muscles in good condition. Short-term rehabilitation efforts can be beneficial in the early stages of the disorder but not in the later stages. Educators should encourage independence to avoid self-esteem problems associated with dependence on others. For successful rehabilitation, normal social opportunities should be encouraged whenever possible.

Counseling can be beneficial for both the student and family members. Many psychological problems resulting from the disability can be overcome. Counseling also helps family members by easing the burden of dealing with muscular dystrophy on their own.

For Further Information

Books

Bigge, J. I. *Teaching individuals with physical and multiple disabilities.*
Charash, L. I., Kutscher, A. H., & Roye, D. P. *Muscular dystrophy and other neuro-muscular disease: Psychological issues.*
Emery, A. *Muscular dystrophy: The facts.*

Siegel, I. M. *Muscular dystrophy in children: A guide for families.*
Stone, K., Tester, C., Blakeney, J., & Howarth, A. *Occupational therapy and Duchenne muscular dystrophy.*
Wolfson, P. *Moonrise: One family, genetic identity & muscular dystrophy.*

Organizations and Agencies

Facioscapulohumeral Muscular Dystrophy (FSHD) Society
3 Westwood Road
Lexington, MA 02420
781-275-7781
781-869-0501
Fax: 781-860-0599
E-mail: info@fshsociety.org
www.fshsociety.org

Muscular Dystrophy Association
3300 East Sunrise Drive
Tucson, AZ 85718-3299
800-344-4863
888-HELP-MDA
Fax: 520-529-5454
E-mail: mda@mdausa.org
www.mdausa.org

Muscular Dystrophy Family Foundation
3951 N. Meridian Street, Suite 100
Indianapolis, IN 46208
317-923-MDFF
317-923-6334
E-mail: mdff@mdff.org
www.mdff.org

National Institute of Child Health and Human Development (NICHD)
National Institutes of Health, DHHS
31 Center Drive, Room 2A32 MSC 2425
Bethesda, MD 20892-2425
301-496-7243
800-241-1044
888-320-6942 (TTY)
Fax: 301-984-1473
E-mail: nidcdinfo@nidcd.gov
www.nidcd.nih.gov

National Institute of Neurological Disorders and Stroke (NINDS)
NIH Neurological Institute
P.O. Box 5801
Bethesda, MD 20824

800-352-9424
301-496-5751
301-468-5981 TTY
www.ninds.nih.gov

National Medical Library Association
65 East Wacker Place, Suite 1900
Chicago, IL 60601-7246
312-419-9094
Fax: 312-419-8950
E-mail: info@mlahq.org
www.mlanet.org

U.S. Department of Health and Human Services (CDCP)
1600 Clifton Road NE
Atlanta, GA 30333
800-311-3435
E-mail: inquiry@cdc.gov
www.cdc.gov

Speech Disorders

Definition

The American Speech-Language-Hearing Association (ASHA, 1993) defines a communication disorder as "an impairment in the ability to receive, send, process, and comprehend concepts or verbal, nonverbal, and graphic symbols systems. A communications disorder may be evident in the process of hearing, language, and or speech" (p. 40).

Background

Communication disorders encompass both language and speech deficits. However, an individual with speech problems has difficulty only with communication skills, whereas a person with a language disorder has difficulty not only with the expression of ideas but also with the reception of language. Speech problems are more prevalent than language problems. The U.S. Department of Health and Human Services estimates that speech disorders affect 10% to 15% of preschoolers and about 6% of children in Grades 1 through 12 (National Dissemination Center for Children with Disabilities, 1990c). It is also estimated that 5 million to 10 million children in the United States need speech training (NICHCY, 1990c), and 10 of every 100 children can be expected to have a speech disorder (NICHCY, 1990c). An average estimate of the number of people in the United States is approximately 7.5 million. Between 8 and 6 million have some form of language impairment (National Institute on Deafness and Other Communication Disorders, 2000). Due to the differences in diagnostic criteria, statistical estimates may vary but they do reflect approximations of the disorders.

An impairment in language affects children differently than adults. Research suggests that exposure to language must begin as early as possible since the first six months of an infant's life are crucial for development of language. The use of spoken language in the family can provide the needed language exposure for the infant. Some children have been deprived of this opportunity. Many other factors are involved in causing a language impairment.

Speech centers are located in the left hemisphere of the brain. However, researchers have found that there is a degree of bilateralism between the left and right hemispheres. Any damage to the brain can lead to a speech disorder. Communication disorders such as autism, cerebral palsy, mental retardation, hearing impairment, and aphasia, which have an organic or physical origin, are treated under separate headings in this book.

The four basic components of speech are *articulation, phonation, resonance,* and *rhythm*. Articulation refers to the ability to make specific sounds, and phonation is the actual utterance of words. Resonance is the reinforcement and prolongation of sounds by vibrations. The rate and timing of speech is the rhythm with which it is spoken.

Speech disorders are common in most children who have or have had a cleft lip or palate. A cleft lip is characterized by the separation of the two sides of the lip. It often includes a cleft in the back of the upper jaw and upper gum. A cleft palate is characterized by an opening in the roof of the mouth from behind the teeth to the nasal cavity, and its severity can vary from child to child.

Both a cleft lip and a cleft palate can be present at birth. In 1989, the American Medical Association (1989) stated that of every nine babies affected, two have only a cleft lip, three have only a cleft palate, and four have both. According to the Cleft Palate Foundation (1988), 1 out of every 700 to 750 babies is born with a cleft lip, a cleft palate, or both (also cited in Lynch, 1989). Because clefts tend to run in families, heredity appears to be a factor.

Children born with clefts often experience problems with articulation and resonance, and their speech development is slower than that of other children. They may also have missing, malformed, or malpositioned teeth that require medical attention. Ear infections, which may lead to hearing loss along with accompanying speech disorders, are also common among these children.

Fortunately, with new surgical procedures, a cleft lip can be repaired when a baby is 3 months old, and a cleft palate can be repaired before a baby is 1 year old. In addition to corrective surgery, the medical profession has also designed appliances to replace the missing palate. With early intervention by medical professionals and therapists, most children are able to compensate for or overcome their speech disorders.

Stuttering, or stammering, is another kind of speech disorder. Stuttering is a fluency disorder that involves a rapid repetition of consonant or vowel sounds at the beginning of words. There can also be a total verbal block. Generally, stuttering in children starts before age 8, and 75% stop stuttering by the time they reach adolescence. It has been estimated that over 3 million Americans stutter and that five times more men than women stutter (Stuttering Foundation of America, n.d.). Stuttering frequently appears in children between the ages of 2 and 6 when they are developing language. Boys are three times more likely than girls to suffer from stuttering.

Although the exact cause of stuttering is unknown, the tendency to stutter runs in families. Some researchers believe it might be the result of a subtle brain damage. Others feel that stuttering is primarily a psychological problem. Stuttering can often be improved by the use of speech therapy, electronic aids, or both.

Characteristics

Many children with speech disorders have characteristics that are common to other children. However, the student with a speech disability often has difficulty combining speech sounds for communication. This leads the person to self-correct and hesitate when trying to convey thoughts.

Articulation problems are common in individuals with speech disorders. Some sounds may be completely omitted during speech, so that instead of saying "I see a bike" a child might say "I ee a ike." Some students with articulation problems may have difficulty pronouncing the letters *l* or *t*, or they may substitute one sound for another. The National Institutes of Health uses the cartoon character Elmer Fudd as an example of someone with an articulation disorder when he talks about the "scwewy wabbit." To accurately repeat a sound, a child must be able to perceive its unique characteristics. Although many speech patterns may be called "baby talk" and be part of a young child's normal development, they can become problems if they are not outgrown.

Students who stutter generally have prolonged speech sounds, repeated hesitation, and a delayed utterance of words. Under stress, their vocal cords go into spasms before speaking. To relax the vocal cords and keep them open, stutterers can prolong their inhalations and exhalations before speaking. Even though a person might stutter while speaking, that person usually has no difficulty singing.

A lack of communication skills may lead to intense feelings of frustration, isolation, discouragement, and possible outbursts of anger. Many children who have severe speech disorders and physical impairments have to contend with not only their speech but other physical disabilities as well.

Strategies for Educators

Because stuttering is the most obvious form of speech disorder that students recognize, the teacher needs to explain to them what stuttering is. It is also helpful to discuss the lives of the many successful people who have overcome their own stuttering. The teacher can read stories about these people to younger students and assign to older students oral and written reports concerning successful people with the disability. The following is a partial list of people who overcame their stuttering problems: Sir Isaac Newton, English mathematician and natural philosopher; Marilyn Monroe, actress; Winston Churchill, prime minister of Great Britain during World War II; Kim Philby, British spy; Raymond Massey, actor; James Earl Jones, actor; Ben Johnson, Olympic runner; Greg Louganis, Olympic diver; Carly Simon, singer; Dave Taylor, former hockey star with the Los Angeles Kings; Lester Hayes, former defensive back with the Oakland and L.A. Raiders; Bo Jackson, football and baseball star; Jimmy Stewart, actor; Peggy Lipton, actress; John "Scatman" Larkin, jazz musician; Bill Walton, former basketball player and current TV commentator; and Mel Tillis, country-western singer.

The Stuttering Foundation of America suggests that a teacher should allow time for the student to adjust to the class. During this time, questions should be asked that only require a few words to respond. When everyone in the class is going to be asked a question, the student who stutters should be questioned early. The longer the wait, the more the student's tension increases as that student waits for a turn. Everyone in the class, not just the student who stutters, should be allowed as much time as they need to answer questions. It is better for all students to think through their answers rather than respond quickly with little thought given to the question.

Reading aloud in the class can be very threatening for a student who stutters. However, if the teacher has the entire class read in unison, the student is not made to feel different and can experience fluency and satisfaction. In time, that student may feel more competent and able to read without this backup. In some cases, the student can be given the reading material to practice reading at home.

To encourage successful communication, the teacher should only concentrate on the content of what is being said and not the manner in which it is said. When the student mispronounces a word, the teacher should not supply the word or request the student to repeat the word correctly. When a child who has a speech disorder hesitates, attempts to hasten the student's speech should be avoided.

The teacher should discourage and, whenever possible, prevent teasing in the classroom on the part of the students who are not disabled. It is very painful for a student who stutters to be teased. If teasing occurs, the teacher should talk privately to the student who was teased and let that student know that you take such behavior seriously and will take steps to correct it. The teacher should also tell the student that most children are teased for many different things at one time or another. It is helpful if the teacher shares personal experiences about being teased. The teacher should also have a private talk with the offending students. Explain to them that the speech disorder is very distressing to the student who stutters and that teasing can exacerbate the stuttering. To help them understand the effects of teasing on an individual, the teacher should focus on the feelings the students had when other students teased them. Punishment should be avoided as it only intensifies the students' negative feelings about the student who stutters and makes the situation worse. The majority of students wants the teacher's approval and, if asked in private, will not only empathize with the student who stutters but also stop teasing their classmate.

Acceptance by peers is essential to the student who stutters. Cooperative learning projects can provide this opportunity. The teacher can also select an understanding and caring person to be the learning "buddy"—someone who can be a special friend to the student who stutters.

The classroom teacher can help the student with a speech disorder by having direct communication with the student's speech and language therapist. Together they can determine what speaking activities in the class are appropriate and beneficial for the student to practice newly learned skills.

A child with a speech disorder needs motivation to communicate, and to communicate successfully, a stimulating and supportive environment is mandatory. Criticism does not help a student overcome a speech disorder. When a child who has a speech disorder has difficulty communicating, others may attempt to hasten the child's speech. This should always be avoided. Patience and consideration are necessary for all students who have a speech disorder.

For Further Information

Books

Adler, S., & King, D. (Eds.). *Oral communication problems in children and adolescents.*

Duffy, J. R. *Motor speech disorders: Substrates, different diagnosis, and management.*

Guitar, G. *Stuttering: An integrated approach to its nature and treatment.*

Hamaguchi, P. *Childhood speech, language, & listening problems: What every parent should know.*

Jeze, M. *Stuttering: A life bound up in words.*

Johnson, K. L., & Heinze, B. A. *The fluency companion: Strategies for stuttering intervention.*

McCormick, L., Schiefelbusch, R. L., & Loeb, D. F. *Supporting children with communication difficulties in inclusive settings.*

McFarlane, S. C., & Von Berd, S. L. *Voice and voice therapy.*

Oyer, H. J., Crowe, B., & Haas, W. H. *Speech, language, and hearing disorders: A guide for the teacher.*

St. Louis, K. O. *Living with stuttering.*

Ysseldyke, J. E., & Algozzine, B. *Teaching students with communication disorders.*

Organizations and Agencies

American Speech-Language-Hearing Association (ASHA)
10801 Rockville Pike
Rockville, MD 20852
800-638-8255
301-897-5700
E-mail: actioncenter@asha.org
www.asha.org

National Stuttering Association
5100 East La Palma, Suite 208
Anaheim Hills, CA 92807
800-364-1677
Fax: 714-693-7554
E-mail: nsastutter@aol.com
www.nsastutterconta.html

Spina Bifida

Definition

Spina bifida is a congenital defect in which part of one or more verte-brae fails to develop completely, leaving part of the spinal cord exposed. According to the Spina Bifida Association of America (n.d.-a), "It is a defect in the bony spinal column where the spine failed to close up to form one piece during the first two months of pregnancy" (n.p.).

Background

Spina bifida is a permanently disabling defect that affects newborns. It occurs with a higher frequency than muscular dystrophy, polio, and cystic fibrosis combined. According to the National Dissemination Center for Children with Disabilities (NICHCY, 2004), approximately 40% of all Americans have spina bifida occulta. Most do not know that they have this disorder. At this time, its exact cause is unknown. It is believed that both genetic and nongenetic factors may be involved. The occurrence in siblings is approximately 3% to 5%. If a woman already has a child with spina bifida, she is 10 times more likely than average to have another child with spina bifida. The incidence increases in the pregnancies of both very young women and older women.

There are four types of spina bifida: *spina bifida occulta, myelocele, meningocele,* and *encephalocele.*

Spina bifida occulta is the most common and least serious form of spina bifida. In spina bifida occulta, there is an opening in one or more of the vertebrae of the spinal column without apparent damage to the spinal cord. There is little external evidence of this form except for a possible dimple or tuft of hair over the underlying abnormality. Approximately 40% of all Americans may have spina bifida occulta (National Institute of Health and Human Development, 1981). Most do not even know they have it because they experience few or no symptoms. This type often goes completely unnoticed in children.

Myelocele, also known as *meningomyelocele,* is the severest form of spina bifida. A portion of the spinal cord protrudes through the back. In some cases the sacs are covered with skin and in others, tissues and nerves are exposed. A child with *myelocele* is generally severely handi-capped and may have other associated abnormalities such as cere-bral palsy, epilepsy, mental retardation, and visual problems. Until recently, most infants with *myelocele* died shortly after birth. Now there is surgery to drain the spinal fluid. This is performed in the first

48 hours of life. Now these children are more likely to live, but they will undergo a series of operations throughout their childhood.

Approximately 70% to 90% of children born with myelocele also have hydrocephalus. Although this condition can occur without spina bifida, the two conditions often occur together. In hydrocephalus, there is a fluid buildup in the brain. This can be controlled by a surgical procedure called shunting. If a shunt is not implanted, pressure builds up and may cause seizures, brain damage, or blindness.

Meningocele is less severe than *myelocele*. The spinal cord remains intact but the meninges, or protective coverings around the spinal cord, have pushed out through the opening in a sac called *meningocele*. This form can be repaired with little or no damage to the nerve pathways.

Encephalocele is a rare type of spina bifida. In this type, the protrusion occurs through the skull and results in severe brain damage.

Twenty years ago, 90% of infants with spina bifida died, but because of advances in medical technology, infants born with this birth defect are now expected to have a normal life span. Because there is no central registry for persons affected by this birth defect, the exact number cannot be accurately stated. However, the Spina Bifida Association is currently working on compiling such a registry.

Characteristics

Depending on the type of spina bifida a child has, that child may be heavily braced or be indistinguishable from other children. According to the Spina Bifida Association of America (n.d.-b), the following general characteristics may be present in students with spina bifida:

- Varying degrees of paralysis
- Weakness in the feet, ankles, legs, or all
- Diminished feeling in the feet, ankles, legs, or all
- Incontinence of both bowel and bladder from nerve damage, resulting in occasional accidents and a probable need for clean intermittent catheterization during school hours
- Shunting of fluid from the brain
- Learning disabilities, perhaps resulting from perceptual difficulties, damage to the brain, or both
- Motor difficulties in the arms and hands, with perhaps some slowness in performing certain tasks
- Possible absence seizures, such as staring into space momentarily, or motor involvement ranging from tremors to spasms of the large muscles

Children with spina bifida are similar to other children in their intellectual ability, ranging from gifted to developmentally delayed. The majority have normal to above-normal intelligence.

Strategies for Educators

Inclusion of a child with spina bifida with students without disabilities—where they are provided a school pattern that is as near normal as possible—is of great value. In some cases, certain changes may have to be made for the school to accommodate the student with spina bifida. Depending on the particular type of spina bifida, special architectural adaptations may need to be made, such as adding elevators or ramps. Special equipment, such as wheelchairs, crutches, or braces, may also be needed.

Assistive devices needed to help the child with spina bifida are always stated on the IEP for the child. The teacher should review with the assistive technology specialist how the devices are to be used by the child. For example, if a wheelchair is used, the teacher should know how to use all the devices on the wheelchair as well as how to lock the wheelchair. When a doctor recommends that the child should be out of the wheelchair for a certain amount of time each day, the teacher needs to be informed by the parents and doctor as to the amount of time. The teacher should also know what type of assistance may be needed when transferring the child out of the chair and back into the chair. There should be ongoing communication between the parents of the child and the doctor who can relay pertinent information to the appropriate school personnel.

The teacher should always plan specific safety measures needed in case of a school emergency, such as a fire. It is essential that the teacher designate specific individuals to help the child. These assistants need to be informed exactly what is required and how the child can be evacuated quickly and safely. Opportunities to practice the procedure should be given so the evacuation progresses smoothly.

Some students with spina bifida may have secondary disabilities, such as seizures, cerebral palsy, learning disabilities, or other disabling conditions.

In the case of a child with hydrocephalus, the teacher needs to make certain that the child with a shunt avoids all physical activity that could knock the shunt out of place. The teacher also needs to be aware of symptoms of shunt failure that may include nausea, vomiting, neck pain, visual disturbances, and possible seizures. If a blocked shunt is suspected, the teacher should immediately contact the school nurse, who contacts the parents and doctor.

When feasible, the child should be allowed to participate in physical education activities. The teacher can assign the student an inactive role, such as being a scorekeeper or using a stopwatch for timing events. If there is a game requiring running, the teacher should assign a designated runner for the student. At all times, the teacher should make every effort to accommodate the child so that child is part of the physical education activity.

Some children with spina bifida have deficits in visual-perceptual and perceptual-motor skills. Any task requiring eye-hand coordination is difficult, so accommodations are needed for any task involving handwriting. Additional time should be allowed for any written task, and the amount of handwriting should be limited. Requiring a student with spina bifida to recopy an assignment should be avoided. Computers and tape recorders can be used for assignments requiring handwriting. Secondary students should be provided with a photocopy of the teacher's lecture or another student's notes. Allowing the student to record the teacher's lecture is also advantageous.

As with many neurological based disabilities, children with spina bifida have difficulty in any social interaction. The teacher can help by modeling the behavior that is considered appropriate for a specific social situation. Role-playing is also very beneficial. Above all, the teacher needs patience and understanding.

The teacher needs to set realistic goals for students that encourage and increase their desire to achieve. Students' strengths should be emphasized and opportunities provided to demonstrate their talents in ways that allow them to be successful and gain the approval of their peers.

Comments and responses to the student should always be phrased in a positive manner. Focusing on the student's abilities and positive aspects of that student's personality strengthens the student's feeling of confidence and self-worth.

The teacher should help the other students in the class recognize the similarities among all students and realize that students with spina bifida are more like them than they are different from them.

For Further Information

Books

Bloom, B. A., & Seljeskog, E. S. *Parent's guide to spina bifida.*
Ferri, L., Rowley-Kelly, F. L., & Regal, J. D. *Teaching the student with spina bifida* [Book and Video].

Icon Health Publications. *A parent's sourcebook on spina bifida: A revised and updated directory for the Internet age.*

Lukenhof, M. *Children with spina bifida: A parent's guide.*

Pieper, E. *The teacher and the child with spina bifida.*

Rowley-Kelly, F. L., & Reigel, D. H. (Eds.). *Teaching the student with spina bifida.*

Sandler, A. *Living with spina bifida: A guide for families and professionals.*

Travis, K. S. *Christal: Coping with spina bifida.*

Organizations and Agencies

Council for Exceptional Children (CEC)
1110 North Glebe Road, Suite 300
Arlington, VA 22201
703-620-5660
866-915-5000 (TTY)
Fax: 703-264-9494
E-mail: service@cec.sped.org
www.cec.sped.org

Easter Seals, National Office
230 West Monroe Street, Suite 1800
Chicago, IL 60606
800-221-6827
312-726-6200
E-mail: info@easter-seals.org
www.easter-seals.org

March of Dimes Birth Defects Foundation
1275 Mamaroneck Avenue
White Plains, NY 10605
E-mail: resourcecenter@modimes.org
www.modimes.org

National Family Caregivers Association
10400 Connecticut Avenue, Suite 500
Kensington, MD 20895-3944
301-942-6430
800-896-3650
www.familycaregiver.org

National Organization for Rare Disorders (NORD)
P.O. Box 1968
55 Kenosia Avenue
Danbury, CT 06813-1968
203-744-0100
800-999-NORD (6673)
www.raredisease.org

Spina Bifida Association of America
4590 MacArthur Boulevard NW, Suite 250
Washington, DC 20007-4226
800-621-3141
202-944-3285
E-mail: sbaa@sbaa.org
www.sbaa.org

National Rehabilitation Information Center
1010 Wayne Avenue, Suite 800
Silver Spring, MD 20910-5632
800-346-2742
301-562-2400
www.naric.com

Spinal Cord Injury

Definition

A spinal cord injury (SCI) is caused by trauma to the 18-inch cylinder of nerve tissue running down the central canal of the spine that damages the nerve fibers.

Background

The spinal cord and the brain constitute the central nervous system, which controls all human performance and behavior. The spinal cord carries messages from the brain to the internal organs, muscles, and skin. These messages inform the body what to do or what to ignore. In turn, messages are sent back to the brain about what is happening to the body—for example, sensations of heat or cold. When the spinal cord is damaged, there is no communication between the brain and the spinal cord, resulting in loss of sensation, muscle weakness, or paralysis. The degree of severity may be mild, serious, or fatal.

According to the National Institute of Health and Human Development (1981), the higher on the spine the injury, the greater the disability. When injury occurs at the neck level, both the arms and legs may be paralyzed. This type of paralysis is referred to as *quadriplegia* or *tetraplegia*. According to the Rehabilitation Learning Center at Harborview Medical Center (1995), the term *tetraplegia* is preferred.

If an individual has an injury at the chest level, the arms are spared but the legs and lower part of the body are affected. This is generally referred to as *paraplegia*, and the individual is considered to be paraplegic. Many use the term *paraplegic* when referring to anyone who has a paralysis.

The American Medical Association (1989) identifies three basic types of force that cause spinal cord injury: longitudinal compression, hinging, and shearing. In longitudinal compression, the vertebrae are crushed, often from a fall. When the spinal column receives extreme bending movement, for example, from a whiplash injury, it is called hinging. Shearing is a combination of both hinging and a twisting motion, generally caused when an individual is hit by a motor vehicle.

The National Spinal Cord Injury Association classifies spinal injury into two main types of injury: complete and incomplete. In a complete SCI, there is no functioning—no sensation and no voluntary movement—below the level of the injury. Both sides of the body are affected. In contrast, an incomplete SCI results in the ability to move one part of the body more than another part of the body that cannot be moved. On one side of the body, there is more of an ability to function than on the other side of the body. In *tetraplegia*, there is injury in the cervical area causing a loss of strength in all extremities. *Paraplegia* refers to injury in "thoracic, lumbar or sacral segment including cauda equine" (National Spinal Cord Injury Association, n.d.).

Injury to the spine occurs immediately at the time of the injury. Bone fragments and disc material may bruise or tear spinal cord tissue. The spine in SCI is seldom severed but can cause spinal fractures and compression of the vertebrae. This can crush and destroy the axons, which are extensions of nerve cells that carry signals between the brain and the rest of the body. In SCI, some or all of the axons are damaged. Some individuals completely recover from this while others may suffer complete paralysis.

Some recover from SCI within a week. Most do regain some functions by six months, but recovery time diminishes after six months. Treatment varies with the type of SCI buy may include surgery, immobilization, bed rest, and physical therapy. Coping with SCI is extremely difficult for the injured person and for his or her family and friends. As stated by the National Spinal Cord Injury Association, "Rehabilitation is a place to find hope, strength, inspiration and the specialized medical care needed for spinal cord rehabilitation."

According to the Spinal Cord Injury Statistical Center, between 721 and 906 of every one million people in the United States have suffered spinal cord injuries. This accounts for between 183,000 and 230,000 persons with spinal cord injuries who are alive today (Spinal

Cord Injury Information Network, 2001). Males between the ages of 15 and 25 sustain spinal injury at the rate of 12 to 15 per 10,000 per year. The majority of people average 19 years of age at the time of spinal cord injury. The primary causes of spinal cord injury include but are not limited to falls, automobile accidents, sports accidents, gunshot wounds, and other acts of violence.

The American Paralysis Association states that in the first few hours after an injury, the spinal cord begins to "self-destruct" (as cited in National Institute of Health and Human Development, 1981). The injury sets off a series of self-destructive cellular occurrences. Swelling, hemorrhaging, and a drop in blood pressure that lowers the blood supply to the injured spinal cord occur. The nerve cells die, leaving a gap in the spinal cord; scar tissue forms, which destroys the connections in the cord; and paralysis sets in.

Until recently, paralysis was considered incurable. Now, because of ongoing, extensive research, there is hope. Areas of research include therapeutic and pharmacological approaches, transplantation to prevent the degeneration of the spinal cord, and the use of natural substances to promote neuronal growth. Much of the research is focused on neural regeneration and recovery for the patient who has a spinal cord injury.

Characteristics

Characteristics of spinal cord injury may include loss of sensation, muscle weakness, loss of bladder and bowel control, and paralysis. Some students with a spinal cord injury have neuromuscular degeneration as well as other disabilities, such as spina bifida, cerebral palsy, or muscular dystrophy.

To suddenly find oneself paralyzed presents many difficulties, and significant psychological and emotional problems may occur in attempting to adjust to the paralysis. Each case of spinal cord injury is different, and the inner strength an individual has to surmount the numerous problems associated with a spinal cord injury varies.

Strategies for Educators

The classroom teacher can expect that some, but not all, students with spinal cord injury exhibit immature behavior. Although some may manifest intellectual impairment, others have a similar degree of intellectual ability as other students.

Because of impaired health, the student with a spinal cord injury may often be absent, and assignments should be adjusted as needed. The teacher should also provide the parent, as well as the support personnel, with the assigned work. This helps the student keep up with academic goals.

As they do for students with other disabilities, teachers need to confer with the other professionals involved with the student. Special arrangements must be made to accommodate the physical needs of the student. Depending on the severity of the injury to the spinal cord, assistive devices such as a wheelchair, tilt table, and so forth may be needed.

The teacher should make use of the many electronic aids that are currently available, such as computers and tape recorders, to provide educational support for the student. Communications technology has also developed many new devices for students with severe disabilities; for example, software is available for computers that allow a student who is unable to hold a book to read the text on the computer screen. A page of text appears on the screen, and the student uses a customized chin switch to enter the commands.

As individuals acquire new skills, the type of assistive device needed may also change. For additional information on assistive devices, teachers should be aware that under the Assistive Technology Act of 1998, every state has an Assistive Technology project. The focus of the project is on providing resource information, systems change and advocacy activities, loan programs, lending libraries, and recycling programs. The Resna Technical Assistance Project can provide contact information for individual states' programs: phone: 703-524-6686; fax: 703-524-6630; e-mail: resn@resna.org; Web site: www.resna.org.

Fortunately, the new advances in technology aids enable individuals with spinal cord injuries to have more mobility and to be able to achieve greater independence. Continued research may one day find a cure for this once-incurable condition.

Howard A. Rusk, one of the world's best-known rehabilitation specialists, states,

> Those who, through medical skill, opportunity, work and courage, survive their illness or overcome their handicap and take their places back in the world have a depth of spirit that you and I can hardly measure. They haven't wasted their pain. (as cited in National Institute of Health and Human Development, 1981, p. 28)

For Further Information

Books

Center for Best Practices in Early Childhood Education. *Building interactive futures: Curriculum guide for young children and technology.*

Doughtery, K. *The spinal cord handbook: For parents and families.*

Hill, J. L. *Meeting the needs of students with special physical and health care needs.*

Karp, G. *Stories of adjustment to spinal cord injury.*

Lela, D. H., & Brown, F. *Persons with profound disabilities.*

Meyer, L., Peck, C., & Brown, L. (Eds.). *Critical issues in the lives of people with severe disabilities.*

Osborne, A. G., & Russo, C. J. *A guide for special education and the law practitioners.*

Reeve, C. *Still me.*

Sternberg, L. (Ed.). *Individuals with profound disabilities: Instructional and assistive strategies.*

Williams, M. *Journey to well: Life after spinal cord injury.*

Organizations and Agencies

American Spinal Injury Association
2020 Peachtree Road NW
Atlanta, GA 30309-1402
404-355-9772
www.asia-spinalinjury.org

Center for Best Practices in Early Childhood Education
Western Illinois University
Horrabin Hall 32
1 University Circle
Macomb, IL 61455
309-298-1634 x 248
Fax: 309-298-2305
E-mail: l-robinson1@wiu.edu

Christopher Reeve Foundation and Resources Center
636 Morris Turnpike, Suite 3A
Short Hills, NJ 07078
973-379-2690
800-225-0292
Fax: 973-912-9433
E-mail: info@christopherreeve.org
www.christopherreeve.org

Clearinghouse on Disability Information
Special Education and Rehabilitation Services
550 12th Street, Room 5153
Washington, DC 20202-5133

202-245-7307
202-205-5637
Fax: 202-245-7636
www.ed.gov/about/offices/list/osers

National Rehabilitation Information Center (NARIC)
4200 Forbes Boulevard, Suite 202
Lanham, MD 20706-4829
301-459-5900
301-459-5984
800-346-2742
Fax: 301-562-2401
www.naric.com

National Spinal Cord Injury Association (NSCIA)
1 Church Street, Suite 600
Rockville, MD 20850
800-962-9629
301-214-4006
Fax: 866-387-2196
www.spinalcord.org

TASH
1025 Vermont Avenue, Floor 7
Washington, DC 20005
202-263-5600
Fax: 202-637-0138
E-mail: Please refer to the e-mail staff directory on the Web site.
www.tash.org

Tourette Syndrome

Definition

According to the Tourette Syndrome Association (1994), Tourette syndrome (TS) is a neurological disorder characterized by tics. The American Psychiatric Association (as cited in Comings, 1990) defines a tic as "an 'involuntary,' sudden, rapid, recurrent, nonrhythmic, stereotyped motor movement or vocalization. It is experienced as irresistible, but can be suppressed for varying lengths of time" (p. 12).

Background

In 1825 there was one reported case in medical literature of a woman who had all the symptoms of TS. The disorder was named after

Gilles de la Tourette, a French neurologist, who in 1885 described it as involving muscle tics, vocal noises, and compulsive swearing. He also noted that the tics were usually of short duration and intermittent, in direct contrast to other similar disorders (U.S. Department of Health and Human Services, 1993).

TS often goes undiagnosed due to the similarity of TS symptoms with those of some other disorders, making it difficult to have an accurate prevalence count for TS. Other factors also make it difficult to obtain an accurate figure as to the prevalence of TS. Since the tics associated with TS often subside or disappear as children mature, the estimates of TS may underestimate the prevalence in adults. Another factor in estimating concerns the individuals with milder symptoms of TS who may never have been diagnosed. However, the National Institute of Health estimates that 100,000 Americans have TS. The Tourette Syndrome Association (1994) states, "[S]tudies suggest that the figure may be as high as one in two hundred of those with chronic multiple tics and/or transient childhood tics are included in count."

Although its exact cause is unknown, researchers believe that TS may be caused by a chemical imbalance in the brain, resulting from an abnormality in the neurotransmitters, the chemicals that carry signals between nerve cells. Current research indicates that the abnormal metabolism of one of the neurotransmitters (dopamine and serotonin) is involved (Tourette Syndrome Association, 1994).

Three times as many males as females have TS, and it is believed that TS is inherited. A person who has a dominant gene carrying the symptoms of TS has a 50% chance of passing the gene on to his or her children. The gene-carrying child of a person with TS is three to four times more likely to be a son than to be a daughter. Children of parents who have TS also have a higher incidence of developing obsessive-compulsive behaviors. In cases where TS is not inherited, the cause remains unknown.

Along with research and studies of genes, medical and science professionals are continuing their investigation in order to understand and to diminish the severity of TS symptoms. Knowledge about TS is being gained from various techniques using neuroimaging, neuropathology, and neurophysiology. Currently, many clinical trials involve both children and adults with TS.

TS is not a degenerative disease. It can begin abruptly with multiple symptoms involving movements and sounds. These symptoms can disappear for months and weeks at a time. A remission sometimes occurs after adolescence, but TS is generally a lifelong, chronic condition. Individuals with TS can live a normal life span.

At present, no blood analysis or other type of neurological testing exists to diagnose TS. The medical profession may order tests to rule out other possible ailments before a diagnosis of TS is made. TS is difficult to diagnose simply by observing behavior because tics are unpredictable and often change in frequency and type. Rating scales and questionnaires are used along with the observable symptoms in the diagnosis. A diagnosis of TS requires the individual to have had both vocal and motor tics for more than a year that either change in severity or increase in duration. The American Psychiatric Association (1994) uses the following criteria for diagnosing TS:

A. Both multiple motor and one or more vocal tics have been present at some time during the illness, although not necessarily concurrently. (A tic is a sudden, rapid, recurrent, non-rhythmic, stereotyped motor movement or vocalization.)

B. The tics occur many times a day (usually in bouts), nearly every day or intermittently throughout a period of more than 1 year, and during this period there was never a tic-free period of more than 3 consecutive months.

C. The disturbance causes marked distress or significant impairment in social, occupational, or other important areas of functioning.

D. The onset is before the age of 18 years.

E. The disturbance is not due to the direct physiological effects of a substance (e.g., stimulants) or a general medical condition (e.g., Huntington's disease or postviral encephalitis). (p. 103)

The tics and behavioral symptoms in the majority of TS cases do not hinder the individual. If the symptoms interfere with normal functioning, medications are sometimes prescribed. Some behavior therapies help the individual to substitute one tic for another that is more acceptable. The disorder is not psychological, but some individuals develop emotional problems trying to deal with the symptoms of TS. Psychotherapy may help an individual and his or her family to cope with the problems associated with TS.

When a child is diagnosed as having TS, it is important to start treatment early because many of the manifestations of the syndrome are considered bizarre and disruptive, and the child may be excluded from many activities and normal interpersonal relationships. At this time, there is no cure for TS.

Characteristics

Tics are categorized as either motor or vocal and simple or complex. The Neuropsychiatric Movement Disorder Staff at the University of Iowa Hospitals and Clinics (as cited in Ottinger & Gaffney, 1995) listed the following characteristics for motor and vocal tics:

- Simple motor tics: eye blinking, eye rolling, squinting, head jerking, facial grimacing, nose twitching, lip smacking, tongue thrusting, mouth opening, leg jerking, arm flexing, or flappings
- Complex motor tics: hitting self or others, jumping, touching self or others, smelling hands or objects, clapping, pinching, touching objects (haphemania), stooping, hopping, kicking, throwing, squatting, skipping, somersaulting, stepping backwards, deep knee bending, foot tapping, foot shaking, foot dragging, chewing on clothes, scratching, kissing self or others, pulling at clothes, or any other combinations of movements done repeatedly
- Simple vocal tics: throat clearing, grunts, sniffs, snorts, squeaking, coughs, humming, screams, spitting, puffing, whistling, honking, stammering or stuttering, hissing, laughing, shouts, barking, moaning, guttural sounds, noisy breathing, gasping, gurgling, squeaking, clicking or clacking, hiccups, "tsk" and "pit" noises
- Complex vocal tics: any understandable words or phrases (may include echoing)

Other associated characteristics of TS, which may or may not be present in all cases, are the following:

- Repeating the speech of others (echolalia)
- Repeating their own words (palilalia)
- Involuntary utterances of obscenities or socially taboo phrases (coprolalia)
- Making obscene gestures (copropraxia)

Individuals with TS may exhibit obsessive-compulsive behaviors—for example, continually washing their hands until they become raw or touching something a certain number of times. Chronic self-touching is very common among TS individuals.

Many people with TS also have AD/HD with the accompanying characteristics. Their problems with impulse control result in aggressive behavior and socially inappropriate acts. Their wide range of behavioral symptoms is often more disabling than the tics. See behavior characteristics and strategies under AD/HD.

Individuals with TS have the same range of intellectual functioning as the general population. Some individuals with TS may also have other disabilities such as emotional disturbances, AD/HD, dyslexia, aphasia, autism, or learning disabilities. Strategies for students with these disabilities can also be useful for students with TS.

Strategies for Educators

Having a student with TS in the class can be very disturbing to the teacher who is unprepared. Because the acts of a TS student are involuntary, patience with and consideration for the student are required on the part of the teacher. Most students with TS can sense when their tics are about to precede a severe outburst and know when they need to leave the classroom. The teacher should preselect a secluded area where a TS student can go before a severe attack begins.

A student with TS should be given opportunities to take occasional short breaks from the classroom routine to release tics. For example, the teacher might send the student on errands to the office or the library to give the student time to regain composure. Often, just allowing the student to leave the room voluntarily for a drink of water is sufficient. Short breaks between activities also give the student time to relieve inner stress.

When giving long-term assignments, the teacher should make certain the student knows well in advance what is expected and when the assignment is due. This eases the stress experienced when the TS student is required to complete an assignment in a short period. Timed tests can be especially stressful for a TS student and can increase the possibility of severe tics. It is always better to allow a student to work at his or her own pace. Using tape recorders, typewriters, and computers can also eliminate some of the classroom stress for the TS student.

Because a TS student is likely to have a very poor self-image, the teacher needs to be accepting and positive in all dealings with the student. If the student's conduct is not disruptive, the teacher should ignore the behavior. However, a teacher's intervention can often help a student with a compulsive behavior. For example, if the student continually taps a pencil on the desk, the teacher might provide the student with a small piece of foam on which to tap the pencil. Without the knowledge of the others in the class, the teacher and student should develop a special signal so that the student knows when personal behavior is inappropriate. Above all, the teacher should not allow the student with TS to use the student's symptoms as a means of control.

Transition times can be occasions for many confrontations among the students in any class. To avoid unnecessary conflict, the student with TS should be allowed to leave a few minutes before the class ends. A younger student with TS should be next to the teacher at the front of the line when leaving the classroom.

Medical research may eventually find a way to prevent TS from being transmitted from one generation to the next. With better understanding and treatment, many individuals with TS now lead very productive and successful lives.

For Further Information

Books

Brill, M. *Tourette syndrome.*
Cohen, B., & Wysocky, L. *Tourette syndrome made me the teacher I never had.*
Defilippo, M. G. *Getting personal: Stories of life with Tourette syndrome.*
Haerle, T. *Children with Tourette syndrome.*
Jensen, E. *Different brains, different learners: How to reach the hard to reach.*
Shimberg, E. F. *Living with Tourette's syndrome.*

Organizations and Agencies

Council for Exceptional Children (CEC)
1118 North Glebe Road, Suite 300
Arlington, VA 22201
888-232-7733
866-915-5000 (TTY)
Fax: 703-264-9494
www.cec.sped.org

National Organization for Rare Disorders (NORD)
55 Kenosia Avenue
P.O. Box 1968
Danbury, CT 06813-1968
203-744-0100
203-797-9590 (TTY)
Fax: 203-798-2291
E-mail: orphan@rarediseases.org
http://www.rarediseases.org

Tourette Syndrome Association, Inc.
42-40 Bell Boulevard, Suite 205

Bayside, NY 11361-0861
800-237-0717
718-224-2999
Fax: 718-279-9596
E-mail: tsa@tsa-usa.org
http://www.tsa-usa.org

Visual Impairment

Visual impairment is the diminishment of the ability to see. The terms *partially sighted, legally blind, low vision,* and *totally blind* are commonly used to describe visual impairments.

Background

It is estimated that more than 40 million people in the world are either totally blind or partially sighted. There are 530,000 legally blind people in the United States, and 47,000 new cases are reported each year. The vast majority of cases occur in people age 65 and older. Approximately 5 in 10,000 children have a visual impairment. The U.S. Department of Education (as cited in Heward, 1996) stated that in 1997–1998, there were 25,834 children receiving special education services because of their visual impairment.

There is a widespread misconception that blindness equals total blackness. This is not true. Both the eye and the brain are involved with vision, and there are many degrees of visual impairment.

A person who is *partially sighted* has lost most of his or her sight, cannot see much more than light or some large shapes, and has central visual acuity of 20/70 to 20/200 in the better eye with correction. A partially sighted person with correction sees at 20 feet what the normal eye sees at 70 to 200 feet.

A person who is *legally blind* has central visual acuity of 20/200 or less with correction in the better eye or has a very limited field of vision such as 20 degrees at its widest point. This means that even with correction, there is no more than 10% normal vision in the better eye and the field of vision is no greater than 20 degrees. A legally blind person sees with correction at 20 feet what the normal eye sees from a distance of 200 or more feet.

Low vision usually refers to a severe visual impairment, but it is not necessarily limited to distant vision. Low vision also applies to all who have difficulty reading newspapers or other reading material, even with correction.

There are many causes of impaired vision. It can result from degeneration of the eyeball, or the optic nerve or nerve pathways connecting the eye to the brain may be impaired, causing loss of vision. Damage to the brain can also cause vision problems. Blindness is often the result of injury or disease. No one is immune from developing a vision disorder.

Some vision disorders are refractive errors that can usually be corrected with proper lenses. Refractive errors include hyperopia, myopia, and astigmatism.

Hyperopia, also called *farsightedness,* is a condition in which light rays focus behind the retina. Vision is better for distant objects than for near objects, which are blurred and unclear. A convex corrective lens before the eye increases the bending of the light rays, thereby aiding in focusing.

Myopia is also referred to as *nearsightedness.* In this case, the light rays are focused in front of the retina. Vision is better for near objects than for far objects, which are blurred. A concave corrective lens refocuses the image on the retina.

Astigmatism results from an irregularity in the curvature of the cornea or lens of the eye. This curvature causes light rays to be refracted unevenly at different planes so that horizontal and vertical rays are focused at two different places on the retina, resulting in blurred or imperfect vision. Astigmatism generally can be corrected with proper lenses.

Dysfunction of the muscles of the eye causes strabismus, heterophoria, and nystagmus.

Strabismus, or "crossed eyes" as it is more commonly called, is caused by lack of coordination of the external eye muscles, making it impossible for the two eyes to focus on the same object. The most common cause of *amblyopia* (also known as "lazy eye") is strabismus.

Heterophoria is the result of one or more muscles of the eye being insufficient to bring two images from the two eyes into one focused image.

Nystagmus consists of rapid, jerky movements of the eyeballs that result in ineffectual vision.

Albinism also causes a loss of visual acuity, as the lack of color in the iris allows too much light to reach the retina. Generally, glasses are prescribed to lessen the effects of strong light. Albinism is a congenital and hereditary condition.

Cataracts are another condition of the eye whereby the crystalline lens or its capsule becomes opaque. Some visual acuity is lost, but it usually can be restored by surgery or other medical processes.

Many other disorders of the eye cause visual impairment or blindness, such as retinitis pigmentosa (an inherited progressive deterioration of the retina) and glaucoma. Blindness can also result from pressure in the eyeball that damages fibers in the optic nerve.

Some people with visual impairment learn to read printed material by using Braille. This method was devised by Louis Braille, who was blind. A system of raised dots are evenly arranged in quadrangular letter spaces or cells and are read using the fingertips. Six dots can be placed in each cell, three high by two wide, and 63 different characters can be formed.

Braille comprises three grades. Grade 1 Braille uses full spelling and consists of letters of the alphabet, punctuation, numbers, and several composition signs that are special to Braille. Uncontracted Braille is known as "English Grade 1." Grade 2 Braille, also known as "English Braille," consists of Grade 1 along with 189 contractions and short-form words. Grade 3 Braille is very specialized and few people use it.

For many people who have visual impairments, mobility is difficult. Some use a white cane to help them gain useful information about their environment. The use of a cane is also helpful in finding stairs and curbs and provides protection from obstacles from the waist to the feet. The strip of red at the bottom of the long white cane identifies the person who carries it as legally blind.

Guide dogs can be trained to be of great value to people with severe visual impairments. Generally, a puppy is chosen at 3 months old to be placed with a 4-H child and raised in a family setting. The dog is returned to a special training school when it is a year old to receive formal guidework training for 3 to 6 months. The person who gets the dog then must live at the school for 28 days, during which time that person is taught how to care for the dog and to give it commands. Bonding takes place between the guide dog and the blind person so that they can work as a team. About 1% to 2% of all blind people have guide dogs.

Characteristics

The effect of visual problems on a child's development depends on the severity, type of loss, the age at which the condition appears, and the overall functioning level of the child. Many children with multiple disabilities may also have visual impairments.

Children with visual impairments have normal growth patterns, although those born with the impairment may have difficulty grasping abstract ideas and concepts that depend on visual stimuli. However, if the child's visual impairment occurs after birth, some visually learned concepts and skills might already have been acquired. It is important to remember that there is no intellectual impairment associated with vision disorders. A person's intelligence is not related to that person's ability to see.

The eyes of some people with visual impairment may look different from other people's eyes. At birth, a baby's eyes may seem blank or look disfigured. Diseases of the eyes also may affect their appearance. Excess pressure in the eyes can cause the eyes to bulge or protrude. Many blind people wear glasses. Some may wear glasses for cosmetic purposes only, whereas others who have usable vision may see a little better with them.

Certain characteristics of a possible visual difficulty may be observed by the teacher if the student

- holds work too close or too far;
- thrusts head forward to see distant objects;
- blinks continually when reading;
- tilts head to see better;
- covers one eye;
- holds body tense when reading or looking at distant objects;
- rubs eyes frequently;
- suffers with crusted, red-rimmed, or swollen eyelids;
- has problems with eyes often watering or appearing bloodshot;
- is sensitive to light;
- has frequent headaches; and
- frowns when looking at printed material.

If the signs continue over a period, the teacher should refer the student for a vision screening.

Strategies for Educators

The general education teacher needs to provide adequate accommodations for a student who is visually impaired to ensure an easy transition to the regular class. Conferring with the resource teacher and others who are responsible for the education of the student provides the teacher with information about the student's academic strengths and weaknesses. This information is helpful in meeting the student's educational goals. Teachers and support personnel should be involved in an ongoing evaluation of the progress and needs of the student.

Although some students with visual impairments may require only a few adaptive materials, others may need special devices. Arrangements should be made to have any special devices the student needs available in the classroom before that student's transition from a restrictive environment to a regular classroom.

Bookstands make it possible for students with visual impairments to bring their work closer to their eyes and prevent postural fatigue. Public libraries and the Library of Congress have large-print books that are available for persons who are visually impaired. The Library Reproduction Service (1977 S. Los Angeles Street, Los Angeles, CA 90011-1096) produces large-print material of educational materials. The American Printing House for the Blind, Inc. (1839 Frankfort Avenue, Louisville, KY 40206-0085) is a nonprofit company that creates educational materials for people with visual impairments. The National Association for the Visually Handicapped (22 West 21st Street, New York, NY 10010) has a free lending library of large-print materials that are available through the mail.

Modern technology has provided the tools that have enabled many people to live far better lives in spite of their disability. One such example is Zoom Text. The Zoom Text software is designed to assist individuals with visual impairments. It is available in two levels. Level 1 provides easy-to-use advanced screen magnification. Any handwritten or printed reading material, as well as pictures, can be displayed on the screen and magnified from 2 times to 32 times its original size, making it easier to read for visually impaired students. Level 2 combines speech synchronization along with the features of Level 1. It speaks all on-screen text, echoes typing, and systematically reads multipage documents. The software enables a student to hear what has been written. The many possibilities for using this software are endless. This assistive technology device improves the functional capabilities of students with visual impairments.

A free trial version can be downloaded from the Ai Squared Web site (http://www.aisquared.com). This software is available for Windows 95, 98, NT, 2000, XP, and Vista, including a DOS version. For additional information, contact Ai Squared (P.O. Box 669, Manchester Center, VT 05255, telephone 802-362-3612).

Students with visual impairments who are unable to read a regular printed page even when it is in large type may need to use the Braille system to read. Samples of the Braille alphabet and numbers should be given to the students. After having the opportunity to feel and identify the different letters on a Braille card, the students can be given a stylus to make their own Braille letters.

If the student is not using Braille, different types of paper should be made readily available. Because it is often difficult to see the lines on regular paper, bold-line paper can be provided. Raised-line paper makes it possible for the student with visual impairments to find the lines by touch and then write on the lines. At times, another student may need to take notes for the student who has a less acute visual impairment. To eliminate the need to recopy the notes, the teacher should provide carbonless paper. This paper allows the one taking the notes to make two copies at once, so that each student can keep a copy.

Students need to become aware of the difficulties inherent in living with visual impairments. Simulations of visual impairments may be done to help other students become aware of the problems facing visually impaired students. Students can be given blindfolds made of different materials. Opaque materials can be used to simulate total blindness whereas other less opaque materials can simulate different degrees of light perception. To demonstrate the loss of peripheral vision, the students can use an empty tube from a roll of paper towels as a sighting tube. Tunnel vision can be demonstrated by looking through a paper with a small pinhole.

Two of the greatest concerns of students with visual impairments are mobility and orientation. This lack of orientation and mobility can be simulated by having students attempt to walk while blindfolded. The teacher should select a guide who assists the blindfolded student. Generally, a guide who is unfamiliar with the needs of the students with visual impairments takes the blindfolded student's arm to assist that student. This procedure is incorrect. A blind person needs to take the arm of the guide. This enables the student to walk confidently and successfully. The teacher should demonstrate the correct way to guide a visually impaired person.

Because orientation is a great concern, the student with a visual impairment should be encouraged to become acquainted with the room arrangement. Once the student is familiar with the room arrangement, it should not be changed unless provisions are made for a visually impaired student to be physically shown the change. The teacher can select a "buddy" who can help guide and assist the student. This serves to foster acceptance of a visually impaired student and to increase self-confidence.

A student with a visual impairment may require more time to complete assigned work. At times, it may be better to shorten the assignments so the student is able to complete the work. Tape-recording teacher presentations and lessons that the student can replay can be helpful. Information about assignments and projects should be communicated to the special education teacher who, in turn, can provide the student with additional help in achieving success.

Many students who have been identified as being visually impaired on their IEP receive help from an itinerant specially credentialed teacher. The itinerant teacher instructs students in special classes at regular, special, nonpublic, or private schools. The instruction includes teaching visual efficiency and the use of specialized equipment, as well as Braille and listening skills. When the vision loss affects learning, the itinerant teacher also provides supportive academic instruction. If students are homebound or hospitalized, they still receive the services of the itinerant teacher. To better help the visually impaired student, the general education teacher should maintain ongoing consultation with the itinerant teacher.

Above all, the teacher should provide a safe and comfortable environment for the student and promote a positive relationship between the student who is visually impaired and the rest of the class. It is important to realize that students with visual impairments have problems reading facial expressions and thus may have greater difficulty developing social skills.

For Further Information

Books

Barraga, N. C., & Erin, J. N. *Visual handicaps and learning.*

Best, A. B. *Teaching children with visual impairments.*

Bishop, V. E. *Teaching visually impaired children.*

Mangold, S. S. *A teacher's guide to the special educational needs of blind and visually handicapped children.*

Rogow, S. *Helping the visually impaired child with developmental problems: Effective practice in home, school, and community.*

Scott, F., Jan, J., & Freeman, R. *A guide for parents and professionals about children who are visually impaired.*

Torres, I., & Corn, A. L. *When you have a visually impaired student in your classroom: Suggestions for teachers.*

Organizations and Agencies

American Council of the Blind
1155 15th Street NW, Suite 720
Washington, DC 20005
800-424-8666

202-467-5081
Fax: 202-467-5085
E-mail: ncrabb@erols.com
http://www.acb.org

American Foundation for the Blind
15 West 16th Street
New York, NY 10011
800-232-5463
212-502-7661
E-mail: afbinfo@afb.org
http://www.afb.org/afb

National Association for the Visually Handicapped
22 West 21st Street
New York, NY 10010
212-889-3141
http://www.navh.org

National Library Service for the Blind and Physically Handicapped
Library of Congress
1291 Taylor Street NW
Washington, DC 20542
202-707-5100
http://www.loc.gov/nls

Recording for the Blind and Dyslexic
20 Roszel Road
Princeton, NJ 08540
800-221-4792
609-452-0606
http://www.rfbd.org

Visual Processing Dysfunction

Definition

Visual processing is the ability to recognize and interpret visual stimuli involving perception, memory, sequencing, and integration. This should not be confused with visual impairment, which deals with only the ability to see. Visual processing, like auditory processing, is not a specific category of disability but rather a dysfunction inherent in many disabilities.

Background

The processing of visual stimuli is a very complex, active, and investigative process. People with a visual processing dysfunction experience difficulty in visually examining the individual details of an object. They are unable to identify the dominant visual cues and integrate them to obtain meaning from the object. They also have difficulty classifying the object in a particular visual category and comparing the resulting visual hypothesis with the actual perceived object.

The central processing of visual stimuli actually begins with the identification of visual cues. Operations such as receiving visual stimuli, orienting the head and eyes to the light source, and scanning the object are involved in the process of perception.

It has been generally accepted that the retina is an outward extension of the cerebral cortex. Optic nerve fibers transmit sensations from the retina in each eye to the occipital cortex of the brain. Researchers believe that one of the important functions of the occipital cortex is the analysis and synthesis of visual stimuli. If there is damage to the occipital lobes, complex discrimination tasks involving size, shape, and color become difficult.

Visual stimuli processing is dependent on efficient ocular-motor performance. Most ocular-motor processing tasks are closely related to school-oriented work in math, reading, and writing. When there is an ocular-motor dysfunction, it is extremely difficult for the child to perform the eye movements necessary to scan the perceptual field.

Studies have indicated that frontal lobe damage interferes with the ability to search, scan, or examine objects. Lesions in the frontal lobes may result in "pathological inertia" of the sensory process. This interferes with the motor scanning aspects of perception and the examination of pictures or objects, because of this passive looking and inability to seek out identifying signs.

The processing of visual stimuli at the higher cortical level requires not only visual analysis but also the integration and synthesis of the stimuli into a recognizable whole. All these cognitive tasks are interrelated and need to be considered in visual processing dysfunctions such as spatial relationship, visual discrimination, and visual agnosia.

Characteristics

A *spatial-relationship* dysfunction may be caused by damage to the occipital cortex and to cortical lesions in the infero-parietal and parietal-occipital areas. With this dysfunction, the individual has difficulty in left–right discrimination and generally avoids crossing the midline of the body with the hand. There is poor depth perception. Reversals and rotations are also noted in the writing. A child with a spatial-relationship dysfunction has difficulty assembling puzzles and objects. The identification of a complete form of partially exposed pictures, words, or letters and numbers is also difficult.

A *figure-ground* deficit, considered caused by damage to certain parts of the brain, makes it difficult to differentiate an object from its general sensory background. This deficit causes problems in isolating a single word or words on a page. It is extremely difficult to scan for a specific letter, word, or fact or use a dictionary, an index, or a telephone. A person with this deficit also has trouble keeping his or her place while reading.

Visual agnosia is the inability to recognize objects even with adequate sensory information input. It is caused by damage to areas of the brain involved in interpretation and memory recall. This makes it difficult to recognize and name objects, even though the person can describe the color, shape, and size of the object. People who are unable to synthesize visual information must learn to compensate for the deficit in processing by converting the visual analysis to verbal analysis.

People with a *visual-sequential memory* dysfunction have problems with storage and retrieval of information. It is difficult for them to remember the order of letters in a word when attempting to spell the word or the correct sequence of events or letters in a series. The student with this visual processing dysfunction has trouble remembering the order of days of the week, months of the year, and number sequences. Revisualization of visual clues is also extremely hard.

Strategies for Educators

In the general education classroom, students with a visual processing dysfunction may have difficulty understanding a teacher's written instructions or assignments. If the teacher presents material only visually, the student experiences frustration. When writing assignments and instructions on the chalkboard, when giving other instructions, and during discussions, the teacher should simultaneously present the information orally.

The student with a visual processing dysfunction benefits from a phonetic or linguistic approach to reading. This does not preclude a multisensory approach, which might also include kinesthetic and tactile methods along with the auditory approach.

The student's difficulty in retrieving information can be alleviated by allowing extra time for the student to respond. The teacher should also consider letting the student make use of electronic equipment that allows the student to answer questionnaires and tests orally.

Much more research is needed to resolve the many questions surrounding visual processing. It is hoped that research will lead to a better understanding of the tasks involved in visual processing and educational, psychological, and medical interventions that are more successful.

Refer to the section on learning disabilities for information on books and organizations.

For Further Information

Books

Kranowitz, C. S. *The out-of-sync child.*
Smith, C. *The sensory sensitive child: Practical solutions for out-of-bounds behavior.*

Organizations and Agencies

Council for Exceptional Children (CEC)
1110 North Glebe Road, Suite 300
Arlington, VA 22201
703-620-3660
866-915-5000 (TTY)
Fax: 703-264-9494
E-mail: service@cec.sped.org
http://www.cec.sped.org

International Dyslexia Association
40 York Road, 4th floor
Baltimore, MD 21204
410-296-0232
410-321-5069
http://www.interdys.org

National Dissemination Center for Children with Disabilities (NICHCY)
P.O. Box 1492
Washington, DC 20013-1492

800-695-0285
202-884-8200
Fax: 202-884-8441
E-mail: nichcy@aed.org
www.nichcy.org

5

Other Health Conditions

An estimated 0.5% to 1% of all school-age children have some physical or health-related disorder. Cerebral palsy accounts for the largest part of this percentage, followed by spina bifida. These particular disabilities have already been covered in this book, along with other major disabilities. It would be impractical to attempt to include coverage of all health disorders in a single book. However, teachers often express concern over several other health-related disorders such as asthma, diabetes, heart disorders, and hemophilia frequently encountered in the regular classroom. These are included in this chapter.

Although some health-related disorders may not necessarily affect the student's learning process, they may affect the activities allowed for the student and be a concern for the teacher. Many of the concerns that an educator may have about health-related problems can be alleviated by direct communication with parents of the students and school health professionals. They can provide invaluable information about the health needs of students. Additional information about students can be gained by examining the school records.

Asthma

Asthma is a common health condition of many students. It affects 1 out of every 10 children (Clayman, 1989). Asthma is a chronic disorder that generally starts in early childhood in many cases and becomes less severe in early adulthood. Symptoms include recurrent attacks of shortness of breath, wheezing, a dry cough, and a tight feeling in the chest.

An asthmatic attack can be brought on by a variety of factors including air pollutants; extreme high or low humidity; allergens such as dust, mold, pollen, feathers, or animal dander; lung infections such as bronchitis; vigorous exercise; or emotional stress. Some attacks may occur for no known reason.

Asthmatic attacks can be very frightening to the child. In a severe attack, the low amount of oxygen in the blood results in cyanosis, bringing on a bluish coloration in the face and lips. If this occurs, medical personnel should be immediately notified. It may be comforting for a teacher to know that most attacks pass unnoticed or are controlled by a bronchodilator.

Depending on a school district's policy, most students who need asthma inhalers while at school may carry and self-administer the bronchodilator. The American Academy of Allergy and Immunology recommends that students with asthma be permitted to possess inhaled medications for the treatment and prevention of asthma symptoms when they are prescribed by that student's physician (Public Resource Center, 2001). The parent or guardian is usually required to sign an authorization form permitting the student to self-administer the medication during school hours. Middle and high school students are capable of carrying and administering their own medication, but elementary school students generally self-administer the medication under the supervision of designated school personnel. If the elementary student is going on a field trip, the teacher should make prior arrangements with the school nurse and administrator.

Because undue emotional stress can be a precipitating cause for some asthmatic attacks, the teacher should provide a nonthreatening, positive learning environment. Although students with asthma generally can participate in athletics, physical activity should be monitored, and excessive exercise should be avoided. When the outside air is of poor quality, it is best for the student with asthma to avoid any outdoor activity.

Certain allergens can provoke an asthmatic attack in some students. When conferring with parents, the teacher can find out which specific allergens might be the cause. The teacher may then be able to take precautions to minimize exposure. In some cases, the appropriate staff can take steps to remove the allergen from the school environment. The teacher may be able to remove specific allergens such as those in art supplies, chemicals, or other agents from the student's immediate vicinity. As with any health reason for absence, arrangements need to be made to allow the student to make up assignments.

Diabetes

According to the National Diabetes Information Clearinghouse (2001), 15.7 million people have diabetes. Each year, 798,000 new cases are diagnosed; 123,000 children under the age of 20 are diagnosed with diabetes, but the figure does not include undiagnosed cases. Many children and adults are unaware that they have diabetes.

Diabetes is a chronic metabolic disorder in which the body does not produce enough insulin to process foods efficiently; as a result, there is not enough insulin for the blood to carry sugar to the cells for nourishment. Diabetes can be kept under control by medication (insulin injections) or regulation of diet and activity or both.

There are two different types of diabetic emergencies. One is insulin shock, which is the result of too much insulin in the blood. Another emergency results from too little insulin and too much sugar. This can result in a diabetic coma.

Insulin reactions and diabetic comas can come on gradually. The educator should be aware of the major signals that are the same for both an insulin reaction and a diabetic coma. These signals include rapid breathing and pulse, sweating, dizziness, drowsiness, and confusion. If a student becomes unconscious, immediate emergency medical treatment should be obtained.

People with insulin-dependent diabetes usually give insulin injections one to four times a day. Some children as early as age 7 can give themselves injections, whereas others are not ready to do this until the age of 12. If the injection is self-administered at school, the nurse must keep track of the injections. Insulin injections help maintain a normal level of blood sugar in the bloodstream.

There may be a need to check the level of sugar in the blood several times a day to make sure the blood sugar level does not drop too low. The student's treatment program will specify the times the blood sugar level should be tested. It consists of taking a drop of blood from a finger and placing it on a coated strip, which is then measured with a glucose meter or by using a color-coded chart. This will indicate the blood sugar level of the student. This test can be done under the supervision of the school nurse or the teacher.

More commonly, first aid for diabetic emergencies simply requires that the student eat or drink a sugar-rich food such as candy, fruit juice, or a nondiet soft drink. The sugar will help a diabetic who has too much insulin in the blood and will not harm one who has too little. A teacher may confer with the parents of a diabetic student and arrange for the parents to provide a supply of sugar-rich candies or drinks that can be made available to the student in the classroom in the event of a diabetic emergency. Often, those who have diabetes will know when something is wrong and will reach for or ask for sugar. If the symptoms do not improve within 5 minutes, emergency medical assistance should be obtained immediately.

A teacher who has in class a student with diabetes has an obligation to make certain all school personnel are informed about the student's medical condition. They should also be knowledgeable of the signs indicating a possible insulin reaction and be informed as to what to do if a diabetic problem occurs.

Heart Conditions

Heart disorders are also a concern for teachers. By examining the health records of students in the class and by conferring with the school health care professionals, a teacher can learn what, if any, physical limitations the student's doctor has prescribed.

A teacher may notice cyanoses in a child when the lips and nail beds turn bluish. This indicates that the child's body has too low a level of oxygen in the body. This generally becomes worse during physical activity. The teacher may also notice extreme breathlessness occurring even with little exercise. The teacher should also be aware of other symptoms that may need teacher intervention such as rest from physical activity. Ongoing two-way communication with the parents or caregivers of a child with a heart condition will be able to provide answers to the questions a teacher may have regarding a child.

In general, many of the children at school may have a congenital heart condition. Many of the abnormalities may already exist when a baby is born. The abnormalities develop early in a woman's pregnancy. One of the abnormalities might include a hole between the walls of the heart. The blood vessels entering or leaving the heart may also be defective. Depending on the defects of the heart, some children with a congenital heart condition may not have restrictions placed on them.

Although there are many types of heart conditions, there is an aspect that a teacher should consider. These children need to be treated the same as all the other children in the class. Although they may need accommodations, they are not different. All children in the class need the teacher's patience and encouragement to be successful in the academic environment.

A heart disorder usually does not affect the learning process unless there are extensive absences from school. Allowances should be made for the student to make up the missed assignments. As with other disorders, some students may occasionally use the heart condition as an excuse to avoid participation in certain school events. Because this is a medical condition, the student's doctor is the only appropriate person to determine which activities should be avoided.

The doctor can also inform the teacher how to recognize the signs and symptoms of possible heart failure. To know what to do in case of an emergency, the teacher should become certified in CPR.

Hemophilia

Hemophilia is an inherited bleeding disorder caused by insufficient levels of blood-clotting factor. According to the National Hemophilia Foundation (as cited in Beiersdorfer, Clements, & Weisman, 1995), 20,000 people in the United States have hemophilia.

Hemophilia is a lifelong disorder that occurs in three levels of severity: mild, moderate, and severe. Mild bleeding can be prolonged bleeding but occurring only after surgeries such as tooth extractions or minor injuries. The Hemophilia Health Services (n.d.) states that a student with mild hemophilia averages one or two bleeds per year. Following a minor trauma such as a sprain or hard fall, moderate bleeding can occur. Those with moderate hemophilia average around 12 bleeds per year. In severe bleeding, episodes are more frequent, can occur with no apparent injury or cause, and may result in bleeding into joints, muscles, or body organs. On an average, people with severe hemophilia will have 52 bleeding episodes per year. Current medical treatment can control the bleeding (Hemophilia Health Services, n.d.).

According to the Hemophilia Health Services (n.d.), children with bleeding disorders can participate in many normal physical activities. Most school sports and playground games are allowed. In any case, the teacher should always check with the parent and the student's hemophilia treatment center to see what activities should be restricted. The teacher should also consider getting a letter from the student's hemophilia treatment center stating what activities are permissible. The student with hemophilia may have to be excluded from some activities (Hemophilia Health Services, n.d.).

The National Hemophilia Foundation (as cited in Beiersdorfer et al., 1995) cautions teachers to be aware of certain activities that may have to be restricted. The foundation cites various examples such as exempting a student from running laps if there is frequent bleeding in the knee or from doing push-ups if the student has an active elbow bleed accompanied with pain. Rough contact sports that may involve risk of head injury should always be avoided. Injuries to the neck and throat are very serious because blood and swelling can block the airway. When the teacher has been informed that the student was recovering from an acute bleeding episode, it may be necessary to temporarily restrict activity of the student.

When a student wishes not to participate in a sport or game, the teacher and all school personnel should accept this. At no time should a teacher force an activity on a student with hemophilia. Children with hemophilia have been taught how to recognize the feelings of an internal bleed. They are the best judges of their need for medical intervention. When internal bleeding is suspected, the parents and the hemophilia treatment center should immediately be notified. If the teacher observes a student limping or not using an arm or hand, or if an area is swollen or hot to the touch, bleeding should be suspected and the parents notified.

For external bleeding from a cut, scrape, or laceration, first aid should be given as would be done for any other child. The teacher should use Universal Infection Control Precautions to prevent blood exposure. The school nurse can provide information on the precautions to take.

Before talking to the class about hemophilia, it is necessary for a teacher to allow parents to decide the approach. In some cases, a student with hemophilia does not want to feel different and does not want classmates to know about the bleeding disorder. On the other hand, some students with hemophilia are very open about their bleeding difficulty and encourage discussions about hemophilia. If this is the case, the student talking about hemophilia puts classmates at ease and allows them to ask questions about hemophilia. Open discussions in the class can be arranged with parents and hemophilia treatment centers to provide much needed information to all.

As with other health disorders, a teacher and school nurse need to have ongoing communication with parents, who can provide current information about their child, as well as the limitations and restrictions needed. It is important to know who to call if the student is injured, shows signs of a bleed, or complains of a problem. The telephone numbers of the parents' home, work, pager, and cellular phone and of the hemophilia treatment center must be kept current.

For Further Information

Books

Britton, H., & Sheen, B. *Hemophilia.*
Buzzard, B., & Beeton, K. (Eds.). *Physiotherapy management of hemophilia.*
Edelwich, J., & Brodsky, A. *Diabetes: Caring for your emotions as well as your health.*
Hanas, R. *Type 1 diabetes: A guide for children, adolescents, young adults and their caregivers.*
Hilgartner, M., & Pochedly, C. (Eds.). *Hemophilia in the child and adult.*
Nichols, D. E., & Cameron, D. E. *Critical heart disease in infants and children.*
Sander, B. *A parent's guide to asthma.*
Scheiner, G. *Carb counting: Featuring the tools and techniques used by the experts.*
Steinmann, M. *A parent's guide to allergies and asthma.*
Zaret, D. L., & Moser, M. *Yale University of medicine heart book.*

Organizations and Agencies

American Diabetes Association
23 East 26th Street
New York, NY 10010
800-232-3472
E-mail: customerservice@diabetes.org
http://www.diabetes.org

Asthma and Allergy Foundation of America, Inc.
1125 15th Street NW, Suite 502
Washington, DC 20005
800-727-8462
202-466-7643
Fax: 202-409-4377
E-mail: info@aafa.org
http://www.aafa.org

National Heart, Lung, & Blood Institute Health Information Center
P.O. Box 30105
Bethesda, MD 20824-0105
800-575-0355
301-592-8573
E-mail: NHLBIinfo@nhlbi.nih.gov
http://www.nhlbi.nih.gov/health/infoctr/

National Hemophilia Foundation
116 West 32nd Street, 11th Floor
New York, NY 10001
800-424-2634
212-328-3700
Fax: 212-328-3777
E-mail: info@hemophilia.org
http://www.hemophilia.org

A Note About Medications

The school health care professionals are responsible for administering any medication that the student may require while the student is at school. The classroom teacher should obtain from the health care professional a schedule that indicates when medication needs to be given to the student as a reminder to release the student from the classroom at the specified time. The teacher should never administer the medication.

One book that everyone should have in their home library is the *Physicians Desk Reference* (PDR). This reference book contains more than 3,000 pages of the latest word on prescription drugs. It provides current information about the usage, possible side effects, and interaction between certain medications. This book is especially useful for educators who have many students on prescription drugs. The PDR is published yearly by Thomson Healthcare Publishing.

Behavior Interventions

The following are characteristic behavior patterns that may be indicative of a larger problem:

- short attention span: difficulty concentrating on one subject long enough to complete the activity
- restlessness or hyperactivity: fidgety, constantly on the move, and acts without previous thought
- listening difficulties: uninterested and does not seem to understand
- poor interaction with other children: knows how to interact only by hurting or avoids interaction
- poor interaction with adults: avoids adults in most situations or clings to the adult

- repetitive behavior: repeats unusual movements or words over and over almost as if unable to stop
- ritualistic or unusual behavior: a fixed or ritualistic way of doing something not usually exhibited by other children of the same age
- resistance to discipline or direction: defiant, resentful, destructive, negative, refuses directions, difficult to manage, or defies without reason
- inappropriate conduct: lies, steals, uses profanity, participates in sex play, undresses, is cruel, or runs away
- unusual bizarre language content: language is bizarre, strange, fearful, or uses jargon
- physical complaints: constantly talks of being sick, hurt, or tired
- repetition of others' words: parrots and uses words but not for communication
- self-aggression or self-derogation: tries to verbally or physically hurt self
- introversion: withdrawn, daydreams, a loner, manipulated easily by others, no friends or peer group, or out of touch with reality
- temperamentalness: moody, sensitive, sad, irritable, or shows extreme emotions
- self-stimulation: tics, shaking, rocking, twirling, and so on
- anxiety: looks for constant reassurance in each task and is preoccupied with death, accidents, or disaster
- nonreponsive behaviors: maintains no eye contact and looks past people
- attachment to objects: preoccupied with objects without regard to their intended use
- immature behaviors: prefers younger playmates and has frequent crying spells

Students benefit from a classroom management program that is structured and consistent in the application of rules and consequences. Students who have behavior problems need guidelines to govern their behavior. These rules can be determined cooperatively. The rules established for the class should be fair, stating the types of behaviors expected to have an orderly classroom. The classroom management plan should clearly state the consequences for students who do not follow the established standards and procedures.

There are several common behavior intervention techniques. For the techniques to be successful, they must be used correctly. The explanations of various techniques help you determine an appropriate plan for your students.

A signaling device is a predetermined cue to the student for the performance of a specified behavior. It can also serve as a warning to cease a behavior or there will be a specified consequence. Signaling devices can be successful if the student knows what the desired behavior means. It must be clearly explained to the student beforehand. The consequences of noncompliance must be understood. The signaling device and the appropriate behavior should be practiced before implementation. This plan is known only to the teacher and student.

Nonexclusionary time-out refers to the removal of a student to stop an undesirable behavior. Removing the student to a quiet area for a short period often helps the student gain composure. The time-out consequence must be clearly defined and explained to the student before its use. The site administrator should know when you are planning on using this method for a particular student. If the time-out period was successful, the student should be praised for any appropriate behavior after returning to class. If time-out is used more than five times per school day, other methods should be considered.

The Prernack Principle is the use of student-preferred activities as reinforcement for activities that are less preferred. It allows you to use reinforcers that exist in the school setting. You can give the student a choice of preferred activity when that student is having a difficult time making the correct decision. This technique helps a student regain control because you are leaving the choice up to the student. This avoids confrontation and teaches the valuable social skill of compromise.

Shaping is the technique of reinforcing successive approximations of a desired behavior each time it occurs. This reinforcement can start with a behavior that currently exists but is not the target behavior. You can prompt the student on the behavior verbally, through modeling, gesturally, or physically. Initially, rewards encourage the desired behavior, but they should gradually be faded out as the target behavior is learned.

Behavior learned by observations is called modeling. It is considered the most natural learning mode. The desired behavior is acted out, or the teacher can model the desired behavior. The peers can also model the correct behavior. When the modeling technique is used, the student should be informed as to what target behavior is to be observed.

Planned ignoring is considered an extinct technique. It should be used only when the behavior is being maintained by teacher attention.

An example of this is that you want a student to raise his or her hand for attention, but instead, the student calls out every time help is needed. Planned ignoring consists of ignoring the calling out and responding only when a student is quiet or raises his or her hand. A point to remember is that the behavior generally increases before it decreases.

Many teachers use contracts that are determined between the teacher and student. A reinforcer is provided contingent upon completion of certain academic or behavioral goals. The reinforcer should reward an accomplishment and must be timely. The terms of the contract must be fair and age appropriate.

Token systems are used when students have failed to respond to praise or other commonly used methods. An advantage of the token system is that tokens can be given to students without interrupting ongoing lessons. The tokens can later be traded in for reinforcers of the student's choice. As with other interventions, the desired behavior must be specific and clear. In using a token system, each student in the class must be able to achieve some success daily if the system is to be successful. At no time should the tokens be removed for negative behavior, since they are intended to be used to reward a specified behavior.

A teacher must maintain control so the environment is conducive to learning. This does not mean that a quiet classroom is the best environment. Meaningful interaction between the students stimulates interest and encourages educational growth.

Resource A

Acronyms

The following acronyms are commonly encountered in special education.

ADD   Attention Deficit Disorder
AD/HD   Attention-Deficit/Hyperactivity Disorder
APE   Adapted Physical Education
APH   Aphasia
AS   Asperger Syndrome
ASHA   American Speech-Language-Hearing Association
ASL   American Sign Language
AU   Autism
AYP   Adequate Yearly Progress
BD   Behavior Disorders
BIA   Bureau of Indian Affairs
BIP   Behavior Intervention Plan
BL   Blind
BP   Bipolar
CATS   Center and Transition Services
CDD   Childhood Degenerative Disorders
CEC   Council for Exceptional Children
CG   Cognitive Delay
CHADD   Children and Adults With Attention Deficit Hyperactivity
           Disorder
CIFMS   Continuous Improvement and Focused Monitoring
           System
CMI   Chronic Mental Illness
COTA   Certified Occupational Therapist Association
CP   Cerebral Palsy

CSPD	Comprehensive System Personnel Development
DBL	Deaf/Blind
DD	Developmental Disability
DEA	Deaf
DH	Developmental Handicapped
D/HH	Deaf/Hard of Hearing
DIS	Designated Instructional Services
DOH	Department of Health
DP	Developmental Disability
DPH	Due Process Hearing
DPHO	Due Process Hearing Office
DSM-IV	*Diagnostic and Statistical Manual IV*
ED	Emotional Disturbance, Emotionally Disturbed
EH/LD	Emotionally Handicapped/Learning Disabled
EI	Early Intervention
ER	Educable Retarded
ESEA	Elementary and Secondary Education Act
FAE	Fetal Alcohol Effects
FAPE	Free Appropriate Education
FAS	Fetal Alcohol Syndrome
FBA	Functional Behavior Assessment
FERPA	Family Education Rights and Privacy Act
FFH	Family Foster Home
FH	Foster Home
FM	Focused Monitoring
GT	Gifted and Talented
HIPAA	Health Insurance Portability and Accountability Act
ICC	Interagency Coordinating Council
IDEA	Individuals with Disabilities Act
IEE	Individual Education Evaluation
IEP	Individualized Education Plan
IFSP	Individual Family Service Plan
IHCP	Individual Health Care Plan
INT/D	Interpreter/Deaf
IPP	Individual Program Plan
ITP	Individualized Transition Plan
IWEN	Individual With Exceptional Needs
LA	Lead Agency
LAS	Language/Speech Impaired, Language and Speech
LD	Learning Disabled
LEA	Local Education Agency
LEP	Limited English Proficiency

LH	Learning Handicapped
LRE	Least Restrictive Environment
MD	Muscular Dystrophy
MGM	Monthly Gifted Minors
MH	Multihandicapped
MPRRC	Mountain Plains Regional Resource Center
MR	Mental Retardation, Mentally Retarded
NCLB	No Child Left Behind
NECTAC	National Early Childhood and Technical Assistance Center
NICHD	National Institute of Child Health and Human Development
NIH	National Institutes of Health
OH/ORT	Orthopedically Handicapped
OHI	Other Health Impaired
OI	Orthopedic Impaired
OSEP	Office of Special Education Program
OT	Occupational Therapy
P&A	Protection and Advocacy
PBD	Pediatric Bipolar Disorder
PD/PH	Physically Disabled/Physically Handicapped
PDD	Pervasive Development Disorders
PL	Public Law
PL94-142	Public Law 94-142 (Reauthorized as IDEA)
PLEP	Present Level of Educational Performance
PPD	Programs for Physically Disabled
PS	Partially Sighted
PT	Physical Therapy
PTIC	Parent Training and Information Center
RSP	Resource Specialist Program
RST	Resource Specialist Teacher
SAT	School Appraisal Tem
SCI	Spinal Cord Injury
SDC	Special Day Class
SEA	State Education Agency
SEAP	State Education Advisory Panel
SED	Severely Emotionally Disturbed
SH	Severely Handicapped
SIP	State Improvement Plan
SLD	Speech and Language Disorders
SLH	Speech and Language Handicap
SLP	Speech Language Pathologist
SST	Student Success Team

TBI	Traumatic Brain Injury
TDD	Telecommunications Device for the Deaf
TMR	Trainable Mentally Retarded
TS	Tourette Syndrome
TTY	Text Telephone
VH/VI	Visually Handicapped/Visually Impaired
VR	Vocational Rehabilitation

Resource B

Public Agencies Offering Assistance to Individuals with Disabilities and Their Families

In 1990 the National Dissemination Center for Children with Disabilities in Washington, DC, listed the following agencies that offer assistance to people with disabilities and their families.

State Education Departments

The state department staff can answer questions about special education and related services in your state. Many states offer special manuals explaining the steps to take regarding educational placement options for individuals with disabilities as well as providing information about available resources. Find out if one is available in your area. Education department officials are responsible for special education and related services programs in their respective states for preschool, elementary, and secondary children.

State Vocational Rehabilitation Agencies

Each state's vocational rehabilitation agency provides medical, therapeutic, counseling, education, training, and other services needed to prepare people with disabilities for work. This agency provides the address of the nearest rehabilitation office where one can discuss issues of eligibility and services with a counselor. It can also refer individuals to an independent-living program in their state. Independent-living programs provide services that enable adults with disabilities to live productively as members of their communities. The services might also include information and referral, peer counseling, workshops, attendant care, and technical assistance.

Office of the State Coordinator of Vocational Education for Disabled Students

States that receive federal funds for vocational education must ensure that such funding is used in programs that include students with disabilities. This office can tell you how your state funds are being used and provide information on current programs.

State Mental Retardation and Developmental Disabilities Agencies

The functions of state mental retardation and developmental disabilities agencies vary from state to state. These agencies' general purpose is to plan, administer, and develop standards for state and local mental retardation and developmental disabilities programs provided in state-operated facilities and community-based programs. They provide information about services available to families, consumers, educators, and other professionals.

State Developmental Disabilities Councils

Assisted by the U.S. Department of Health and Human Services' Administration on Developmental Disabilities, state councils plan and advocate improvement in services for people with developmental disabilities. In addition, funding is available for time-limited demonstration and stimulatory grant projects.

State Mental Health Agencies

The functions of state mental health agencies vary from state to state. The general purposes of these offices are to plan, administer, and develop standards for state and local mental health programs such as those in state hospitals and community health centers. They can provide information about mental illnesses and a resource list of contacts to which you can go for help.

Protection and Advocacy Agencies and Client Assistance Programs

Protection and advocacy systems are responsible for pursuing legal, administrative, and other remedies to protect the rights of people who are developmentally disabled or mentally ill, regardless of their age. Protection and advocacy agencies may provide information about health, residential, and social services in your area. Legal assistance is also available.

The Client Assistance Program assists individuals seeking and receiving vocational rehabilitation services. These services, provided under the Rehabilitation Act of 1973, include assisting in the pursuit of legal, administrative, and other appropriate remedies to ensure the protection of the rights of individuals with developmental disabilities.

Programs for Children With Special Health Care Needs

The U.S. Department of Health and Human Services' Office of Maternal and Child Health and Resource Development provides grants to states for direct medical and related services to children with disabling conditions. Although services will vary from state to state, additional programs may be funded for training, research, special projects, genetic disease testing, and counseling services.

University-Affiliated Programs

The University-Affiliated Programs, a national network of programs affiliated with universities and teaching hospitals, provide interdisciplinary training for professionals and paraprofessionals. It also offers programs and services for children with disabilities and their families. Some programs provide direct services for children and families. Individual university-affiliated programs have staff with expertise in a variety of areas and can provide information, technical assistance, and inservice training to agencies, service providers, parent groups, and others.

You can obtain a listing of all individual university-affiliated programs by contacting the National Center for Education in Maternal and Child Health, 2000 15th Street North, Suite 701, Arlington, VA 22201-2617, telephone 703-524-7802. Additional information about university-affiliated programs can be obtained by contacting the American Association of University-Affiliated Programs for Persons With Developmental Disabilities, 8630 Fenton Street, Suite 410, Silver Spring, MD 20910, telephone 301-588-8252.

Directory of National Information Sources on Disabilities (NIS)

The NIS, published by the U.S. Department of Education, provides information, referral, or direct services relating to disabilities. Although regional and local resources are not always included, it does include nationwide resources. Information about this directory can be obtained from the National Institute on Disability and Rehabilitation Services, 400 Maryland Avenue SW, Washington, DC 20202, telephone 800-346-2742.

The NICHCY State Resource Sheet for your state can help you locate organizations and agencies within your state that address disability-related issues. Included on NICHCY state sheets are the following:

- state senators
- state governors
- state agencies serving children and youth with disabilities
- state chapters of disability organization and parent groups
- parent training and information projects

The Web site is http://www.nichcy.org/states.htm.

The National Association of State Boards of Education provides hyperlinks to all state education agencies. The Web site is http://www.nasbe.org.

Resource C

Children's Books About Disabilities

The following list of children's books about disabilities was provided by the ERIC Clearinghouse on Disabilities and Gifted Education. Current updates can be found on their Web site (http://www.ericec.org).

Key to Age Group or Grade Level

AC   *Adult Read to Children.* For Pre–K to Grade 3; ranging from 10 to 30 pages with illustrations; typically designed for parents to read to their children

JE   *Juvenile Easy Reader.* For children who are beginning to read on their own such as those in Grades 1 and 2; ranging from 30 to 80 pages; illustrations are included to break up the text

JF   *Juvenile Fiction.* Children's fiction or chapter books; for children in Grades 2 to 6; ranging from 60 to 200 pages, the books are generally divided into chapters, contain fewer illustrations, and have more complicated plots or concepts than either AC or JE books

YA   *Young Adult.* For young adults in Grades 5 to 12; more complicated plots and topics of general interest to the young adult population

A   *Adult.* Contains language or content that may be unsuitable for young adults

Aphasia

Title: *Look Inside Your Brain*
Author: Heather Alexander
Publisher: Penguin Putnam, 1991
Story Profile: It has wonderful illustrations and demonstrates how the brain controls everything you do including speech, learning, and memory.
Reading level: JE

Title: *Nana's Stroke*
Author: Barbara Baird
Publisher: Interactive Therapeutics, 1997
Story Profile: A counseling storybook for children
Reading Level: YA

Asthma

Title: *Luke Has Asthma, Too*
Author: Alison Rogers
Publisher: Waterfront Books, 1987
Story Profile: Luke has an older cousin who teaches him some aspects of asthma management and serves as a general role model.
Reading Level: AC

Asperger Syndrome

Title: *All Cats Have Asperger Syndrome*
Author: Kathy Hoopman
Publisher: Jessica Kingsley Publishers, 2006
Story Profile: This takes a playful look at Asperger syndrome through the eyes of a cat. All pictures of cats have captions.
Reading Level: JF

Attention-Deficit/Hyperactivity Disorder

Title: *Eukee: The Jumpy Jumpy Elephant*
Authors: Clifford L. Corman and Esther Trevino
Publisher: Specialty Press, 1995
Story Profile: Eukee is a smart little elephant who likes to chase butterflies, blow bubbles, and do cartwheels. He always feels jumpy

inside, however, and can never finish the march at school. Unhappy that he doesn't have any friends, he consents to a visit to the doctor, where he learns he has AD/HD.
Reading Level: AC

Title: *Eagle Eyes: A Child's View of Attention Deficit Disorder*
Author: Jeanne Gehret
Publisher: Verbal Images Press, 1991
Story Profile: Ben, a boy with attention deficit disorder, describes the frustrations and feelings associated with his initially unidentified syndrome.
Reading Level: JF

Title: *First Star I See*
Author: Jaye Andras Caffrey
Publisher: Verbal Images Press, 1997
Story Profile: Paige is a young girl with ADD who is trying to win a school writing contest.
Reading Level: JF

Title: *Zipper: The Kid With ADHD*
Author: Caroline Janover
Publisher: Woodbine House, 1997
Story Profile: Zachary (nicknamed Zipper), a fifth-grader who has attention-deficit/hyperactivity disorder (AD/HD) has trouble concentrating and controlling himself until a retired jazz musician recognizes his talent, believes in him, and gives him the motivation to start trying to do better.
Reading Level: JF

Title: *Views From Our Shoes: Growing Up With a Brother or Sister With Special Needs*
Author: Donald Meyer, Editor
Publisher: Woodbine House, 1997
Story Profile: Forty-five siblings share their experiences. The children whose essays are featured range in age from 4 to 18 and have siblings with a variety of special needs, including autism, cerebral palsy, developmental delays, attention deficit disorder, hydrocephalus, visual and hearing impairments, Down syndrome, and Tourette syndrome.
Reading Level: YA

Title: *Shelley: The Hyperactive Turtle*
Author: Deborah M. Moss
Publisher: Woodbine House, 1988
Story Profile: Shelley is a young hyperactive turtle who faces difficulties due to his inability to sit still and his frequent behavior problems that lead to problems at school and on the bus, at home and with friends, eventually leading to a poor self-image and depression. After a visit to a neurologist, he no longer thinks of himself as a bad turtle, and this condition gradually improves.
Reading Level: JE

Title: *Otto Learns About His Medicine: A Story About Medication for Hyperactive Children*
Author: Matthew Galvin
Publisher: Magination Press, Brunner-Mazel, 1995
Story Profile: Otto, a fidgety young car that has trouble paving attention in school, visits a special mechanic who prescribes a medicine to control his hyperactive behavior.
Reading Level: AC

Autism

Title: *Andy and His Yellow Frisbee*
Author: Mary Thompson
Publisher: Woodbine House, 1996
Story Profile: Sarah is a new girl at school who is curious about why Andy spins his yellow Frisbee every day by himself on the playground. When Sara tries to talk to Andy, Rosie, Andy's older sister, watches and worries about how her brother may react. Rosie knows that Andy is in his own world most of the time and that he has trouble finding the words to express himself.
Reading Level: AC

Title: *Having a Brother Like David*
Author: Cindy Dolby Nollette
Publisher: Minneapolis Children's Medical Center, Early Childhood Center, 1985
Story Profile: Marty's brother, David, is autistic. Marty explains that David looks a lot like other children but has special needs.
Reading Level: AC

Title: *Ian's Walk: A Story About Autism*
Author: Laurie Lears
Publisher: Albert Whitman, 1998
Story Profile: Tara feels frustrated while taking a walk with her autistic brother, Ian. After she becomes separated from him, she learns to appreciate the way Ian experiences the world.
Reading Level: AC

Title: *Russell Is Extra Special: A Book About Autism for Children*
Author: Charles A. Amenta, III
Publisher: Brunner-Mazel, 1992
Story Profile: This portrayal of an autistic boy and his family is designed to help children (ages 4 to 8) and their parents understand this serious developmental disorder.
Reading Level: AC

Title: *Talking to Angels*
Author: Esther Watson
Publisher: Harcourt Brace, 1996
Story Profile: Christa is an autistic girl who is described in this picture book by her sibling. Her behavior is described and illustrated in mixed media, including her favorite sounds and textures, occasional staring and fixation on stimuli, and interactions with others.
Reading Level: AC

Title: *Joey and Sani*
Authors: Illana Katz and Edward Ritvo
Publisher: Real Life Story Books, 1993
Story Profile: Sam is 5 and has autism, and Joey is his 6-year-old brother. They describe an ordinary day at home and at school, showing some of the ways they are different and alike.
Reading Level: JE

Title: *Are You Alone on Purpose?*
Author: Nancy Werlin
Publisher: Houghton Mifflin, 1994
Story Profile: This novel focuses on the lives of two Jewish families, one including an autistic boy and his academically gifted sister, the other featuring a bully who suffers a severe spine injury in a diving accident and is paralyzed from the waist down.
Reading Level: YA

Cerebral Palsy

Title: *I'm Joshua and "Yes I Can"*
Author: Joan Lenett Whinston
Publisher: Vantage, 1989
Story Profile: Joshua, a young boy with cerebral palsy, describes his fears and insecurities about his disability on his first day in first grade.
Reading Level: JF

Title: *A Smile From Andy*
Author: Nan Holcomb
Publisher: Jason and Nordic Publishers, 1989
Story Profile: Andy, who has cerebral palsy, is very shy. One day he meets a girl who helps him discover something that he can do to reach out to others in his own special way.
Reading Level: JE

Title: *Can't You Be Still?*
Author: Sarah Yates
Publisher: Gemma B. Publishing, 1992
Story Profile: Ann, who has cerebral palsy, attends school for the first time.
Reading Level: JE

Title: *Andy Opens Wide*
Author: Nan Holcomb
Publisher: Jason and Nordic Publishers, 1990
Story Profile: Andy, a young boy with cerebral palsy, is frustrated by his inability to open his mouth wide enough for his mother to feed him easily.
Reading Level: JE

Title: *Here's What I Mean To Say ...*
Author: Sarah Yates
Publisher: Gemma B. Publishing, 1997
Story Profile: Ann (age 9), who has cerebral palsy, takes us through her struggles with everyday activities.
Reading Level: JF

Title: *Howie Helps Himself*
Author: Joan Fassler

Publisher: Albert Whitman, 1975
Story Profile: Howie has cerebral palsy. He gets around in a wheelchair, or rather, other people get him around in his wheelchair. More than anything, Howie wants to move that chair himself.
Reading Level: JF

Title: *Don't Stop the Music*
Author: Robert Perske
Publisher: Abingdon Press, 1986
Story Profile: Follow our teen hero and heroine (with cerebral palsy) through thrills, romance, and adventure all rolled into this "whodunnit."
Reading Level: YA

Title: *Under the Eye of the Clock: The Life Story of Christopher Nolan*
Author: Christopher Nolan
Publisher: St. Martin's, 1988
Story Profile: The author, a 21-year-old Irishman severely disabled by cerebral palsy, tells the story of his childhood and how he must cope with his handicap, revealing the thoughts and realities of his world.
Reading Level: A

Title: *Danny and the Merry-Go-Round*
Author: Nan Holcomb
Publisher: Jason and Nordic Publishers, 1987
Story Profile: Danny, who has cerebral palsy, visits the park with his mother and watches other children playing on a playground. He makes friends with a young girl after his mother explains cerebral palsy to her and points out that it is not contagious.
Reading Level: AC

Title: *Rolling Along: The Story of Taylor and His Wheelchair*
Author: Jamee Riggio Heelan
Publisher: Rehabilitation Institute of Chicago, Dixon Education and Training Center, 2000
Story Profile: A young boy enjoys his new mobility with his first wheelchair.
Reading Level: AC

Title: *We Can Do It!*
Author: Laura Dwight
Publisher: Checkerboard Press, 1992

Story Profile: The daily activities of five children who each have either cerebral palsy, blindness, spina bifida, or Down syndrome. Color photographs show the children engaging in their favorite pastimes at home and at school, with family members and with peers.
Reading Level: JE

Diabetes

Title: *Sarah and Puffle: A Story for Children About Diabetes*
Author: Linnea Mulder
Publisher: Henry Holt, 7992
Story Profile: Sarah feels resentful of the limitations the disease places on her activities until a stuffed animal (Puffle) comes to life and offers her encouraging rhymes about coping with diabetes.
Reading Level: JE

Down Syndrome

Title: *Be Good to Eddie Lee*
Author: Virginia Fleming
Publisher: Putnam, 1993
Story Profile: Eddie Lee, a young boy with Down syndrome, follows the neighborhood children into the woods to find frog eggs. They are resentful and try to make him stay home.
Reading Level: AC

Title: *Big Brother Dustin*
Author: Alden R. Carter
Publisher: Albert Whitman, 1997
Story Profile: Dustin, a young boy with Down syndrome, learns that his parents are expecting a baby.
Reading Level: AC

Title: *Russ and the Almost Perfect Date*
Author: Janet Elizabeth Rickert
Publisher: Woodbine House, 2001
Story Profile: Recent book in a series about Russ, a boy with Down syndrome, who has a great day going to school and playing with friends. He takes responsibility for a mistake and feels good about himself when he does the right thing.
Reading Level: AC

Title: *Russ and the Apple Tree Surprise*
Author: Janet Elizabeth Rickert
Publisher: Woodbine House, 1992
Story Profile: Russ, a 5-year old boy with Down syndrome, longs for a swing set. All his backyard has to offer is an apple tree. When his grandparents visit, Russ discovers the job of picking apples and making them into apple pie. He decides that his apple tree may be just as good as a swing set.
Reading Level: AC

Title: *Russ and the Fire House*
Author: Janet Elizabeth Rickert
Publisher: Woodbine House, 1992
Story Profile: Russ is a young boy with Down syndrome whose everyday life experiences—not his disability—are the subject of books in this series. Russ goes "on duty" with his uncle, a fireman. Their shift includes a full inspection of the fire equipment, including keeping it clean. He also encounters Spark, the firehouse dog. At the end of this exciting day, all the firemen thank Russ for his hard work and invite him back for another visit.
Reading Level: AC

Title: *Keith Edward's Different Days*
Author: Karen Melberg Schwier
Publisher: Impact Publishers
Story Profile: Keith meets a variety of people with differences, including Down syndrome and physical differences, and learns that being different is okay.
Reading Level: AC

Title: *Buddy's Shadow*
Author: Shirley Becker
Publisher: Jason and Nordic Publishers, 1991
Story Profile: Buddy, a 5-year-old boy with Down syndrome, purchases a puppy.
Reading Level: JE

Title: *Charlie's Chuckle*
Author: Clara Widess Berkus
Publisher: Woodbine House, 1992
Story Profile: Charlie, a 7-year-old boy with Down syndrome, has an infectious laugh and enjoys bicycling around his neighborhood. On one

such excursion, he inadvertently wanders into a disputatious city council meeting and brings humor and harmony to the argumentative adults.
Reading Level: JE

Title: *Cookie*
Author: Linda Kneeland
Publisher: Jason and Nordic Publishers, 1989
Story Profile: Molly, a 4-year-old girl with Down syndrome, has difficulty talking. Her frustration with communication difficulties is relieved when someone comes to teach her sign language.
Reading Level: JE

Title: *Thumbs Up, Rico!*
Author: Maria Testa
Publisher: Albert Whitman, 1990
Story Profile: Rico is a boy with Down syndrome who loves basketball. The story describes his relationship with a neighborhood boy named Caesar, his older sister Nina, and his art class.
Reading Level: JE

Title: *The Hangashore*
Author: Geoff Butler
Publisher: Tundra Books, 1998
Story Profile: This is a Newfoundland story of a young man with Down syndrome who displays courage and kindness toward a judgmental government official.
Reading Level: JE

Title: *We'll Paint the Octopus Red*
Author: Stephanie Stuve-Bodeen
Publisher: Woodbine House, 1998
Story Profile: Emma is a little girl who has a new baby brother with Down syndrome.
Reading Level: JE

Title: *Where's Chimpy?*
Author: Berniece Rabe
Publisher: Albert Whitman, 1988
Story Profile: Misty, a young girl with Down syndrome, misplaced her stuffed monkey and reviews her day with her father to try to remember where she left him.
Reading Level: JE

Title: *My Sister Annie*
Author: Bill Dodds
Publisher: Boyds Mills Press, 1989
Story Profile: Charlie is an 11-year-old boy who attempts to cope with growing up in the shadow of an older sister with Down syndrome.
Reading Level: JF

Title: *Bus Girl*
Author: Gretchen Josephson
Publisher: Brookline Books, 1997
Story Profile: Gretchen, through poetry, describes her emotional development toward independence and adult relationships.
Reading Level: YA

Title: *Idea Man?*
Author: Karen Melberg Schwier
Publisher: Diverse City Press, 1997
Story Profile: Erin is angry when her parents leave her overnight with family friends. The family's older son, Jim, has Down syndrome, and Erin doesn't want to be seen with him because he's known as the Dork, but kids from school witness Jim giving her a hug. She realizes she misjudged him after he helps her with a homework assignment.
Reading Level: YA

Dyslexia

Title: *How Dyslexic Benny Became a Star: A Storm of Hope for Dyslexic Children and Their Parents*
Author: Joe Griffith
Publisher: Yorktown Press, 1998
Story Profile: Benny, who has dyslexia, struggles while his fifth-grade classmates' skills improve. He is suddenly terrified when he is called on by his teacher to read aloud.
Reading Level: JF

Title: *Happy Birthday Jason*
Authors: C. Jean Cutbill and Diane Rawsthorn
Publisher: IPI Publishing, 1984
Story Profile: A delightful story that helps children better understand their world by understanding Jason's. His story reveals that children with learning disabilities are more similar to other children than they are different.
Reading Level: AC

Title: *Kevin's Story*
Author: Dvora Levinson
Publisher: IPI Publishing, 1984
Story Profile: Kevin exhibits reading problems and is referred for testing with a psychologist who explains reading and learning disabilities to him and his family.
Reading Level: JE–JF

Title: *Josh: A Boy With Dyslexia*
Author: Caroline Janover
Publisher: Waterfront Books, 1988
Story Profile: The life and adventures of Josh, who has dyslexia, as he moves to a new town and school.
Reading Level: JF

Title: *My Name Is Brain Brian*
Author: Jeanne Betancourt
Publisher: Scholastic, 1993
Story Profile: Brian, a sixth-grade boy, is diagnosed as having dyslexia. His initial trepidation at being singled out for attention and diagnosis is gradually replaced by enthusiasm.
Reading Level: JF

Title: *The Worst Speller in Jr. High*
Author: Caroline Janover
Publisher: Free Spirit Publishing, 1995
Story Profile: Katie Kelso, an adolescent girl with dyslexia, describes her struggles with issues of peer acceptance, dating, and academic achievement, all of which are complicated by her dyslexia.
Reading Level: YA

Epilepsy

Title: *A Season of Secrets*
Authors: Alison Cragin Herzig and Jane Lawrence Mali
Publisher: Little, Brown, 1982
Story Profile: Benji is a 6-year-old who has been fainting at school, and Brooke and Jason, his teenage sister and brother, wonder all summer long what is wrong with him.
Reading Level: JF

Head Injury

Title: *My Friend Ben*
Author: Wanda Gilberts Kachur
Publisher: Peytral Publications, 1997
Story Profile: Narrated through the eyes of a classmate, this story tells of Ben, a boy with traumatic brain injury, who is included in a general education, third-grade class.
Reading Level: JF

Hearing Impairment

Title: *A Thousand Lights*
Author: Hope Benton
Publisher: Open Minds, 1996
Story Profile: Two brothers, Will and Donnie, one with a severe hearing impairment, climb Mount Fuji in Japan.
Reading Level: YA

Title: *A Very Special Friend*
Author: Dorothy Hoffman Levi
Publisher: Gallaudet University Press, 1989
Story Profile: Frannie, a lonely little girl, discovers a new friend when a deaf girl her age moves in next door.
Reading Level: AC

Title: *Silent Observer*
Author: Christy MacKinnon
Publisher: Gallaudet University Press, 1993
Story Profile: Christy MacKinnon is a young girl born in 1889 on a farm on Cape Breton Island, Nova Scotia, Canada, who became deaf after having whooping cough. She describes her life in adjusting to deafness, her relationships with family, and her problems in trying to understand and be understood by hearing individuals.
Reading Level: AC

Title: *When I Grow Up*
Author: Candri Hodges
Publisher: Jason & Nordic Publishers, 1995
Story Profile: Jimmy is a deaf youth who takes a field trip and encounters various careers of deaf individuals.
Reading Level: JE

Title: *Ludwig van Beethoven. Musical Pioneer*
Author: Carol Greene
Publisher: Children's Press, 1990
Story Profile: The life of Beethoven is chronicled from his despair over his worsening deafness to his deepening commitment to his music.
Reading Level: JF

Title: *The Flying Fingers Club*
Author: Jean F. Andrews
Publisher: Kendall Green, 1988
Story Profile: Donald is a third grader who is bitter about repeating it when he meets Matt, who comes to class with an interpreter because he is deaf; they become fast friends.
Reading Level: JF

Title: *Annie's World*
Author: Nancy Smiler Levinson
Publisher: Gallaudet University Press, 1990
Story Profile: The adjustment of 16-year-old Annie to her family move that necessitates her becoming mainstreamed into a public high school.
Reading Level: YA

Title: *Tell Me How the Wind Sounds*
Author: Leslie D. Guccione
Publisher: Scholastic, 1989
Story Profile: Amanda is 15 when she meets Jake on Clark's Island. She is angered at every encounter with him until he tells her he's deaf.
Reading Level: YA

Title: *The Silents*
Author: Charlotte Abrams
Publisher: Gallaudet University Press, 1996
Story Profile: Charlotte writes her autobiography about day-to-day life with her deaf parents. She describes the communication challenges they faced as a Jewish family overcoming the Depression and the hardships of World War II, as well as the additional challenge and fear the mother faced when she found out she was going blind.
Reading Level: A

Title: *Thomas Alva Edison: Great Inventor*
Author: Nancy S. Levinson
Publisher: Scholastic, 1996
Story Profile: Thomas Edison's life and his many inventions, despite his deafness, that shape our lives today.
Reading Level: AC

Title: *A Very Special Sister*
Author: Dorothy Hoffman Levi
Publisher: Gallaudet University Press, 1992
Story Profile: Mixed feelings are experienced by Laura, a young deaf girl, on finding out her mother will soon give birth. Her initial excitement is displaced by worries that the new child, if able to hear, would be more lovable.
Reading Level: AC

Learning Disabilities

Title: *What Do You Mean I Have a Learning Disability?*
Author: Kathleen M. Dwyer
Publisher: Walker and Company, 1991
Story Profile: Ten-year-old Jimmy is having problems at school and believes he is stupid. After a parent-teacher conference, he is tested and found to have a learning disability.
Reading Level: AC

Title: *Trouble With School: A Family Story About Learning Disabilities*
Authors: Kathryn Boesel Dunn and Allison Boesel Dunn
Publisher: Woodbine House, 1993
Story Profile: A family's real-life experiences with learning disabilities follows Allison and her mother as each tells her side of the story of diagnosing and adjusting to Allison's special learning needs.
Reading Level: JF

Title: *The Best Fight*
Author: Anne Schlieper
Publisher: Albert Whitman, 1995
Story Profile: Jamie is an adolescent boy who has learning disabilities that impair his reading. Frustration at his low reading ability combines with alienation due to his placement in special classes. His mixed emotions toward his teachers, friends, and family are explored.
Reading Level: JF

Title: *Wrongway Applebaum*
Author: Marjorie Lewis
Publisher: Coward-McCann, 1984
Story Profile: Stanley is in fifth grade when his awkwardness and inability to tell left from right conflict with his family's interest in baseball.
Reading Level: JF

Title: *Probably Still Nick Swansen*
Author: Virginia Euwer Wolff
Publisher: Holt, 1988
Story Profile: Nick is 16 and in special education classes with "Down" kids and some "hyperactive" students, too. He can't figure out if there's a word for his placement in special education.
Reading Level: YA

Title: *Reach for the Moon*
Author: Samantha Abeel
Publisher: Pfeifer-Hamilton Publishers, 1997
Story Profile: Samantha, a 13-near-old girl with a learning disability in understanding mathematical concepts, provides a collection of illustrated poems and stories. She writes about her difficulties in middle school, including coping with her disability and the accompanying emotional challenges and the encouragement received by her English teacher to develop her writing talent.
Reading Level: YA

Title: *A Zebra Named Al*
Author: Wendy Isdell
Publisher: Free Spirit Publishing, 1993
Story Profile: Julie is an eighth-grader who has trouble in math. Frustrated, she rests her head on her book . . . and is awakened by an Imaginary Number who suddenly appears in her room. When she follows the Number through a mysterious portal, she enters a strange land of mathematics, where she meets a zebra named Al.
Reading Level: JF

Mental Retardation

Title: *My Sister Is Different*
Author: Betty Ren Wright
Publisher: Steck-Vaughn Company, 1990
Story Profile: Carlo tells us what it is like to have an older sister with mental retardation.
Reading Level: JE

Title: *At the Back of the Woods*
Author: Claudia Mills
Publisher: Four Winds, 1982
Story Profile: Davey is a young boy with mental retardation who is at a special care facility. His sister, Clarisse, and his parents come to visit him.
Reading Level: JF

Title: *Wish on a Unicorn*
Author: Karen Hesse
Publisher: Penguin, 1991
Story Profile: A sixth-grade girl, Mags, lives in a trailer and has a younger sister named Hannie with mental retardation. Hannie finds an old stuffed unicorn and believes it is magical when strange things start to happen.
Reading Level: YA

Title: *Emily Good as Gold*
Author: Susan Goldman Rubin
Publisher: Harcourt Brace, 1993
Story Profile: Emily, a 13-year-old girl with mental retardation, experiences adolescence.
Reading Level: YA

Title: *My Brother, Matthew*
Author: Mary Thompson
Publisher: Woodbine House, 1992
Story Profile: David is a young boy who describes life with his younger brother who was born with a mental disability.
Reading Level: AC

Title: *Retarded Isn't Stupid, Mom!*
Author: Sandra Z. Kaufman
Publisher: Brookes, 1988
Story Profile: The mother of a child diagnosed as mildly retarded at age 2 recounts experiences of the child's growing up into an adult.
Reading Level: YA

Muscular Dystrophy

Title: *Extraordinary People With Disabilities*
Authors: Deborah Kent and Kathryn A. Quinlan
Publisher: Children's Press, 1996
Story Profile: Nearly 50 well-known men and women with mental or physical disabilities are profiled in this collection, including an Indian chief with muscular dystrophy.
Reading Level: YA

Speech Disorders

Title: *Sarah's Surprise*
Author: Nan Holcomb
Publisher: Jason and Nordic Publishers, 1990
Story Profile: Six-year-old Sarah, who is unable to talk, has used a picture board to communicate. She is now ready for an augmentative communication device. With the help of her speech therapist, she gives everyone a surprise at her mother's birthday party.
Reading Level: JE

Title: *The Bob (Butterbean) Love Story*
Authors: Terry Page and Bob Love
Publisher: Boo Books, 1995
Story Profile: Bob's autobiography tells his story: a famous basketball player with a speech impediment.
Reading Level: JE

Title: *The Summer Kid*
Author: Myrna Neuringer Levy
Publisher: Second Story Press, 1991
Story Profile: Karen, a 10-year-old girl who stays at a summer cottage with her grandmother, encounters Tommy, a 9-year-old boy with a severe language disorder.
Reading Level: JF

Title: *Armann and Gentle*
Author: Kristin Steinsdottir
Publisher: Stuttering Foundation of America, 1997
Story Profile: A 6-year-old boy named Armann stutters when he is frustrated.
Reading Level: AC

Title: *Cat's Got Your Tongue?*
Author: Charles E. Schaefer, PhD
Publisher: Brunner-Mazel, 1992
Story Profile: Anna, a kindergartner, is diagnosed as an electively mute child.
Reading Level: AC

Spina Bifida

Title: *Margaret's Moves*
Author: Bernice Rabe
Publisher: Dutton, 1987
Story Profile: Margaret is 9 years old and has problems with the fact she is in a wheelchair and blames it for slowing her down.
Reading Level: JF

Title: *Patrick and Emma Lou*
Author: Nan Holcomb
Publisher: Jason and Nordic Publishers, 1994
Story Profile: Three-year-old Patrick has cerebral palsy. He is having a hard time managing his new walker, but with the help of a new friend, Emma Lou, who is 6 and has spina bifida, they both discover something very important about each other.
Reading Level: JF

Title: *We Can Do It*
Author: Laura Dwight
Publisher: Checkerboard Press, 1997
Story Profile: The daily activities of five children who each have either cerebral palsy, blindness, spina bifida, or Down syndrome. Color photographs show the children engaging in their favorite pastimes at home and at school, with family members and with peers.
Reading Level: JE

Tourette Syndrome

Title: *Adam and the Magic Marble*
Authors: Adam Buehrens and Carol Buehrens
Publisher: Hope Press, 1991
Story Profile: Adam, Chris, and Matt are often harassed by bullies until they discover a magic marble.
Reading Level: JF

Title: *Hi, I'm Adam: A Child's Story of Tourette Syndrome*
Author: Adam Buehrens
Publisher: Hope Press, 1991
Story Profile: Adam, a 10-year-old boy diagnosed with Tourette syndrome, wrote this book to help children with Tourette syndrome understand that they are not alone and that other children are experiencing similar difficulties.
Reading Level: JF

Visual Impairment

Title: *Springtime*
Author: Virginia L. Kroll
Publisher: Boyds Mills Press, 1987
Story Profile: Naomi tells us of the signs of spring though the mind of the blind.
Reading Level: JE

Title: *See You Tomorrow, Charles*
Author: Miriam Cohen
Publisher: Bantam, 1997
Story Profile: Charles is a first-grader who is adjusting to school as a blind student.
Reading Level: JE

Title: *The Night Search*
Author: Kate Chamberlin
Publisher: Richard S. McPhee, Jason and Nordic Publishers, 1997
Story Profile: Heather, who is blind, resists using her white cane until her puppy wanders off.
Reading Level: JE

Title: *A Picture Book of Helen Keller*
Author: David A. Adler
Publisher: Scott Foresman, 1992
Story Profile: Some salient details in the life of Helen Keller are described in this pictorial biography: her frustration and untamed behavior and the radical changes effected by Anne Sullivan Macy.
Reading Level: AC

Title: *Knots on a Counting Rope*
Authors: Bill Martin and John Archambault
Publisher: Henry Holt, 1997
Story Profile: A boy is told a story by his grandfather of a boy born blind.
Reading Level: AC

Title: *Stevie Wonder*
Author: John Swenson
Publisher: Harper & Row, 1994
Story Profile: Stevie Wonder's life from his birth in Saginaw, Michigan, in 1950 through his rapid rise as a Motown artist in the early 1960s and up to his present-day work.
Reading Level: YA

Title: *Luna and the Big Blur: A Story for Children Who Wear Glasses*
Author: Shirley Day
Publisher: Magination Press, 1995
Story Profile: Luna resents the fact that she needs glasses to correct her nearsightedness.
Reading Level: JE

Resource D

Associations to Contact

The following is a list of associations that provide information about the health-related problems discussed in this book. In addition, you will want to refer to Resource B: Public Agencies Offering Assistance to Individuals with Disabilities and Their Families.

American Diabetes Association	800-582-8323
American Heart Association	800-242-8721
American Kidney Fund	800-638-8299
American Psychological Association	800-374-2721
American Speech-Language-Hearing Association (ASHA)	800-638-8255
The Arc of the United States	800-433-5255
Asthma and Allergy Foundation of America	800-727-8463
Autism Society of America	800-328-8476
CDC National AIDS Clearinghouse	800-458-5231
CHADD Children and Adults with Attention Deficit/Hyperactivity Disorder	800-233-4050
Children's Craniofacial Association	800-535-3643
Council for Exceptional Children	888-232-7733
Cystic Fibrosis Foundation	800-344-4823
Epilepsy Foundation	800-332-1000
Human Growth Foundation	800-451-6434
International Dyslexia Association	800-223-3123
Learning Disabilities of America	888-300-6710
Leukemia Society of America	800-955-4572
Muscular Dystrophy Association	800-572-1717
National Aphasia Association	800-328-8476

National Clearinghouse for Alcohol and Drug Information	800-729-6686
National Dissemination Center for Children with Disabilities	800-695-0283
National Down Syndrome Congress	800-232-6372
National Easter Seal Society	800-221-6827
National Heart Lung Blood Institute	800-575-0355
National Hemophilia Foundation	800-328-8476
National Institute on Deafness and Other Communication Disorders	800-241-1044
National Jewish Center for Immunology and Respiratory Medicine	800-222-5864
National Organization for Albinism and Hypopigmentation	800-473-2310
National Organization for Rare Disorders	800-999-6673
National Reve's Syndrome Foundation	800-233-7393
National Spinal Cord Injury Association	800-962-9629
National Tuberous Sclerosis Association	800-225-6872
Sickle Cell Disease Association of America	800-421-8453
Spina Bifida Association	800-621-3141
United Leukodystrophy Foundation	800-728-5483

Resource E

Similarities and Differences: ADHD and Early Onset Bipolar Disorder

By F. Russell Crites

Some characteristics of ADHD and Bipolar Disorder look the same, but have different motivations.

Others show the same type of behavior, but it is more or less intense in some way.

This is not an exhaustive list of the characteristics of ADHD or Bipolar Disorder. However, it is a good start for those trying to get a handle on which disorder seems to be most evident. These characteristics are documented in the works of Papolos and Papolos (2002), Geller (1997), Popper (1996), Miklowitz (2002), and others.

Breaks Things

An ADHD child breaks things carelessly while playing (non-angry destructiveness).

A Bipolar child breaks things as a result of anger. He has severe temper tantrums where he releases extreme amounts of physical and emotional energy. Aggression towards others and physical property damage sometimes occurs.

Anger

An ADHD child usually calms down in twenty to thirty minutes (maybe less).

A Bipolar child may continue to feel and act angry for up to four hours or more.

Regression

An ADHD child rarely regresses, e.g., displays disorganized thinking, language, and body position.

A Bipolar child regresses and often has disorganized thinking, language and body position during the episode.

Forgets the Event

An ADHD child does not lose memory of events.

A Bipolar child may lose memory of the tantrum or event.

Trigger Events

An ADHD child is typically triggered by a lack of structure.

A Bipolar child overreacts to limit-setting, is triggered by anxiety (look for PTSD issues), or by sensory or emotional over-stimulation.

Sleeping and Waking Up

An ADHD child usually arouses quickly and attains alertness within minutes. However, they are tired and often do not get a good night sleep . . . especially hyperactive-impulsive students.

A Bipolar child often stays up late, and is irritable upon early morning arousal. He may have slow arousal and have irritability, fuzzy thinking, or somatic complaints when he gets up (may last for a few hours).

Getting Tired

An ADHD child seems to wear himself out and get tired during the day (this may be a medication issue).

A Bipolar child is not usually tired during the day.

Reality and Judgment

An ADHD child can see reality for what it is. He can make good judgments, but he just doesn't take the time to do so.

A Bipolar child is grandiose and believes that he can do things that he can't do (impaired judgment). Doesn't think things through, and even if he does, it is often flawed thinking.

Nightmares

An ADHD child may destroy the bed covers, but he does not have excessive nightmares or night terrors.

A Bipolar child often has severe nightmares or night terrors. Themes of explicit gore and bodily mutilation are often reported.

Mood Swings

An ADHD child will not have significant shifts in mood, e.g., depressed to manic.

A Bipolar child will often have mood shifts during the day, or at the least during the week.

Misbehavior

An ADHD child misbehavior is often accidental and usually caused by inattention, impulsivity, or over-activity.

A Bipolar child will intentionally provoke or misbehave. Some are seen as the "bully on the playground."

SLEEP

An ADHD child may sleep 5–9 hrs. However, he will often be tired because he doesn't get good REM (rapid eye movement) sleep.

A Bipolar child has a decreased need for sleep (3–6 hrs), e.g., may stay up late and get up early and not seem to have any bad effects from it.

Racing Thoughts

An ADHD child has racing thoughts that are fragmented; bits and pieces of hundreds of things that distract or draw his attention.

A Bipolar child often has racing thoughts. Will usually give concrete answers to describe his thoughts, e.g., "I need a stoplight up there." "My thoughts broke the speed limit." Can tell you about a specific "topic" he is racing about. His speech is usually goal directed.

Risk Taking

An ADHD child may engage in behavior that can lead to harmful consequences without being aware of the danger.

A Bipolar child is often a risk, or sensation seeker.

Sexual Behaviors

An ADHD child is often immature for his age. As a result, sexuality comes along at a slower pace because of psychosocial or developmental delays.

A Bipolar child tends to have strong early sexual interest and behavior. He may be sexually inappropriate for age, e.g., use explicit sexual language, sexual pictures.

Reality Testing

An ADHD child usually does not have psychotic symptoms or reveal a loss of contact with reality.

A Bipolar child may exhibit gross distortions in perception of reality or in the interpretation of emotional events.

Elation

An ADHD child will be elated (giggle, excited, extremely "happy") when special events occur.

A Bipolar child will be elated for no apparent reason, e.g., giggling in the classroom when peers are not, laughing for no apparent reason, etc. At the same time he may be sensitive or easily irritated.

Restlessness

An ADHD child may have restless tension as seen in an inability to keep his legs, hands, etc. still. This occurs all day long.

A Bipolar child will have the same problem with restlessness, but it may cycle through the day, often getting worse at night (depends on type of bipolar).

Impulsivity

An ADHD child can be impulsive and react to his environment, not so much his inner turmoil.

A Bipolar child will be impulsive due to a swing in moods. If hypomanic, judgment fades. If depressed he may have a need to find a way to reduce his depression or energize himself.

Inattention and Poor Focus

An ADHD child will probably be inattentive or distractible all day long, every day of the week (pending medication).

A Bipolar child may be inattentive for a time and then become attentive as he pulls out of his depression. If he goes too far into the manic side he will lose attention again. Attention is often cyclical . . . may be hour by hour or day by day.

Self-Centered

An ADHD child may be self-centered, but is usually so because of a sense of frustration at being unable to focus.

A Bipolar child seems to be unable to see others perspective in a situation. He will do whatever is necessary to justify his position. Very irritable.

Suicidal Thinking and Suicide

An ADHD child may talk of suicide as a control issue. Usually there is no intention, plan, etc. for follow through.

A Bipolar child may have a morbid fantasy about death, hurting others, etc. Suicide is the leading cause of death of people with Bipolar Disorder.

Injury to Self or Others

An ADHD child would rarely intentionally hurt self or others. If something were to occur it would be more of an accident due to inattention.

A Bipolar child will intentionally hurt self or others with purpose. This purpose will often seem to be malevolent or grandiose in nature, i.e., creative ways to hurt someone who has offended him.

Rages

An ADHD child will have nondirective meltdowns. They are usually short in duration.

A Bipolar child will go into a rage and direct it at a person, or some available target. It is deliberate and intentional in nature. He may attack those in authority.

Talks a Lot

An ADHD child may speak out of turn (even have a lot to say), but can be redirected to task.

A Bipolar child, when in a manic state, will have a verbal outpouring, speaking without stopping even when someone tries to stop him.

If your child has more characteristics on the bipolar side of this chart, you may want to consider the possibility that your child may have bipolar disorder instead of ADHD. Consult with your doctor to discuss what may need to be done.

SOURCE: Used with permission from F. Russell Crites, from his work titled *Bipolar or ADHD*.

Bibliography

Aefsky, F. (1995). *Inclusion confusion.* Thousand Oaks, CA: Corwin Press.

Alexander Graham Bell Association for the Deaf. (1970). *Speech and hearing checklist.* Washington, DC: Author.

Alltman, L. K. (1990). *Nerve protein raises hope for paralyzed: Progress in research.* Springfield, NJ: American Paralysis Association.

American Council of the Blind. (1989, January). *Resources for parents of blind and visually impaired children.* Washington, DC: Author.

American Paralysis Association. (1989a). *The APA spinal cord hot line: A special report.* Springfield, NJ: Author.

American Paralysis Association. (1989b). *Facts about the American Paralysis Association and paralysis.* Springfield, NJ: Author.

Association for Retarded Citizens. (1991, February). *Fetal alcohol syndrome: Fact sheet.* Atlanta, GA: Author.

Association for Retarded Citizens. (1993, September). *Question and answer page.* Retrieved from http://www.thearc.org

Banbury, M., & Trice, C. (n.d.). *Mainstreaming: From intent to implementation* (Grant No. G007901295). New Orleans, LA: University of New Orleans.

Barkley, R. (1990). *Attention deficit hyperactivity disorder: A handbook for diagnosis and treatment.* New York: Guilford.

Batshaw, M. (1991). *Your child has a disability.* New York: Little Brown.

Bauer, S. (2001, February). *Asperger syndrome: Through the lifespan.* Retrieved from http://aspenn.org/bauer.html

Baum, S. (1997). *Gifted but learning disabled: A puzzling paradox.* Retrieved March 20, 2008, from http://www.ldonline.org

Baum, S., Owen, S. V., & Dixon, J. (1991). *To be gifted and learning disabled: From identification of practical intervention strategies.* Mansfield Center, CT: Creative Learning Press.

Better Hearing Institute. (1982). *Hearing impairment in children.* Washington, DC: Author.

Biklen, D. (1993). *Communication bound.* New York: Teachers College Press.

Birch, J. L., & Reynolds, M. C. (1981). *Teaching exceptional children in all America's schools.* Reston, VA: Council for Exceptional Children.

Blanck, P. D. (1994, December). Celebrating communications technology for everyone. *Federal Communications Law Journal.* Retrieved from http://www.law.indiana.edu/fclj

Braille Institute. (n.d.). *Are you nervous because I'm blind?* Los Angeles: Author.

Britannica. (1996a, May). *Coma.* Retrieved May 19, 2008, from http://www.britannica.com/eb/article-9024905/coma

Britannica. (1996b, May). *Diabetes mellitus.* Retrieved May 19, 2008, from http://www.britannica.com/ebc/article-9362655

Britannica. (1996c, May). *Diabetes statistics.* Retrieved May 19, 2008, from http://www.eb.com.180

Britannica. (1996d, May). *Hemophilia.* Retrieved May 19, 2008, from http://www.eb.com.180

Britannica. (1996e, May). *Hypoglycemia.* Retrieved May 19, 2008, from http://www.britannica.com/ebc/article-9367691

Brody, L. E., & Mills, C. J. (1997, May/June). *Gifted children with learning disabilities: A review of the issues.* Retrieved February 21, 2008, from http://www.ldonline.org

Brucker, P. O. (1994). The advantages of inclusion for students with learning disabilities. *Journal of Learning Disabilities, 27*(9), 581–582.

Buckmann, S., & Pratt, C. (2000). *Supporting students with Asperger's syndrome who present behavioral challenges.* Bloomington: Indiana Resource Center for Autism.

Canadian Down Syndrome Society. (1999). *Resource catalogue.* Calgary, Alberta, Canada: Author.

Carroll, S. (1998). *ADHD look-alikes.* Bethesda, MD: National Association of School Psychologists.

Center for Study of Autism. (1995). *Autistic savant.* Retrieved from http://autism.org/savant.html

Chasnoff, I. J. (1988). *Drugs, alcohol, pregnancy, and parenting.* London: Kluwer Academic.

Deakin, D. (1981, June). *The national head and spinal cord injury survey* (NIH No. 81-2240). Bethesda, MD: National Institutes of Health.

Dembart, L. (1988, May 29). Kids on the couch: How psychotherapists are helping children to succeed at the difficult job of growing up. *Los Angeles Times Magazine,* pp. 9–15, 35–36.

Dyslexia Institute. (2001). *How can I help the dyslexic pupils while I teach everyone?* Retrieved March 20, 2008, from www.dyslexia-inst.org.uk/articles/howcani.htm

Educational Leadership. (1996, February). *Students with special needs.* Alexandria, VA: Author.

Elliott, B., & Riddle, M. (1992). *An effective interface between regular and special education: A synopsis of issues and successful practices.* Unpublished manuscript, Indiana University.

First, P. F., & Curcio, J. L. (1993). *Individuals with disabilities: Implementing the newest laws.* Thousand Oaks, CA: Corwin Press.

Fowler, M. (1991, September). *Attention deficit disorder: Briefing paper.* Washington, DC: National Dissemination Center for Children with Disabilities.

Frost, L. (1994). *Focus on autistic behavior: The picture-exchange communication system* (Vol. 9). Newark, NJ: Pyramid Educational Consultants.

Geller, and Del Balla. (2006). *Bipolar disorder in children and early adolescence.* New York: Guilford Press.

Geralis, E. (1991). *Children with cerebral palsy: A parent's guide.* Rockville, MD: Woodbine House.

Getlin, J. (1989, July 24). Legacy of a mother's drinking. *Los Angeles Times,* pp. V1, V6.

Glass, R. M., Christiansen, J., & Christiansen, J. L. (1982). *Teaching exceptional students in the regular classroom.* Boston: Little Brown.

Greene, L. (1951–1952). *Emotional factors in children with muscular dystrophy: Proceedings of the first and second medical conference of MDAA.* New York: Muscular Dystrophy Association of America.

Handicap News. (1996, March). *Dyslexia diagnosis.* Retrieved from http://www.inform.umd.eous/Journals/dyslexia

Harrie, R. P. (1984). *What is dyslexia?* Reston, VA: Council for Exceptional Children.

Healey, B. (1997, November). *Helping parents deal with the fact that their child has a disability.* Retrieved February 21, 2008, from http://www.ldonline.org

Health Resource Center. (1993–1994). *National clearinghouse on postsecondary education for individuals with disabilities.* Washington, DC: American Council on Education.

Heinrichs, P. (1992, October 3). Experts slam disabled charade. *Sunday Age,* p. 1.

Hollister, W. G. (1959, September). *A bridge of feelings.* Washington, DC: National Educators Association.

Howard, J. (1994, March 23). Sports: A constant battle with Tourette's. *Washington Post,* p. C1.

Imaizumi, S. O. (1990). *Prenatal factors and their influences on neonatal outcome: Identifying the needs of drug-affected children.* Rockville, MD: U.S. Department of Health and Human Services.

International Dyslexia Association. (2000, January). *Multisensory teaching* (Fact Sheet No. 969). Baltimore: Author.

Internet Mental Health. (1996, April). *Antisocial personality disorder.* Retrieved from http://mentalhealth.com/

Kagan, J. (1998). *Gale encyclopedia of childhood and adolescence.* Farmington Hills, MI: Gale Group.

Kalina, N. (1999). *The puzzle of lifestyle planning.* Bloomington: Indiana Resource Center for Autism.

Kannemann, F. (1994, April 17). *Frequently asked questions about attention deficit disorder.* Retrieved from use http://www.ncf.ca/ip/sigs/life/disability/faq/attn

Kay, K. (Ed.). (2000). *Uniquely gifted: Identifying and meeting needs of the twice exceptional student.* Gibson, NH: Avocus Publishing, Inc.

Kilbey, M., & Asghar, K. (Eds.). (1991). *Methodological issues in controlled studies on effects of prenatal exposure to drug abuse* (Research Monograph No. 114). Rockville, MD: National Institute on Drug Abuse.

Kirk, S. A., Gallagher, J. J., & Anastasiow, N. J. (2000). *Educating exceptional children* (9th ed.). Boston: Houghton Mifflin.

Kolata, G. (1989, December 5). Understanding Down syndrome: A chromosome holds the key. *New York Times,* p. C3.

Latson, S. R. (1995, January/February). *Preventing parent burn-out: A model for teaching effective coping strategies to parents of children with learning disabilities.* Retrieved February 21, 2008, from http://ldonline.org

Levine, M. (1984, September). Learning abilities and disabilities: The medical form. *Harvard Medical School Health Letter,* 2(11).

Los Angeles Unified School District. (1999, January 7). *Student Health & Human Services bulletin* (No. Z-19 rev.). Los Angeles: Author.

Los Angeles Unified School District. (2000, April). *Special education compliance guide.* Los Angeles: Author.

March of Dimes Birth Defects Foundation. (1989). *Fetal alcohol syndrome.* White Plains, NY: Author.

Mathias, R. (1992, January/February). *Developmental effects of prenatal drug exposure may be overcome by postnatal environment* (Publication No. ADM 92-1488). Rockville, MD: National Institute on Drug Abuse.

McDonnell, L., McLaughlin, M., & Morrison, P. (Eds.). (1997). *Educating one and all students with disabilities and standards-based reform.* Washington, DC: National Academy Press.

Mellma, S. L. (2002). *Childhood apraxia of speech resource guide.* New York: Thomson Delmar Learning.

Meyers, A. (1994). *Serving clients with Tourette syndrome.* Bayside, NY: Tourette Syndrome Association.

Mother's little helper. (1996, March 18). *Newsweek,* pp. 51–58.

National Aphasia Association. (1988a). *Communicating with people who have aphasia: Some do's and don'ts.* New York: Author.

National Aphasia Association. (1988b). *The impact of aphasia on patients and family: Results of a CREEDS survey* (Publication No. 4). New York: Author.

National Aphasia Association. (2001). *Primary progressive aphasia.* New York: Author.

National Center for Stuttering. (1981). *Fact sheet.* New York: Author.

National Clearinghouse for Alcohol and Drug Information. (1995). *Effects of paternal substance abuse.* Rockville, MD: Author.

National Dissemination Center for Children with Disabilities. (1988, September). *Down syndrome.* Washington, DC: Author.

National Dissemination Center for Children with Disabilities. (1990a, June). *Epilepsy.* Bethesda, MD: Author.

National Dissemination Center for Children with Disabilities. (1990b, March). *Spina bifida.* Bethesda, MD: Author.

National Dissemination Center for Children with Disabilities. (1990c, October). *Visual impairments.* Washington, DC: Author.

National Dissemination Center for Children with Disabilities. (1991, April). *Autism.* Washington, DC: Author.

National Dissemination Center for Children with Disabilities. (1992, March). *Learning disabilities.* Washington, DC: Author.

National Dissemination Center for Children with Disabilities. (1992, May). *Cerebral palsy.* Washington, DC: Author.

National Dissemination Center for Children with Disabilities. (1995, June). *Traumatic brain injury* (Fact sheet No. 18). Washington, DC: Author.

National Dissemination Center for Children with Disabilities. (2000a, April). *Autism and pervasive developmental disorder* (Fact Sheet No. 1). Retrieved February 21, 2008, from http://www.ucp.org/

National Dissemination Center for Children with Disabilities. (2000b, May). *General information about cerebral palsy.* Retrieved May 19, 2008, from http://www.kidsource.com/NICHCY/cerebral_palsy.html

National Down Syndrome Congress. (1993). *Resources on integration.* Park Ridge, IL: Author.

National Head Injury Foundation. (1992). *Traumatic brain injury newsletter.* Washington, DC: Author.

National Information Center for Handicapped Children and Youth. (1988, September). *The least restrictive environment: Knowing one when you see it.* Washington, DC: Author.

National Institute of Diabetes and Kidney Diseases. (1996, May). *Statistics.* Retrieved from http://www.niddk.nih.gov/NIDDKHomePage.html

National Institute of Health and Human Development. (1980, December). *Cerebral palsy: Hope through research* (No. 81-159). Bethesda, MD: Author.

National Institute of Health and Human Development. (1988, March). *Developmental speech and language disorders* (No. 88-2757). Bethesda, MD: Author.

National Institute of Health and Human Development. (1990, October). *Aphasia* (No. 91-391). Bethesda, MD: Author.

National Institute of Mental Health. (2005). *Surgeon general.* Retreived from http://www.surgeongeneral/library/mentalhealth/chapter3/sec4.html

National Institute of Neurological Disorders and Stroke. (1990). *Aphasia: Hope through research.* Bethesda, MD: Author.

National Institute of Neurological Disorders. (1993, September). *Hope through research* (No. 93-159). Bethesda, MD: Author.

National Institute of Neurological Disorders and Stroke. (1995, February). *Tourette syndrome* (MH Publication No. 95-2163). Bethesda, MD: Author.

National Mental Health Association. (2001, September). *Mental illness and the family: Mental health statistics.* Retrieved from http://www.nmha.org/infoctr/factsheets/15.cfm

Orlansky, M. D. (1977). *Mainstreaming the visually impaired child.* Austin, TX: Learning Concepts.

Orton Dyslexia Society. (1988). *How is dyslexia assessed?* Baltimore: Author.

Orton Dyslexia Society. (1989a). *What is dyslexia?* Baltimore: Author.

Orton Dyslexia Society. (1989b). *Where can I find help?* Baltimore: Author.

Ottinger, B. (1995, September). *Modifications for students with Tourette syndrome, attention-deficit disorder and obsessive-compulsive disorder.* Retrieved from http://www.uihealthcare.com/topics/neurologicalhealth/tourette syndrome.html#modifications

Powers, M. D. (1989). *Children with autism.* Rockville, MD: Woodbine House.

Reisner, H. (1988). *Children with epilepsy: A parent's guide.* Kensington, MD: Woodbine House.

Robinson, F. B. (1964). Introduction to stuttering. Englewood Cliffs, NJ: Prentice Hall.

Robinson, S. M., Braxdale, C. T., & Colson, S. E. (1985). *Focus on exceptional children.* Denver, CO: Love.

Rolland, A. (1991, June). *Some thoughts on future needs and directions for research and treatment of Aphasia: Vol. 2.* Washington, DC: U.S. Department of Health and Human Services.

Rosen, L., & Weiner, L. (1984). *Alcohol and the fetus: A clinical perspective.* New York: Oxford University Press.

Rovner, S. (1989, July 2). America unkind to mentally ill children. *Los Angeles Times,* pp. 13, 126.

Rynders, J. E. (1983, October). *Mainstreaming children with Down syndrome: Cooperative paddling works particularly well when the waters get rough.* Park Ridge, IL: Down Syndrome Congress.

Sarno, M. T., & Hook, O. (1980). *Aphasia, assessment and treatment.* Stockholm: Almquist & Wikell.

Scott, E., Jan, J., & Freeman, R. (1994). *A guide for parents and professionals about children who are visually impaired* (3rd ed.). Austin, TX: Pro-Ed.

Shames, G., & Wiig, E. (1986). *Human communication disorders.* Columbus, OH: Merrill.

Shore, K. (1998). *Special kids problem solver.* Paramus, NJ: Prentice Hall.

Silver, L. (1988). *The misunderstood child: A guide for parents of learning disabled children.* New York: McGraw-Hill.

Smith, S. (1981). *No easy answers.* New York: Bantam.

Spina Bifida Association of America. (n.d.-a). Alphafetoprotein blood screening and amniotic testing. Rockville, MD: Author.

Spina Bifida Association of America. (n.d.-b). *Emerging issues in spina bifida: Secondary disabilities.* Rockville, MD: Author.

Spina Bifida Association of America. (1990a). *Not-so-trivial pursuit of information about spina bifida.* Rockville, MD: Author.

Spina Bifida Association of America. (1990b, January/February). *Task force keys on quality health care, special needs for teens, adults: Insights.* Rockville, MD: Author.

Spina Bifida Association of Nova Scotia. (1996). *About spina bifida.* Retrieved February 21, 2008, from http://www.sbhans.ca/

State Medical Society of Wisconsin. (2001). *Autistic savant.* Retrieved from http://www.wismed.org/foundation/SavantSyndrome.html

Stolov, W. C., & Clowers, M. R. (1981). *Handbook of severe disability.* Seattle: University of Washington Press.

Svoboda, W. B. (1979). *Learning about epilepsy.* Baltimore: University Park Press.

Talent, B. K., & Busch, S. G. (1982, February/March). Epilepsy. *Today's Education,* pp. 8, 34.

Tanenhaus, J. (1990, Winter). *Computers and Down syndrome: NDSS update.* New York: National Down Syndrome Society.

Tisdale, S. (1990, June). Neither morons nor imbeciles nor idiots: In the company of the mentally retarded. *Harper's,* pp. 47–56.

Tourette Syndrome Association. (1992). *Questions and answers on Tourette syndrome.* Bayside, NY: Author.

Truitt, C. J. (1954, October). *Personal and social adjustments of children with muscular dystrophy: Clinical management of patients. Symposium at the third medical conference.* New York: Muscular Dystrophy Associations of America.

Turnbull, A. P. (1993). *Coping, families, and disability.* Baltimore: Brooks.

Understanding learning problems. (1984, March). *Current Health,* pp. 3–7.

United Cerebral Palsy Association. (1989). *What is cerebral palsy?* New York: Author.

United Cerebral Palsy Association. (1993, December). *Cerebral palsy: Facts and figures.* New York: Author.

United Cerebral Palsy Association. (2000, November). *Cerebral palsy: Facts & figures.* Retrieved February 21, 2008, from http://www.ucp.org

U.S. Department of Health and Human Services. (1990, January). *Fetal alcohol syndrome and other effects on pregnancy outcome: Alcohol and health* (Publication No. RP0756). Rockville, MD: Author.

U.S. Department of Health and Human Services. (1991, July). *Fetal alcohol syndrome: Alcohol alert.* Rockville, MD: Author.

U.S. Department of Health and Human Services. (2001, September). *Administration for children and families.* Retrieved February 21, 2008, from http://www.acf.dhhs.gov/

Van Ripper, C. (1973). *The treatment of stuttering.* Englewood Cliffs, NJ: Prentice Hall.

Walton, J., Beeson, P. B., & Scott, R. B. (1986). *Diabetes* (Vol. 1). New York: Oxford University Press.

Weiner, L., & Morse, B. A. (1989). *Drugs, alcohol, pregnancy and parenting.* Boston: Kluwer Academic Publishers.

Weiner, L., Morse, B. A., & Garrido, P. (1989). FAS/FAE: Focusing prevention on women at risk. *International Journal of the Addictions, 24,* 385–395.

Weisenburg, J., & McBrider, K. E. (1973). *Aphasia.* New York: Hofner.

Wender, P. M. (1987). *The hyperactive child, adolescent, and adult.* New York: Oxford University Press.

Willard-Holt, C. (1999, May). *Dual exceptionalities.* Retrieved March 11, 2008, from http://www.ericdigests.org/2000-1/dual.html

Williams, D. (1992). *Nobody nowhere.* New York: Times Books.

Williams, D. (1994). *Somebody somewhere.* New York: Times Books.

Wing, L. (1980). *Autistic children: A guide for parents and professionals.* Secaucus, NJ: Citadel Press.

Wobus, J. (1996). *Autism: Frequently asked questions.* Retrieved March 11, 2008, from http://www.autism-resources.com/autism.faq.full.html

Wright, P. W. D., & Wright, P. D. (2004). *Wrightslaw: Special Education Law* (2nd ed.). Hartfield, VA: Harbor House Law Press. Retrieved from http://www.wrightslaw.com

References

Albert, M. L., & Velez, A. (2000, Spring). *Aphasia therapy/research: Annual update* (Vol. 12, no. 1). New York: National Aphasia Association.

Allen, D., & Affleck, C. (1985). Are we stereotyping parents? A postscript to Blacher. *Mental Retardation, 23,* 200–202.

Alper, S., Schloss, P. J., Etscheidt, S. K., & Macfarlane, C. A. (1995). *Inclusion: Are we abandoning or helping students?* Thousand Oaks, CA: Corwin Press.

American Medical Association. (1989). *American Medical Association home medical encyclopedia* (Vol. 1, No. 2). New York: Random House.

American Psychiatric Association. (1994). *Diagnostic and statistical manual of mental disorders* (4th ed.). Washington, DC: Author.

American Psychiatric Association. (2000). *Diagnostic criteria for Asperger's syndrome.* Washington, DC: Author.

American Psychiatric Association. (2000). *Diagnostic and statistical manual of mental disorders* (*DSM-IV-TR*). Washington, DC: Author.

American Speech-Language Hearing Association. (1993). *Definitions of communication disorders and variations.* Rockville, MD: Author.

ARC. (1987, March). *Introduction to mental retardation.* Arlington, TX: Author.

Atwood, T. (1998). *Asperger's syndrome: A guide for parents and professionals.* London: Jessica Kingsley.

Autism Research Review International. (1999). *Major medical, political developments fuel furor over vaccines* (Vol. 13, No. 3). San Diego, CA: Author.

Autism Research Review International. (2000). *Concerns rise over mercury in vaccines* (Vol. 14, No. 3). San Diego, CA: Author.

Autism Society of America. Rutgers University. Retrieved May 19, 2008, from http://www.autism-society.org

Beiersdorfer, W. A., Clements, M. J., & Weisman, C. (1995). *The student with hemophilia: A resource for the educator.* New York: National Hemophilia Foundation.

Burke, C. (with McDaniel, J. B.). (1991). *A special kind of hero: Chris Burke's own story.* Garden City, NY: Doubleday.

Cahill, S. (2007, February 12). *Understanding extreme irritability in children.* Available at http://www.nih.gov/news/research_matters/february2007/02122007children.htm

Chalfant, J. C., & Scheffelin, M. A. (1969). *Central processing dysfunctions in children: A review of research* (Contract No. PH-434-67-761). Bethesda, MD: National Institute of Neurological Diseases and Stroke.

Cicero, T. J. (1994). Effects of paternal exposure to alcohol and other drugs. *Alcohol Health and Research World, 18*(1), 37–41.

Clayman, C. B. (Ed.). (1989). *The American Medical Association home medical encyclopedia* (Vols. 1–2). New York: Random House.

Cleft Palate Association. (1988). *Information about the dental care of a child with cleft lip/palate.* Pittsburgh, PA: Author.

Comings, D. E. (1990). *Tourette's syndrome and human behavior.* Duarte, CA: Hope.

Comprehensive Epilepsy Program of the University of Minnesota. (1980). *Epilepsy and the school-age child* (Contract No. 1-NS-5-2327). Minneapolis, MN: Author.

Cook, P. S., Petersen, R. C., & Moore, D. T. (1990). *Alcohol, tobacco, and other drugs may harm the unborn.* Rockville, MD: U.S. Department of Health and Human Services.

DeVane, C. L. (1991). *Pharmacokinetic correlates of fetal drug exposure: Methodological issues in controlled studies on effects of prenatal exposure to drug abuse* (Research Monograph No. 114). Rockville, MD: National Institute on Drug Abuse.

Dorris, M. (1989). *The broken cord.* New York: Harper & Row.

Dunn, David W. (April 2002). Teacher assessment of behavior in children with new-onset seizures [Abstract]. Accession number 024732. The National Epilepsy Library. Seizures, 2002

Education for All Handicapped Children Act, Pub. L. 94-142, 20 U.S.C. at 1401 et seq., and the federal implementing regulations at 34 C.F.R. at 300 (1975).

Epilepsy Foundation of America. (1985a). *Epilepsy school alert.* Landover, MD: Author.

Epilepsy Foundation of America. (1985b). *Recognizing the signs of childhood seizures.* Landover, MD: Author.

Epilepsy Foundation of America. (1987). *Children and epilepsy: The teacher's role.* Landover, MD: Author.

Epilepsy Foundation of America. (1988). *Seizure recognition and first aid.* Landover, MD: Author.

Gifted and Talented Children's Act of 1978, Public Law 95-561. Title IX, section 902.

Gillingham, G. (1995). *Autism: Handle with care.* Arlington, TX: Future Education.

Grandin, T. (1995). *Thinking in pictures, the expanded edition, My life with autism.* Garden City, NY: Doubleday.

Grandin, T. (with Scariano, M.). (1986). *Emergence: Labeled autistic.* Novato, CA: Arena.

Hemophilia Health Services. (n.d.). *Understanding students with bleeding disorders.* Nashville, TN: Author.

Heward, W. L. (1996). *Exceptional children: An introduction to special education* (6th ed.). Upper Saddle River, NJ: Prentice Hall.

Honig v. Doe, 479 U.S. 1084, 107 S. Ct. 1284, L. Ed. 2d 142 (1988).

Hsieh, L. P. (2001). Comparison of epilepsy and asthma perception among preschool teachers in Taiwan [Abstract]. Accession number 023133 Epilepsia. Vol. 42, no. 5, pp. 647–650.

Individuals with Disabilities Education Act, Pub. L. 101-476, 20 U.S.C. at 1400-1485 (1990).

International Dyslexia Association. (2000a). *Dyslexia basics* (Fact Sheet No. 62). Baltimore: Author.

International Dyslexia Association. (2000b, January). *Multisensory teaching* (Fact Sheet No. 69). Baltimore: Author.

Johnson, T. (1986). *The principal's guide to the educational rights of handicapped students.* Reston, VA: National Association of Secondary School Principals.

Kankirawatana, P. (2002). Epilepsy awareness among school teachers in Thailand [Abstract]. Accession number: 019464. Epilepsia, April 1999, vol. 40, no. 497–501.

Kingsley J., & Levitz, M. (1994a). *Count us in: Growing up with Down syndrome.* Orlando, FL: Harcourt Brace.

Kingsley, J., & Levitz, M. (1994, April). Role models. *Exceptional Parent,* pp. 17–20.

Luckasson, R., Coulter, A., Polloway, E. A., Reiss, S., Schalock, R. L., Snell, M. E., et al. (1992). *Mental retardation: Definition, classification, and systems of supports.* Washington, DC: American Association on Mental Retardation.

Maaker, C. J., & Udall, A. J. (n.d.). *Giftedness and learning disabilities.* Retrieved February 21, 2008, from http://www.ldonline.org

Manzo, K. K. (1998, March 11). Study finds distinctive brain patterns in people with dyslexia. *Education Week,* p. 6.

Mattis, S. (1978). *Dyslexia syndromes: A working hypothesis.* New York: Oxford University Press.

McCroskery, M. (2000). *Asperger's syndrome: A developmental puzzle.* Bloomington: Indiana Resource Center for Autism.

National Dissemination Center for Children with Disabilities. (1990a, July). *Emotional disturbance.* Washington, DC: Author.

National Dissemination Center for Children with Disabilities. (1990b, June). *Epilepsy.* Bethesda, MD: Author.

National Dissemination Center for Children with Disabilities. (1990c, July). *General information about speech and language disorders.* Washington, DC: Author.

National Dissemination Center for Children with Disabilities. (1995, June). *Traumatic brain injury.* Washington, DC: Author.

National Dissemination Center for Children with Disabilities. (2000a, April). *General information about epilepsy.* Washington, DC: Author.

National Dissemination Center for Children with Disabilities. (2000b, April). *Learning disabilities* (Fact Sheet No. 7). Washington, DC: Author.

National Dissemination Center for Children with Disabilities. (2004). *Spina bifida* (Fact Sheet No. 12). Washington, DC: Author. Available from www.nichcy.org/pubs/factshe/fs12txt.htm

National Dissemination Center for Children with Disabilities. (2005). *Reading and learning disabilities* (Fact Sheet No. 17). Washington, DC: Author.

National Down Syndrome Congress. (1988a). *Down syndrome.* Park Ridge, IL: Author.

National Down Syndrome Congress. (1988b, February). *Facts about Down syndrome.* Park Ridge, IL: Author.

National Down Syndrome Society. (1993a). *Down syndrome myths and truths.* New York: Author.

National Down Syndrome Society. (1993b). *Questions and answers about Down syndrome.* New York: Author.

National Down Syndrome Society. (2001, April). *Incidence of Down syndrome.* Retrieved February 21, 2008, from http://www.ndss.org

National Head Injury Foundation. (1989). *Basic questions about head injury and disability.* Bethesda, MD: Author.

National Information Center on Deafness, Gallaudet University. (1989). *Deafness: A fact sheet.* Washington, DC: Author.

National Institute of Health and Human Development. (n.d.). *Muscular dystrophy.* Bethesda, MD: Author.

National Institute of Health and Human Development. (1981, February). *Spinal cord injury* (Publication No. 81-160). Bethesda, MD: Author.

National Institute of Health and Human Development. (1993, April). *Dyslexia* (Publication No. 93-3534). Bethesda, MD: Author.

National Institute of Mental Health. (2001, September). *Mental disorders in America.* Retrieved from http://www.ninih.nih.gov/publicat/numbers.cfm

National Institute of Neurological Disorders and Stroke, Interagency Head Injury Task Force. (1989, February). *Facts, causes, costs.* Bethesda, MD: Author.

National Institute on Deafness and Other Communication Disorders. (2000). Retreived from www.nidcd.nih.gov/health/statistics/vsl.asp

Neergaard, L. (2007, March 20). Brain region study may shed light on attention disorders. *Ventura County Star,* p. A3.

New clue to cause of dyslexia seen in mishearing fast sounds. (1994, August 16). *New York Times,* pp. C1, 7–10.

Newson, K. (2006, December 30). Brain's emotional center linked to autism. *Ventura County Star,* p. A9.

Online Asperger Syndrome Information and Support. (2001a, March). *Asperger information: Specially designed instruction for educators.* Retrieved February 21, 2008, from http://www.udel.edu/bkirby/asperger

Online Asperger Syndrome Information and Support. (2001b, March). *Diagnostic rating scales for Asperger syndrome.* Retrieved February 21, 2008, from http://www.udel.edu/bkirby/asperger/DX_scales.html

Ottinger, B., & Gaffney G. R. (1995). *Tourette syndrome.* Retrieved July 30, 2008, from www.uihealthcare.com/topics/neurologicalhealth/tourette syndrome.html

Papolos, Demitri. (2006). *Bipolar child.* New York: Broadway.

Phillips, B. (1993). *Book of great thoughts.* Wheaton, IL: Tyndale House.

Pierangelo, R., & Jacoby, R. (1996). *Parents' complete special education guide.* West Nyack, NY: Center for Applied Research in Education.

President's Committee on Mental Retardation. (2001). Presidential services for the mentally retarded. Washington, DC: Retrieved July 18, 2008, from http://www.acf.hhs.gov/programs/pcpid/pcpid_about.html

Public Resource Center. (2001, September). *Tips to remember: Childhood asthma.* Retrieved February 21, 2008, from http://www.aaaai.org/patients/publicedmat/tips/childhoodasthma.stm

Pyramid Educational Consultants. (n.d.). *Picture-exchange communication system.* Newark, DE: Author.

Rehabilitation Act. Pub. L. 93-112, 29 U.S.C. at 794 (1973).

Rehabilitation Learning Center, Harborview Medical Center. (1995). *SCI classifications and terminology.* Retrieved February 21, 2008, from http://uwmedicine.washington.edu/PatientCare/LOC/Neurosurgery/conditions/SpinalCordInjury/index.htm

Reynolds, C. R., & Fletcher-Janzen, E. (Eds.). (1999). *Encyclopedia of special education* (2nd ed.). New York: John Wiley.

Seay, B. (2001). *The ADDed brain: A biological marker for ADHD.* Retrieved July 18, 2008, from http://user.cybrzn.com/kenyonck/add/seay/Stanford_NIH.htm

Shapiro, J. P. (1992, July 27). See me, hear me, touch me. *U.S. News and World Report,* pp. 63–64.

Simpson, J. (2000). *Parenting a child with cerebral palsy* [Electronic version]. Washington, DC: United Cerebral Palsy Foundation.

Singh, N. N., & Ellis, C. R. (1993). *Effects of school, child and fancily variables on drug responsiveness of children with ADHD.* Washington, DC: Office of Education and Rehabilitation Services.

Spina Bifida Association of America. (n.d.-a). *Spina bifida makes them this way.* Rockville, MD: Author.

Spina Bifida Association of America. (n.d.-b). *Spina bifida: What the teacher needs to know.* Rockville, MD: Author.

Spinal Cord Injury Information Network. (2001, May). *Spinal cord injury: Facts and figures at a glance.* Retrieved February 21, 2008, http://www.spinalcord.uab.edu/show.asp?durki=21446

Sternfeld, L. (1988, April 4). *History of research in cerebral palsy.* Washington, DC: Cerebral Palsy Association.

Stratton, A., & agencies. (2007, November 12). Ritalin of no long-term benefit, study finds. *Guardian Unlimited.* Retrieved May 19, 2008, from http://www.guardian.co.uk/news/2007/nov/12/uknews.health

Stuttering Foundation of America. (n.d.). *Fact sheet about stuttering.* Memphis, TN: Author.

Suplee, C. (1998, March 3). Clue to dyslexia found. *Washington Post,* pp. 2–3.

Tourette Syndrome Association. (1994). *Questions and answers about Tourette syndrome.* Retrieved February 21, 2008, from http://www.mentalhealth.com/book/p40-tour.html

Turner, L. (2006, October 20). Study reveals risks, benefits of Ritalin. *Ventura County Star,* p. A9.

University of California Office of the President. (1996, March). *President's report* (Vol. 4, No. 5). Oakland, CA: Author.

University of Michigan Health System. (2004, May 11). *International trial shows cooling cap prevents brain injury in newborns* (Press release). Ann Arbor: Author. Retrieved from www.med.umich.edu/opm/newspage/2004/coolingcap.htm

U.S. Department of Education. (1993). *National excellence: A case of developing America's talent*. Washington, DC: Author.

U.S. Department of Education, National Institute of Education. (1984). *What is dyslexia?* (Publication No. 1432). Washington, DC: Author.

U.S. Department of Education, Office of Educational Technology. (2000). *Parent's guide to the Internet*. Washington, DC: Government Document Service.

U.S. Department of Health and Human Services. (1993). *Fact sheet: Tourette syndrome* (Rev. ed.). Bethesda, MD: Author.

Vellutino, F. R. (1987, March). Dyslexia. *Scientific American, 256*(3), 34.

Wolkenberg, F. (1987, October 11). Out of the darkness. *New York Times Magazine*, pp. 29–32.

Wong, P. C. M., Skoe, E., Russo, N. M., Dees, T., & Kraus, N. (2007, April). Musical experience shapes human brainstem encoding of linguistic pitch patterns. *Nature Neuroscience 10*, 420–422.

Zametkin, A., Mordahl, T. E., Gross, M., King, A. C., Semple, W. E., Rumsey, J., et al. (1990, July 12). Cerebral glucose metabolism in adults with hyperactivity of childhood onset. *New England Journal of Medicine, 323*(2), 1361–1366.

Index